ACTA UNIVERSITATIS UPSALIENSIS
Studia Historica Upsaliensia

Utgivna av
Historiska institutionen vid Uppsala universitet
genom Rolf Torstendahl,
Torkel Jansson och Jan Lindegren
182

Dag Blanck

Becoming Swedish-American

The Construction of an Ethnic Identity in the
Augustana Synod, 1860–1917

UPPSALA 1997

Dissertation for the Degree of Doctor of Philosophy in History
presented at Uppsala University in 1997

ABSTRACT

Dag Blanck (1997). Becoming Swedish-American. The Construction of an Ethnic Identity in the Augustana Synod, 1860–1917. Acta Universitatis Upsaliensis. *Studia Historica Upsaliensia* 182. 240 pp. Uppsala. ISBN 91-554-4027-4.

This dissertation examines the construction of an ethnic identity in the Swedish-American community around the turn of the century 1900. It takes its starting points in discussions of the nature of ethnic identity, the role of ethnic leadership, and the process of nation-building and nationalism in 19th-century Europe and America.

The study focuses on the largest organization founded by Swedish immigrants in the United States, the Lutheran denomination the Augustana Synod, and examines its role for the creation of an ethnic identity. Three fundamental questions are posed: How did an ethnic identity develop in the Augustana Synod, what did it consist of, and why did it come into being. Three main empirical areas are used to analyze the development and contents of the Swedish-American identity: the Synod's largest institution of higher education, Augustana College in Rock Island, Illinois; the Synod's publishing house, the Augustana Book Concern; and the way in which a Swedish-American history was fashioned within the Synod.

The results of the study show how a Swedish-American identity was constructed by a cultural leadership in the Augustana Synod. This idealized and romanticized identity included Swedish, Swedish-American, and American cultural elements. An awareness of a Swedish-American culture, separate from both Sweden and the United States, developed in which the construction of a Swedish-American history played an important role, emphasizing an early Swedish presence on the American continent and significant Swedish and Swedish-American contributions to the American republic. The reasons for the creation of the identity are seen in the light of the nature of American nationalism, which made it possible for European immigrant groups to develop and maintain ethnic identities and still be loyal Americans.

Key words: American history, ethnic identity, immigration, Swedish-American history.
Dag Blanck, Department of History, Uppsala University, S:t Larsgatan 2, SE-753 10 Uppsala, Sweden

ISSN 0081-6531
ISBN 91-554-4027-4

Typesetting: Rätt Satt Hård & Lagman HB, Bjärka Säby
Printed in Sweden by Reklam & Katalogtryck AB, Uppsala 1997
Distributor: Uppsala University Library, Uppsala, Sweden

Table of Contents

Preface

This study has been carried out on both sides of the Atlantic, and over the years I have incurred a number of debts to both individuals and institutions. In Sweden, I would like to recognize the unfailing support of my supervisor Docent Hans Norman as well as that of Docent Harald Runblom, both of Uppsala University. Without their support, criticism, and friendship, this study would never have been completed. Professor Torkel Jansson of the History Department at Uppsala University has read and made important comments on my manuscript, for which I am grateful. For the last ten years, I have been fortunate enough to be affiliated with the Centre for Multiethnic Research in Uppsala, and I thank the staff of the Center, past and present, for providing an unusually stimulating work environment. The cooperation with the Swedish-American literature project at the Department of Literature in Uppsala has been of great significance to me and I especially thank Dr. Anna Williams from that group. I also thank Professors Jan Lindegren and Rolf Torstendahl of Uppsala University's history department for their readings of the text.

During my frequent stays in the United States, I have benefitted greatly from my association with Augustana College in Rock Island, Illinois. It was during my student years at Augustana that I discovered Swedish America and it has been as a staff member at the college that I have gotten to know America. In particular Larry Scott, Professor of Scandinavian, Thomas Tredway, Professor of History and President of the College, and Michael Nolan, Assistant Professor of English have been constant sources of discussions, support, and friendship and have taught me to understand much about both Swedish-American and American life and history, without whose insights this study would have been poorer. Michael Nolan and Larry Scott have also read the entire manuscript and commented on its content and language during its final stages, for which I thank them especially. At Augustana, I would also like to recognize my colleagues and friends at the Swenson Swedish Immigration Research Center, Christina Johansson, Vicky Oliver, and Jill Seaholm, as well as Kermit Westerberg, presently of New Haven. Elsewhere in the United States, Professor H. Arnold Barton of Southern Illinois University has generously read and commented on my work with great insight for many years, Professor Rudolph Vecoli of the Immigration History Research Center at the University of Minnesota received me on two prolonged occasions as a guest researcher, and Professor Philip Anderson of North Park College in Chicago has been helpful for my thinking about Swedish-American religion.

In addition, I would like to recognize the following persons who have been of great importance, both privately and professionally: Tania and Herman Blanck, Stockholm, Åsa Blanck, Amsterdam, Monica Blom, Uppsala, Kathleen Neils Conzen, Chicago, Daniel Culver, Rock Island, Tordis and Urban Dahllöf, Uppsala, Ingrid Edsman, Stockholm, Janina Erlich, Rock Island, Dana Freund, Stockholm, Gunlög Fur, Växjö, Lars Furuland, Uppsala, Nils Hasselmo, Minneapolis, Eric Johannesson, Luleå, Angela and Bruce Karstadt, Minneapolis, Charles Mahaffey, Rock Island, Annika Markesjö, Stockholm, Marie Clark Nelson, Linköping, Per Nordahl, Umeå, Nils William Olsson, Winter Park, Florida, Ann-Sofie Ohlander, Örebro, Jörgen Olsson, Stockholm, John Rogers, Uppsala, Arne Selbyg, Rock Island, Harold Sundelius, Rock Island, Mary and David Swanson, Minneapolis, Maria Södling, Stockholm, Eva Tedenmyr, Stockholm, Mariann Tiblin, Minneapolis, Kate Tredway, Rock Island, Mattias Tydén, Stockholm, Barbara Doyle-Wilch, Rock Island, Henrik Williams, Uppsala, Erik Åsard, Uppsala, and Eva Österberg, Lund.

The following institutions have supported my work financially, which is gratefully acknowledged: American-Scandinavian Foundation, New York, Knut och Alice Wallenbergs Stiftelse, Stockholm, Kungl. Gustav Adolfsakademien, Uppsala, Kungl. Vetenskapsakademien, Stockholm, Lars Johan Hiertas Minnesfond, Stockholm, Sverige-Amerika Stiftelsen, Stockholm, and Uppsala University. I also extend my recognition to the following archives and libraries where I have received professional and courteous help: The Swedish Emigrant Institute, Växjö, the Royal Library, Stockholm, and the Uppsala University Library, all in Sweden and the Augsburg-Fortress Publishing House, Minneapolis, Minnesota, the Augustana College Library and its Special Collections, Rock Island, Illinois, the Minnesota Historical Society, St. Paul, Minnesota, the Swenson Swedish Immigration Research Center, Rock Island, Illinois, the University of Minnesota Library, Minneapolis, Minnesota, and the Evangelical Lutheran Church in America, Chicago, Illinois, all in the Unites States.

Finally, a very special recognition goes to my wife Agneta Emanuelsson Blanck, whose help, comments and insights, especially during the final hectic year, have been of the greatest importance to me.

It should lastly be noted that all the translations from Swedish are my own, and that throughout the text "America" will be used interchangeably with "the United States."

June 1997
Dag Blanck

Chapter One

Introduction

Between 1850 and 1930, some 1.3 million Swedes emigrated to North America, primarily to the United States. This movement of Swedes across the Atlantic was a part of a general mass migration from Europe to the United States that came to include some 33 million persons between 1820 and 1930. In absolute numbers the Swedes were one of the smaller groups among the European immigrants to America, dwarfed by other groups such as the Germans, the Italians, the Irish, and the British. If the number of emigrants is put in relationship to the size of the population of the sending country, however, the Swedes, together with the British, are in third place. Only Ireland and Norway sent more emigrants relative to the countries' population to North America.

The effects of the emigration were felt on every level of Swedish society. The thousands of personal contacts and ties established across the Atlantic are but one example. In addition, emigration became a pressing issue in Swedish political debate, as the political and economic leaders of the country suddenly realized that people were leaving by the hundreds of thousands. A virtual "America fever" swept across Sweden, and even though the cities had the greatest emigration frequency in relation to their population, the greatest number of emigrants came from the rural areas.

The initial Swedish settlements were in the Midwest, and like Vilhelm Moberg's Karl Oskar and Kristina many became farmers. By the turn of the century, however, the majority of the Swedish immigrants lived and worked in the rapidly growing American urban areas, including substantial numbers on the East and West Coasts. By 1910 a Swedish-American middle class was also taking shape, consisting of teachers, lawyers, physicians, and other professional groups, as well as merchants and shopkeepers. By this time, too, a significant group of American-born, second-generation Swedish Americans had come onto the scene.

Soon after the arrival of large numbers of Swedish immigrants, a Swedish-American community developed, helping the immigrants and their children to meet their various needs in the new country, to adjust to American society, and yet also to keep a sense of distinctiveness in the new multi-ethnic environment. By the turn of the century, the term "Swedish America" had been coined to describe this Swedish presence in the United States.[1] Swedish America consisted of many different groups, reflecting the social diversity of the community and addressing the community's varying needs.

One central issue facing the newcomers dealt with the question of their identity in the new land. Who were they? Were they Swedes or Americans? Or were they perhaps, a combination of both? Was it possible to be Swedish in America, and if so, what did this mean? This study seeks to answer these questions and others of a similar nature. In particular, the construction of a Swedish-American ethnic identity will be discussed: the way in which this identity was established, what it consisted of, and why it came into being.

The answers to these questions will be provided by examining the Augustana Synod, a Lutheran denomination founded by a group of ministers from the Church of Sweden in 1860 and which became the largest organization founded by Swedish immigrants in the United States. The Augustana Synod developed into an institution serving both religious and other needs of Swedish immigrants and their children, and by the turn of the century it encompassed well over a thousand congregations across the entire North American continent, colleges, a seminary, academies, newspapers, magazines, a publishing house, bookstores, children's homes, hospitals, and old people's homes.

Although religion obviously was a fundamental aspect of the Synod's life, concerns for a sense of Swedishness in America were also visible, and in 1901 one pastor declared that if the Augustana Synod had not existed, "Swedish culture and education [in America] would have been virtually dead,"[2] suggesting that the Synod played an important role in maintaining a Swedish distinctiveness in America. Because Swedish America was such a diverse community, consisting of a great number of different, and at times competing, factions. It is possible to speak of a cultural struggle within the Swedish-American community, where Augustana's answer to the question of what it meant to be Swedish in America was one of many, albeit the dominant one.

Swedish immigrants in the United States were not alone in struggling with these kinds of questions. Nationalism and nation-building were important processes both throughout Europe and in the United States in the nineteenth century, and the construction of national and ethnic identities was thus of significance in both the country the emigrants left and the one in which they settled. The emergence of a Swedish-American identity should thus also be seen in this larger context, and by focusing on a fairly small and well defined Swedish-American community, it will also be possible to contribute to the general discussion of the nature of both national and ethnic identities.

---

[1] Beijbom 1980, 257.

[2] "Om Augustana-synoden icke hade varit, vad hade då svenskarna i Amerika varit?" *Augustana*, 12 June 1902.

Previous Research

The historiography of Swedish immigration to North America has a long tradition and a large body of literature, of which Arnold Barton has observed that the Swedes in North America have "one of the richest historical literatures that exists for any migrant group."[3] As a number of good historiographical overviews already exist, this section does not seek to provide a comprehensive account of this body of literature. Rather, it will first sketch some general patterns of Swedish-American historical scholarship and then will discuss the existing work on Swedish-American identity. This will be followed by a more detailed discussion of some important concepts dealing with ethnicity and ethnic identity, that form the theoretical starting point for this study. The literature on ethnicity and ethnic identity is extensive and inter-disciplinary, including practitioners from such varied fields as anthropology, sociology, ethnology, and history. The concept of ethnicity has been defined in a number of different ways,[4] yet it remains in the words of one student "an enduring enigma."[5] Some aspects of this discussion that are relevant and that form the starting points for this study will be presented here. The intention is not to develop new theoretical constructs about ethnicity: that discourse is already suggestive enough.[6] Instead, a number of the central concepts in this study will be clarified and discussed, sharpening and making the explanatory tools more precise. Finally, a more detailed presentation of the questions to be addressed will be given.

Swedish Migration to and Settlements in America.
A Brief Overview

The first historical accounts of Swedish America were written by and for members of the Swedish-American community itself, often highly celebratory and with little critical perspective.[7] Many are chronical accounts of various Swedish settlements throughout the U.S.; histories of congregations, denominations, organizations, or clubs; or accounts of contributions by Swedish immigrants to American life.[8] Today they are chiefly valuable as primary

---

[3] Barton 1978, 3.
[4] Cf. Isajiw 1974.
[5] Kivisto 1989, 11.
[6] Cf. Malcolm Chapman, Mary McDonald & Elizabeth Tonkin who state that "[ethnicity] is ... a term that invites endless and fruitless definitional argument among those professional intellectuals who think that they know, or ought to know, what it means." (Chapman, McDonald & Tonkin 1989, 11).
[7] Barton 1978, Beijbom 1980.
[8] Selected examples include Grönberger 1879, Johnson & Peterson 1880, Norelius 1891 & 1916, Nilsson & Knutson 1898, Peterson 1898, Olson, Schön & Engberg 1908, Severin 1919, Skarstedt 1917.

sources, and the term "filio-pietistic" is often used to describe these works.[9]

The academic study of the Swedish migration to America began in earnest during the first decades of the twentieth century, and up until approximately 1960 a small group of scholars on both sides of the Atlantic were active from disciplines such as history, geography, religion, and ethnology.[10] Noticeable contributions were made by George Stephenson, whose magisterial examination of the growth of the Swedish religious communities in the U.S., *The Religious Aspects of Swedish Immigration*[11] from 1932 remains a landmark study in the field. Other contributions from this phase come from historians such as Fritiof Ander, Emory Lindquist, and Conrad Bergendoff, and deal with the history of different Swedish-American individuals, institutions, and settlements.[12] The establishment of the Swedish Pioneer Historical Society in 1950 and its journal *Swedish Pioneer Historical Quarterly* (today *Swedish-American Historical Quarterly*) were also important developments in the field in the U.S.

The Swedish academic community was only marginally interested in the emigration and Swedish America during this early phase. Still, as official Sweden began to perceive the sustained emigration as a major societal problem by the beginning of the twentieth century, a Royal Commission of Inquiries (Emigrationsutredningen) under the leadership of the statistician Gustav Sundbärg was established in 1907.[13] Emigrationsutredningen was primarily concerned with the reasons behind the emigration, and the major part of its massive 21-volume report include an exhaustive analysis of the economic conditions in Swedish society, especially those in the rural sector that, in the Commission's opinion, had resulted in the mass emigration. A minor part of the Report was also devoted to the conditions of the emigrants in America. Additional work was also done by the church historian Gunnar Westin and the geographer Helge Nelson, dealing with Swedish-American religious conditions and settlement patterns, respectively.[14]

With the increased interest in social history after 1960, the volume of scholarship increased significantly. Attention was now directed to previously "hidden" people and groups in society, such as African-Americans, women, and workers. Immigrants were also studied, and "immigration history" experienced a tremendous upswing in the U.S. in the decades after 1960. In a bibliography of American dissertations dealing with immigration and ethnic life in

[9] Cf. Saveth 1948, chapter 8.

[10] For more detailed and systematic overviews of academic research on Swedish migration to North America see Barton 1978, Ostergren 1986, Norman & Runblom 1988b, Anderson & Blanck 1991b, and Blanck 1996.

[11] Stephenson 1932.

[12] Ander 1931, Lindquist 1953, Bergendoff 1969.

[13] For the background to Emigrationsutredningen, see Kälvemark 1971.

[14] Westin 1932, Nelson 1943.

the U.S. between 1885 and 1983, almost 80 per cent of the titles were written after 1960, and the 1970s stand out as a particularly productive decade, with more than half of these dissertations being published between 1960 and 1970.[15]

For the first time, Swedish historians entered the field in earnest, following Frank Thistlethwaite's 1960 challenge to European historians not to leave the history of the European trans-Atlantic migration solely to American historians,[16] and there was a new, systematic interest in the homeland for the history of emigration. Much of the work was centered around the so-called Uppsala project that yielded a great number of studies, but work was also done elsewhere in Sweden, in the other Nordic countries, and in the U.S. In accord with the general tendency of social history, much of the focus of this work was quantitative in nature. Questions that were studied included the demographic, economic, and social aspects of the migration process both in Sweden and the United States and the internal structure and development of the Swedish immigrant community. Issues such as who emigrated, how many they were, from where they came and why, where they settled, and social and economic circumstances in the New World stood out as particularly important. Some attention was also given to the patterns of return migration.[17]

From the mid-1970s, emphasis has shifted towards more qualitative aspects of the history of the Swedish immigrant and ethnic group in the U.S.[18] The previous interest in quantification, social structure, and social mobility has now been replaced with a concern for such issues as cultural and linguistic persistence, organizational and religious life, literary and artistic activities, politically radical Swedes, and the role of women. Efforts have also been made to integrate the history of the Swedish ethnic group in the United States with that of general American ethnic history. Some comparative work has also been attempted, especially concerning the Swedish immigrant urban experience. In addition, the way in which Swedes and Swedish Americans viewed each other has been discussed.[19] For the first time, for example, the creative literary output among Swedish Americans has been systematically analysed from the perspective of the sociology of literature and been placed in the con-

[15] Hoglund 1986.

[16] Thistlethwaite 1960, 32–60.

[17] Examples of Swedish work from the period include Beijbom 1971, Lindmark 1971, Ljungmark 1971, Norman 1974, and Tedebrand 1972. The Uppsala project is summarized in Runblom & Norman 1976. Cf. also Nordstrom 1978, Rice 1978, and Ostergren 1988 for work done in the U.S.

[18] For some assessments of the situation after 1976 see Runblom & Tedebrand 1979, and Beijbom 1983.

[19] Some examples of this new emphasis are individual contributions in the following edited volumes: Anderson & Blanck 1991a, Beijbom 1993, Blanck & Runblom 1991, and Lovoll 1985 & 1993. See also Barton 1994, Beijbom 1986, Beijbom 1990a, Estus & McClymer 1994, Hasselmo 1974, Hasselmo 1978, Nordahl 1994, Scott 1991.

text of literary traditions, reading habits, and canon building in different social spheres in Sweden and Swedish America during the late nineteenth century.[20]

A Swedish-American Identity

In this extensive body of scholarly literature, the specific question of Swedish-American identity has received relatively little attention. It is not until recent years that the question has been more specifically discussed, and then often in the context of Swedish-American culture. The analyses of Swedish-American cultural life have shown how, while obviously being very much rooted in cultural traditions from Sweden, it was also shaped by the American context in which it existed. Swedish-American cultural patterns thus exhibit a duality, and it is possible to speak of an identity drawing on cultural elements from both Sweden and the United States, while at the same time maintaining a distance from both.[21] Birgitta Svensson, Gunnar Thander, and Anna Williams also explicitly deal with the formation and contents of a Swedish-American identity in their respective analyses of a Swedish-American literature.[22]

The question of what it meant to be Swedish-American in different contexts is one leading theme in several works by Arnold Barton,[23] and Ulf Beijbom has discussed different aspects of the content and development what he calls the "Swedish-Americanism" or "Swedish ethnicity," as well as comparing them to Swedish ethnicity in Australia.[24] Nils Hasselmo also raises the question of a Swedish-American identity in conjunction with his studies of the Swedish language in America,[25] and the Swedish-American identity has also been dealt with in the contexts of religion, political radicalism, education, and art in Swedish America.[26] The specific nature of the Swedish-American identity in the Augustana Synod, finally, has been discussed by Conrad Bergendoff, Birgitta Svensson, and myself.[27]

---

[20] Furuland 1991a, Johannesson 1991b, Svensson 1994, Thander 1996, Williams 1991, Wendelius, 1990. See also the special issue of *Swedish-American Historical Quarterly*, 43 (July 1992) on literary and cultural life in Swedish America.

[21] Williams 1991, 212–14, Barton 1992, 5–18.

[22] Svensson 1994, Thander 1996, Williams 1991.

[23] Barton 1984, Barton 1994.

[24] Beijbom 1990a, chapter 6, Beijbom 1988.

[25] Hasselmo 1974.

[26] Erickson 1996, Nordahl 1994, Anderson et al. 1995, Swanson 1996.

[27] Bergendoff 1968, Svensson 1994, esp. chapters 3, 5 and 8, Blanck 1982, 1989, 1993.

Theoretical Points of Departure

Ethnicity, Ethnic Identity, and Ethnic Groups

All humans have multiple social identities. Each such identity helps define who we are, varying both in different social contexts and in degree and significance. Ethnic identity is one of these. At one level ethnic and other identities are deeply personal and a part of an individual's psyche. In the present study, however, the focus is on the collective level of the ethnic group. One general definition states that an ethnic group "is a segment of a larger society whose members are thought, by themselves or others, to have a common origin and to share important segments of a common culture, and who in addition, participate in shared activities in which the common culture and origin are significant ingredients."[28]

In the extensive discussion of ethnicity in America, some scholars have emphasized the primeval and enduring nature of ethnicity and ethnic identity, arguing that it is something so deeply rooted in human nature that it remains static and unchangeable.[29] Others, however, have underscored its changing nature and content, and have emphasized how ethnicity has been used in different ways, depending on the context, describing ethnic groups as "interest groups" mobilizing to achieve certain goals.[30] One should not, however, exaggerate the dichotomy between the primordial and situational approaches. Some aspects of ethnic identity seem more difficult to shed than others and obviously are more important to an individual's conception of self.[31] For example, the maintenance of one's language seems to have been a more important component in the American ethnic identities than, say, the eating of certain foods. The primordial approach also seems to be more relevant for discussions of individual identities, and as the focus of this study is on collective representations, the situational perspective on ethnicity will form a basic starting point.

James McKay and Frank Lewins distinguish between ethnic categories and ethnic groups, a conceptualization which also points to how ethnicity can vary in significance.[32] Ethnic categories are groups of people who share certain characteristics. Examples of such characteristics include religion, race, language, and national origin. According to these authors, these ethnic characteristics are but a few of, and no more meaningful than, many other cultural, social, and physical traits that group members exhibit. Instead, McKay and

---

[28] Yinger 1994, 3.

[29] Isaacs 1975 is one example of this view.

[30] Conzen et al. 1992, 4. For further elaborations of this discussion and extensive bibliographical references, see Lange & Westin 1981, 243. See also Patterson 1975, Yancey et al. 1976, and Fischer 1986.

[31] Cf. Smith 1984a, 283–305.

[32] The following section is based on McKay & Lewins 1978, 413–22.

Lewins maintain that it is the degree of what they call ethnic identification that is significant for membership in the ethnic group.[33] When a certain number of people "meaningfully interact" on the basis of shared ethnic characteristics, then a consciousness of kind and a sense of belonging develops, or, in the terminology of McKay and Lewins, an ethnic group.

Anthony Smith also distinguishes between ethnic categories and communities.[34] The population making up ethnic categories only has a "dim consciousness that they form a separate collectivity" because it lacks "a myth of common origins, shared historical memories, a sense of solidarity or an association with a designated homeland." Ethnic communities, on the other hand, are characterized exactly by the presence of these attributes, even though these convictions may only be held by a segment of the population and even if some of the attributes "are more intense and salient than others at a given period."

The strength of the ethnic community is related to the degree to which the population shares these attributes. The degree of ethnic identification that individuals exhibit can thus vary, from weak identifications to more fully developed ethnic identities, and although the strength of ethnicity in part depends on the criteria used, it is clear that a range of degrees of identifications exists, all the way from a full to a minimal ethnic identity.[35]

It is important to underscore that this study focuses on the institutional rather than the individual level and is concerned with a collective self-representation, concentrating on one segment of a population associated with a particular organization—the Augustana Synod—and assuming some sense of ethnic identification among its members. We are thus dealing with what we could call an "ethnic institution" and its role for the creation of a Swedish-American ethnic identity. The part played by ethnic institutions in the establishment of ethnic communities was recognized early in American immigration history research, and was strongly emphasized in one of the very first studies of ethnic life in the U.S., *The Polish Peasant in Europe and America* (1918–1920).[36] This emphasis has continued ever since.[37]

The role of ethnic institutions for ethnic identity has also been discussed by Raymond Breton, who has advanced the concept of "institutional completeness."[38] He argues that there is a relationship between the degree of ethnic identity expressed and the number of institutions, both formal and informal, that exist within the ethnic community to serve the different needs of its mem-

[33] This point is also made forcefully by Fishman & Nahirny 1965.
[34] For the following, see Smith 1991, 20–21.
[35] Yinger 1994, 3–5.
[36] Thomas & Znaniecki 1985, 239–55.
[37] See, e.g., Bodnar 1985, 120–30 for an overview of the role of ethnic fraternal organizations.
[38] Breton 1964.

bers. The more "institutionally complete" the community is, Breton states, the stronger the sense of ethnic identity can be expected to be, and Edward Kantowicz has suggested that the Polish Americans in Chicago are one example of an institutionally complete American ethnic community.[39] A parallel situation can be found among Germans in Milwaukee, while the Irish in the same city did not create a sufficient number of institutions to develop an ethnic community, and instead tended to identify themselves along class lines.[40]

Thus it can be said that the more needs that the Augustana Synod could fulfill for its members, the stronger the identification of Swedish Americans would be with the identity that Augustana represented. Becoming a member in one of the various congregations, attending an Augustana Synod school, or reading an Augustana Synod publication might be indicators of a high degree of identification with Augustana's ethnicity. Still, as the ethnic element was only one dimension of the activities of the Augustana Synod, it is difficult to determine exactly the degree to which Swedish Americans have identified with the Augustana version of what it meant to be Swedish in America. There may of course have been other reasons than Augustana's Swedish profile for joining one of its churches or attending one of its schools. This observation means that, although this study argues that the Augustana Swedishness was the dominant in the struggle for defining a Swedish-American ethnic identity, it is the construction, contents, and maintenance of this ethnic identity that will be in focus, not the exact degree to and manner in which it was spread throughout and received in Swedish America.

The close link between religion and ethnicity has long been recognized, and Milton Yinger has, for example, called attention to the "close and...natural affinity between ethnicity and religion."[41] Several studies of American immigrant and ethnic groups have also shown the central role that religion has played for the development and shape of ethnicity in the United States, something also noted by Martin Marty who has called religion "the skeleton of ethnicity in America."[42]

As will be shown, the maintenance of a particular form of Lutheranism was a paramount reason for the establishment of the Augustana Synod. Still, as the denomination's religious roots were found in Sweden and as the vast majority of the membership were either Swedish-born or descendants of Swedish immigrants, ethnicity also shaped the Synod's life in important ways. The relationship between religion and ethnicity varied over time, and it will be one of the questions that will be addressed in this study.

---

[39] Kantowicz 1977, 184.
[40] Conzen 1976, 225–28.
[41] Yinger 1994, 255.
[42] Marty 1972. See also Abramson 1980 and Smith 1978.

The Invention of Ethnicity

The nature of ethnic identities has been the subject of extensive scholarly discussion in American immigration history. Oscar Handlin's *The Uprooted* is the classic statement of a position which argues that the immigrants severed their cultural and social ties with the Old Country and that the new, often urban, American environment shaped the immigrants' lives and behavior in the United States.[43] The rise of the "new social history" and "the ethnic revival" in the 1960s saw a break with this view, and many studies concluded that instead of being uprooted, the immigrant groups experienced a cultural continuity in the U.S. The first formulation of this view was Rudolph Vecoli's article *"Contadini* in Chicago: A Critique of *The Uprooted"* which showed how south Italian peasants in Chicago resisted assimilation and Americanization and instead maintained their traditional behavior and value systems.[44]

A further development of this discussion has suggested that the ethnic identities and cultures in America depended on a combination of both Old and New World contexts and that new cultural forms were created in the immigrant and ethnic communities in the United States, specific to the groups' needs there. As David Gerber has put it: "Immigrants cannot be said to possess some primordial consciousness of themselves as members of an ethnic group. Nor can it be said that a feeling of ethnic identity arises suddenly, *ex nihilo*, upon emigration." Rather, "the immigrants' internal understanding of possessing a group identity comes as a result of existential fusing of its Old World cultural inheritance (language, religion, values, beliefs and expressive symbols) and New World experiences."[45] Ethnicity is thus seen as changing or "emerging,"[46] a process that several scholars also have labelled "ethnicization."[47]

This emphasis on the novelty of ethnic cultures, on ethnicization, or invention, can also be traced to discussions of the invention of ethnicity, which originated with the publication of Werner Sollors' *Beyond Ethnicity* and *The Invention of Ethnicity*, in which ethnicity is seen as invented or culturally constructed.[48] The best application of Sollors' ideas on American immigration history comes from a group of American immigration historians, including Kathleen Conzen and Rudolph Vecoli. They maintain that the invention of ethnicity is a useful explanatory term, but that it needs to be placed in an historical context, and they do so by pointing to various historical factors that

---

[43] Handlin 1951.
[44] Vecoli 1964.
[45] Gerber 1989, 118.
[46] Yancey et al., 1976.
[47] Greene 1975, 3–5, Sarna 1978.
[48] Sollors 1986, Sollors 1989.

affect the development of an invented ethnicity. They see ethnicity as developing in a continuous relationship with American society and conclude that it is "a process of construction or invention which incorporates, adapts, and amplifies preexisting communal solidarities, cultural attributes, and historical memories. That is, it is grounded in real life context and social experience."[49]

Consequently, Conzen and her colleagues also speak of struggles for cultural hegemony within ethnic groups, as different factions of the groups try to establish control over the contents of ethnicity.[50] Raymond Breton makes a similar point when he suggests that the "symbolic order" created within an ethnic community is best seen as a "negotiated order" or the "outcome of struggles and accommodations among contradictory cultural-symbolic interests."[51]

The Creation of National Identities

As noted in the introduction, processes of nation-building were important in nineteenth-century Europe. Proceeding at different speeds and in greatly varying social, political, and cultural contexts, nations and national identities were being formed.[52] There are many parallels between the construction of ethnic identities and national identities,[53] and the concept of inventing an ethnic identity can also be found with regard to national identities. In 1983 Eric Hobsbawm advanced his now well-known term "invention of tradition," pointing to the novelty and creation of a number of traditions and customs of seemingly much older date. Hobsbawm also suggests that these inventions occur when rapid societal change "weakens or destroys the social patterns for which 'old' traditions had been designed."[54] Hobsbawm's concept of "invented traditions" shows great similarities with the ethnic identities of American immigrant groups, emerging when the old social patterns no longer were available and functioning as a unifying ideology for the group.

Nineteenth-century Sweden also experienced nation-building. As Torkel Jansson has suggested, the nature of the Swedish "nation" was discussed during the first half of the nineteenth century, often couched in the language of political liberalism and only affecting a small group of the population. Towards the end of the century, Swedish nationalism was expressed in conserva-

---

[49] Conzen et al. 1992, 5.

[50] Conzen et al. 1992, 16.

[51] Breton 1992, 13–14.

[52] Cf. Hroch 1985 and Hobsbawm 1990.

[53] Yinger 1994, 10–16. Yinger also makes the point that there is extensive "overlap" in their meanings and usage (13), and that a "substantial literature nearly equates nation and ethnic group." (12). Cf. also Smith 1992.

[54] Hobsbawm 1983, 1–4. Quotation from p. 4.

tive and patriotic terms, largely due to the increased strength for Swedish conservatives as a result of the break-up of the union with Norway.[55] The establishment of a compulsory elementary school was of great importance in this process, and, as Lars Furuland has shown, the reader *Läsebok för folkskolan*, which was widely used in Swedish elementary schools, was very significant in installing a sense of national feeling among large strata of the Swedish population, as a "patriotic canon of persons and events" was created.[56]

The 1890s are often seen as a high period for a conservative kind of nationalism, during which period a national romanticism was advanced, in which selected parts of the Swedish culture and past played an important role. Attention was, for example, given to Swedish folk and local culture, to which the establishment of the two ethnographic and folk life museums Nordiska Museet and Skansen in Stockholm are two examples.[57]

The question of to what degree the Swedish emigrants were affected by these attempts to create a Swedish national feeling is, of course, difficult to answer. We know relatively little about the growth of the Swedish national feeling in the nineteenth century, but it was a complex phenomenon, affecting, for example, social strata of the Swedish population differently. Because the course of the emigration ran during a significant part of the nineteenth and early twentieth centuries, there is clearly a temporal dimension to be considered, suggesting that those emigrants who left after the turn of the century must have been much more exposed to the Swedish national feeling than those who left during the decades after the mid-nineteenth century.

Thus, it can be assumed that the sense of Swedish nationality was fairly weakly developed among those Swedes who arrived in America, especially during the first several decades of emigration. The identity that these immigrants brought with them instead seems to have been much more regional or local in nature, and it was in the U.S. that a sense of national identity emerged, something which also was a general phenomenon among European immigrant groups in nineteenth and early twentieth-century America.[58] Two leading Swedish-American journalists and observers of Swedish America also made this point. In 1898 C.F. Peterson claimed in Sweden the immigrants had been more or less provincial, "an *östgöte, västgöte, smålänning* or *skåning* first, then a Swede," whereas in America, he continued, one becomes "first of all a Swede."[59] Fourteen years later Johan Person wrote that when most of his fellow Swedish Americans had left their homeland, it was hardly possible to

---

[55] Jansson 1985, 65–71, Jansson 1990, 344, Jansson 1994, 32–33.
[56] Furuland 1991b, 72.
[57] Björck 1946, 38–69, Elvander 1961, 341–50, 419–24. Cf. also various contributions in Medelius & Rentzhog 1991.
[58] Connor 1990, 93–95. Cf. also Glazer 1954, 160–70.
[59] Peterson 1898, 448.

speak of a "Sweden," except as a political and geographic entity,[60] as the country was divided in as many "nations" as its twenty-four provinces. In America, however, these provincial loyalties had been overcome, and "[D]uring the eight days of the Atlantic crossing," Person writes, "the foundations were laid for the making of a Swedish-American people, which thus separates them from the Swedes in Sweden, who consist of at least twenty-four."[61]

The growth of a national identity in the United States proceeded from a different set of assumptions than in Sweden or Europe. It has been argued that the United States was the "first new nation,"[62] meaning that it was the first major European colony to successfully break away from colonial rule and establish itself as a "new nation." In the case of the United States, this new nation was founded on a set of abstract political and philosophical ideas, codified in such central documents as the Declaration of Independence and the Constitution, and the U.S. was thus what Wilbur Zelinsky has called an "ideological construct," making it different from other "old" nations in that it lacked "strong historical or territorial traditions" or common "cultural bonds" such as a common religion or language.[63] Except for the vague sense of "the New World," America was not, as Sacvan Berovitch has put it, "a territorial definition" but "the symbol of ideological consensus."[64] Moreover, as Nathan Glazer has recently argued, there is an "avoidance" of "specific ethnic references" in the "founding documents" and in the debates on the American revolution, as the framers of the Constitution "did not define their Americanness as an ethnic characteristic," but rather emphasizing its universality.[65] To be sure, a sense of national identity also increased in the United States after 1776, replete with national symbols, heroes, and celebrations, a process which seems to have become especially marked during the second half of the nineteenth century.[66] Still, most of these ingredients were rooted in the political dimension of American nationality, which at times has also been referred to as American civic culture or civil religion.[67]

For immigrants coming to the United States, this "ideological quality" of American nationalism became, in Philip Gleason's words, "of decisive importance." Becoming American did not require a particular national, linguistic, religious, or ethnic background, but, Gleason has argued, was a matter of

---

[60] Person 1912, 114–15.
[61] Person 1912, 116.
[62] Lipset 1963.
[63] Zelinsky 1988, 17, 223.
[64] Bercovitch 1978, 161.
[65] Glazer 1997, 99.
[66] Zelinsky 1988 chapters 2 and 3, Kammen 1991, chapter 5. Cf. also Karsten 1978, chapter 5, who traces the emergence of what he calls American "patriot-heroes".
[67] Fuchs 1990, 4–5, Zelinsky 1988, 232–45.

committing to the abstract political ideals of liberty, equality, and republican-ism. The universalist and ideological character of American nationalism meant "that it was open to anyone who willed to become an American."[68]

Still, the American nationality was not open to all groups, as some Ameri-cans, such as the African Americans, had been brought to the country as slaves, or, in the case of the Native Americans, had been subdued by European settlers. Lawrence Fuchs makes this point in his discussion of the role of American nationality for the formation of ethnic identities in the United States, in advancing the concept of "voluntary pluralism." According to Fuchs, as long as European immigrants, who had voluntarily migrated to the U.S. em-braced the political dimension of American nationalism, they could maintain and promote their own cultures and religion. They were, in Fuchs' words, "free ... to choose to be ethnic" if they so wished, a choice which was "sanc-tioned and protected" by American "civic culture."[69] According to this interpretation, which has also been advanced in slightly different terms by Nils Hasselmo,[70] it was thus not only possible for European immigrant groups to maintain their own cultural traits, but the persistence of ethnic identities was, in fact, a central ingredient of American nationalism itself. In this way, Euro-pean immigrant groups were able to combine a pride in their separate antece-dents, while at the same time claiming a stake in the political American civil culture.

According to Fuchs, voluntary pluralism only applied to European immi-grants. Non-European groups, such as African Americans, Native Americans, and Mexicans who had not been given a choice of belonging to the new American nation, were instead subjected to "coercive pluralism." This policy kept them outside the American polity, making it impossible to develop their own cultural patterns within the larger framework of American nationalism, and thus denying them the rights that the European immigrants had.[71]

The Role of Generational Change and the Significance of History

The role of different generations has attracted much attention in the discussion of the changing nature of ethnic identity among American ethnic groups. One early and influential formulation is Marcus Lee Hansen's "third-generation hypothesis," which states that "what the son wishes to forget, the grand-son wishes to remember," and maintains that the American-born children of the immigrant generation showed little interest in maintaining an ethnic identity

[68] Gleason 1980, 32.
[69] Fuchs 1990, 5.
[70] Hasselmo 1974, 38–39.
[71] Fuchs 1990, 77–79.

and that a concern for ethnic maintenance can instead be found in the third generation, the immigrants' grand-children.[72] This thesis has been challenged and discussed throughout the years, and if taken literally can be proven incorrect.[73]

What is finally significant in Hansen's argument, however, is the notion of the dynamic nature of ethnicity, its capacity to wax and wane and assume different characteristics and serve different purposes at different points in time and in different historical contexts. This important point is also made by sociologists Joshua Fishman and Vladimir Nahirny who point to the difference in the nature of ethnic identification among different generations of American ethnic groups. They suggest that to those members of the ethnic group who have no experience of the ancestral culture, the ethnic heritage becomes "a usable past" out of which a "transmuted" ethnic ideology emerges, based not on the immediate memories from the old country, but embracing "the intangible values" of the ancestral past.[74] The historical authenticity of idealized versions of the ethnic pasts is not important, and it is instead the way these elements of the past were used to construct the ethnic identity, or ethnic ideology as they also call it, which deserves attention. Fishman and Nahirny also underscore that the issue of in which generation this change occurs is not of central importance, pointing instead to the "elective affinity" which results in the "transmuted past."[75]

The significance that Fishman and Nahirny and others attach to the role of history for the content of these ethnic identities is worth noting. Anthony Smith has underscored that one of the defining characteristics of an ethnic group is "the role of myths of descent and historical memories" and that "historical memories [are] essential to their continuance," while Abner Cohen has observed that as ethnic groups construct culture, "the past is a resource used by groups in the collective quest for meaning and community."[76] Other scholars have also emphasized the role played by a sense of a common history and culture in the creation of national identities both in Europe and the United States.[77]

Seen from this perspective, a sense of history is an active ingredient in the formation of an ethnic identity and is one which is used for specific purposes. In the introduction to a volume on history and ethnicity, a group of British

[72] Hansen 1938, 9.

[73] See Kivisto & Blanck 1990, for an assessment of Hansen and further discussions of the roles of generations in American immigrant history. Attempts to "test" the Hansen hypothesis include Appel 1961, and Lazowitz & Rowitz 1964.

[74] Fishman & Nahirny 1965, 321.

[75] Fishman & Nahirny 1966, 350.

[76] Smith 1991, 20, Cohen 1985, 99.

[77] For a recent discussion of Europe, see Hobsbawm 1990, esp. chapters 2 and 4, for the U.S. see Appleby, Hunt & Jacob 1994, chapter 3. Cf. also Smith 1984b.

social anthropologists also point to the way history is put to use by ethnic groups for their present needs by posing the question "How did the present create the past," rather than the more traditional way of phrasing the problem, namely "How did the past create the present?"[78] The parallel to Hobsbawm's discussion of "invented traditions" is worth noting, as he maintains that a prominent characteristic of "invented traditions" is that "as far as possible" history is used as a "legitimator of action and cement of group cohesion."[79]

The notion of ethnicity as invented or created acknowledges both the Old World heritage as well as the conditions under which the immigrants lived in the New World, by analyzing how an ethnic identity based on the Old World culture was created in the New World. In the present study we are thus talking of the construction of a specifically Swedish-American identity, a process in which American society sets the boundaries and in which selected aspects of a Swedish cultural repertoire are used.

The Cultural Content of Ethnicity and the Role of Ethnic Leaders

In 1969 anthropologist Fredrik Barth advanced the argument that ethnicity is a boundary construction process, delineating cultural lines between groups. This means that, in Barth's words, it is "the ethnic *boundary* that defines the group, not the cultural stuff that it encloses."[80] With regard to American conditions, Werner Sollors has commented that Barth's theory can "easily accommodate the observation that ethnic groups in the United States have relatively little cultural differentiation, that the cultural *content* of ethnicity (the stuff that Barth's boundaries enclose) is largely interchangeable and rarely historically authenticated."[81] Other scholars have also joined in this "relativization" of the significance of the "cultural stuff" for ethnic groups in the United States. Nathan Glazer and Daniel Patrick Moynihan point out that "the cultural *content* of each ethnic group, in the United States, seems to have become very similar to that of others, but that the emotional significance of attachments to the ethnic group seems to persist."[82]

In recent years, however, scholars have shown a new interest in focusing scholarly attention on the "cultural stuff," and less on the boundaries. For example, in her presidential address to the Immigration History Society in 1991, Kathleen Conzen defended studying the "cultural stuff" of ethnic groups, maintaining that in past scholarship it has been the fact of "cultural

---

[78] Chapman, McDonald & Tonkin 1989, 4–5.
[79] Hobsbawm 1983, 12.
[80] Barth 1969, 15.
[81] Sollors 1986, 28.
[82] Glazer & Moynihan 1975, 8.

preservation" rather than the "actual contours of a particular culture" that has been studied, and that the scholarly concern has been the "demarcation of ethnic boundaries, not defining the core."[83]

Conzen instead advocates a focus on ethnic cultures, but with a different emphasis.[84] In this context "culture" is not viewed as baggage "to be unpacked or packed, uprooted or transplanted," but rather in "the Geertzian sense as the socially produced structures of meaning engendered by and expressed in public behaviors, language, images, institutions." If immigrant and ethnic cultures are seen as "the publicly constructed meanings in and through which that life is lived," she concludes, then the study of these cultures means that we can "begin to explore directly how those meanings are constructed and constantly reconstructed over time."

This latter position, arguing that it is both possible and of scholarly interest to study the "cultural stuff" of immigrant cultures, forms an important starting point for analyzing the development of the Swedish-American ethnic identity among the Augustana Swedish Americans.

One consequence of viewing ethnicity from this perspective is that the ethnic leadership comes into focus. Ethnic leaders played an important role in the creation and invention of a "new" ethnicity that was specific and useful to the groups' experiences in the new land. In the words of John Higham, the American social structure was characterized by "pervasive mobility and ... shifting, multiple allegiances," leaving the ethnic leaders with the task of "focus[ing] the consciousness of an ethnic group and in doing so mak[ing] its identity visible."[85] The ethnic leaders became what Victor Greene has called "agents of their groups' adjustment in America," assigning them the dual roles of preservers of tradition through their efforts to maintain the old country heritage and to promote their people's participation in American life.[86]

For the present study, the role of the ethnic leadership means that attention will be focused on the sometimes self-styled group of Swedish-American intellectuals, authors, journalists, educators, and ministers. They constituted the elite within Swedish America that helped formulate the competing versions of Swedishness that emerged around the turn of the century. This was a small group of persons, and few of them could make a living from their cultural work alone. In her study of the Swedish-American journalist and author Jakob Bonggren, Anna Williams uses the term "literary leader" to describe his role in the Swedish-American community, and Victor Greene has also called attention to the significance of T.N. Hasselquist and Johan Enander, leading

---

[83] Conzen 1991, 10–11.
[84] The following paragraph is based on Conzen 1991, 11–12.
[85] Higham 1980, 642.
[86] Greene 1987, 4–16. Quotation from p. 4.

persons within the Augustana Synod.[87] Attempts to identify the Swedish American canon of writers by the writers themselves is another interesting example of the fact that a self-awareness of belonging to a particular stratum existed among Swedish-American intellectuals.[88] Their work was often unrewarding, and they were frequently met with little understanding among their fellow Swedish Americans.

For example, two of the most ambitious cultural undertakings by the Augustana Synod, the literary calender *Prärieblomman* (The Prairie Flower) and the journal *Ungdomsvännen* (The Friend of Youth), included many of these cultural leaders as contributors and editors. Both publications eventually had to be discontinued due to lack of interest among the audience, and their influence on rank-and-file Swedish Americans is thus hard to determine exactly. Still, Conzen's observation with regard to a similar group of German-American cultural activists—that the discussion that took place in "German-American books and journals of opinion" hardly was representative of the mass of German Americans, the "ethnic rank and file," but that the group was nevertheless influenced by these discussions—seems relevant for the Swedish Americans as well. Moreover, as Conzen concludes, those German Americans who rejected these formulations by the ethnic leader-ship "rejected the only formal ethnic identity Germans in America ever achieved,"[89] a statement which seems equally valid for the Swedish Americans.

A Continuum of Ethnic Identities

Ethnic identities in America have operated on different levels. David Gerber points to two, at times overlapping, levels, where the first is the ways in which "the foundations of the inherited culture of daily life" are maintained, and the second, the "formalistic group activities" through which different institutions seek to establish the group's identity. In a similar vein, Raymond Breton has called attention to ethnic identities both as "spontaneous creations from below" and "consciously created from above."[90] In a discussion of the variety of Swedish-American cultural expressions, Nils Hasselmo distinguishes between the "little" and "great" cultural traditions, the former dealing with the culture of daily life, while the latter is concerned with an elite culture, which Hasselmo also calls an "ideology." [91] Ulf Beijbom, finally, also makes a similar distinction is his discussion of "Swedish-Americanism," in which he contrasts the

---

[87] Williams 1991, 209, Greene 1987, 76–80.
[88] Johannesson 1991.
[89] Conzen 1985, 134.
[90] Gerber 1989, 119, Breton 1992, 13.
[91] Hasselmo 1974, 37–38.

attempts by a Swedish-American cultural leadership to create an elite culture with the everyday ethnicity of the rank-and-file Swedish Americans.[92]

Thus, it is possible to speak of a continuum of ethnic identities, stretching from what can be called an "everyday" level to a "higher," more elite level. The everyday ethnicity from below can be said to include aspects that shape the way people live their daily lives, such expressions as food habits, folk traditions, holiday celebrations, residence patterns, marriage preferences, the friends one keeps and associates with, and so on. These dimensions of ethnicity and ethnic identities are often rooted in the ethnic neighborhoods, with their informal networks providing immigrants with an opportunity to meet their own.

At the other end of the continuum, there is the actively constructed or invented ethnic identity, which to a large degree was formed by, in this case, a Swedish-American cultural leadership, including various opinion shapers, such as pastors, educators, writers, and cultural activists. This ethnicity was intended to be national, transcending the neighborhoods and regionalism of Swedish America. As opposed to the "everyday ethnicity," this Swedish Americanism or Swedish-American identity, as both contemporary leaders and later scholars have called it, emphasized "high culture" focusing on literature, history, the arts, etc., and was promulgated in America through the Swedish-American schools, books, newspapers, and journals, and through public manifestation such as jubilees and celebrations.

It is thus within the tension between these extremes on the continuum that various versions of what it meant to be Swedish in America were created and recreated, and this study will deal with one end of the continuum of ethnic identities, exploring how a "high culture" Swedish-American identity was shaped within the Augustana Synod and focusing on the qualitative expressions of this ethnic institution.

Questions to Be Addressed and Outline of the Study

When the Augustana Synod celebrated its fiftieth anniversary in 1910 a memorial volume was published, reflecting on the history of the denomination. The chapter entitled "The Significance of the Synod's Activities" stated that the Synod had been "of enormous importance for intellectual developments in Swedish America" as a "vanguard for an independent Swedish-American culture."[93] What did it mean when a fiftieth anniversary volume

---

[92] Beijbom 1990a, 146–49, 153–55. Cf. also Posern-Zielinski 1978, 105–25 for an interesting discussion on the relationship between folk culture and Polish-American ethnic identity.

[93] Minnesskrift 1910, 477.

speaks of the Synod's work as a "vanguard" for a "Swedish-American culture?" This question is one aspect of the fundamental problem that this study addresses: first how a Swedish-American ethnic identity was constructed within the Augustana Synod, second what this identity consisted of, and third why it came into being.

As already noted, the nineteenth century was a period of nation-building and nationalism in both Europe and the United States. The construction of an ethnic identity in the Augustana Synod can be seen in the light of this general process, and the ethnic experiences of the Augustana Synod will provide an example of how one well-defined part of an ethnic community of European origin in the United States dealt with the issue of its identity.

The study covers the period from 1860 to 1917, with a special emphasis on the decades around the turn of the century. The Augustana Synod was established in 1860 and the entry of the United States in World War I in 1917 radically changed circumstances for American ethnic groups. A variety of primary sources, both in English and Swedish, will be used. They include official records, such as minutes of the Synod, Augustana College, and the Augustana Book Concern, and the Synod's official organ *Augustana*. In addition college and book catalogs, historical accounts, speeches, newspapers and periodicals, Swedish-language books of different kinds published in America, etc., will be used. Archival material from organizations and private letters from significant individuals will supplement the printed materials.

Based on the discussion on the nature of ethnicity and ethnic identities above, the starting points of this study include a view of a Swedish-American ethnic identity as a cultural construct, and how this "Swedish-Americanism" as it was often called was invented or shaped by an ethnic leadership. This also means that the cultural contents of ethnicity will be central to the analysis and that the focus will be on the Augustana Synod as an ethnic institution and especially its deliberately formulated elite-level ethnicity. The malleable nature of the ethnic identity will be emphasized, with special attention paid to the role of the passing of time and change in generations. The duality of the Swedish-American identity will also be underscored, and particular attention will be paid to the ways in which the new American context shaped the way in which Augustana's ethnic identity was configured, and the process through which selected Swedish cultural elements were transplanted to America and given new meaning in their new circumstances.

Chapter two provides a general overview of the Swedish-American community and places the Augustana Synod in this context. In chapter three, the way in which a Swedish-American identity emerged and what it consisted of at Augustana College, the oldest and largest of the Synod's colleges, will be examined. As the Synod's leading educational institution, the college played a central role in educating the members of the Augustana Synod, and special attention will be devoted to the role and content of Swedish in the college's academic curriculum, and on a number of Swedish-related activities outside of the curriculum, such as student organizations, festivities, etc. The student body at the college will also be analysed, with focus on who the students at Augustana were and the role they played in the Swedish-American community.

Chapter four is devoted to an analysis of the Swedish-language publishing and literary endeavors of the Augustana Synod, and the role they played for the Synod's ethnic identity. As will be shown, a considerable body of Swedish-language reading matter was published in and imported to Swedish America. The chapter will discuss what was read and published both in Swedish America in general and in the Augustana Synod in particular. Schoolbooks and a few publications that specifically addressed the cultural identity of the Swedish Americans will be of special interest in an analysis of how Augustana's publishing activities also contributed to the group's ethnic identity.

The role of history for ethnic identities has already been underscored. In chapter five, the forging and use of a Swedish-American history will be discussed. What did Augustana's view of history consist of? What historical persons and symbols were important? Special emphasis will also be given to how a Swedish-American history was formulated by leading persons in the Augustana Synod. Chapter six, finally, is a conclusion where the results of the study are discussed and placed in a larger perspective.

Chapter Two

The Augustana Synod was the largest Swedish-American organization, and played a significant role in the Swedish-American community, so much so that the well-known Swedish-American journalist and author Vilhelm Berger asked rhetorically in 1933 if it was "possible to imagine a Swedish America without the Augustana Synod?"[1] In this chapter the Augustana Synod and the role it played in Swedish America will be addressed in greater detail. The chapter will also attempt to define the Augustana Synod in relationship to other parts of the Swedish-American community and to Sweden. As a background, the course of Swedish immigration to the United States and the organizational complexity of Swedish America will be discussed.

Swedish Immigration to the United States— Causes and Numbers.

The Swedish mass migration to the United States in the nineteenth and early twentieth centuries was a part of the economic and social transformation that affected both Europe and North America from about 1800. Sharp population growth and the rise of an industrial and capitalist economic system were important factors behind the European overseas migration, which between 1850 and 1950 saw fifty million Europeans settle in non-European areas, the majority in the United States.[2]

The course, composition, and causes of Swedish emigration to the United States have been discussed extensively by many scholars, and it is not my intention to further add to that discourse.[3] Suffice it to say that the mass exodus of often young and healthy men and women during the nineteenth and early twentieth centuries was fundamentally due to the limited outlook and

---

[1] Berger 1933, 8.

[2] Taylor 1971 and Bodnar 1985 provide general overviews of the European trans-Atlantic movement.

[3] Runblom & Norman 1976 and Norman & Runblom 1988a are general overviews of the history of Swedish migration to North America. Both books contain extensive bibliographies.

economic opportunity available in Sweden. A combination of so-called push and pull factors on either side of the Atlantic, as well as the establishment of migratory links are other important factors that more precisely determined the scope and course of the migration patterns. The trans-Atlantic mass exodus must also be considered one of the major dimensions of Swedish history during the last two centuries, with important and long-lasting consequences.

Swedish mass emigration to the U.S. began in earnest in the mid-1840s, when a number of pioneers, often migrating as groups, established an emigration tradition between certain sending areas in Sweden and particular receiving locales in the United States.[4] Examples of colonies founded by these group migrants include settlements in western Illinois, Iowa, central Texas, southern Minnesota, and western Wisconsin.

When the American Civil War broke out, ending the pioneer period of Swedish immigration, the federal Census recorded some 18,000 Swedish-born persons in the U.S.[5] Ten years later, following the first heavy peaks of Swedish immigration in 1868–69, largely due to crop failures in Sweden, the figure was almost five times higher, or 97,332. The rapid increase of Swedish immigration continued. By 1880, the figure had more than doubled to 194,337, and in 1890, following the single decade of the largest Swedish immigration, 478,041 Swedes were living in the U.S. During the 1880s alone, some 330,000 persons left Sweden for the United States, the peak year being 1887 with over 46,000 registered emigrants.

The pace of immigration remained high after 1890. Well over 200,000 Swedes landed in the U.S. during both the 1890s and the first decade of this century. By 1910, the U.S. Census recorded over 665,000 Swedish-born persons in the U.S. Just as the Civil War had restricted the number of foreigners who could enter the U.S., World War I curtailed the number of immigrants during the 1910s. A little fewer than 100,000 Swedes arrived in the U.S. during the 1910s, and by 1920 the number of Swedish-born in the U.S. declined for the first time, and stood at 625,000. The peak year of 1923, when over 26,000 Swedes left for the U.S., represents the end of some eight decades of sustained mass migration from Sweden to the U.S.

As the decades of Swedish immigration to the U.S. progressed, a second generation of Swedish Americans entered the scene. For the present purposes the second generation is defined as persons born in the U.S. to at least one

---

[4] For the following paragraphs on the general course and composition of the migration, see Runblom & Norman 1976, and Norman & Runblom 1988a.

[5] The following figures for the number of Swedes in the U.S. are based on the U.S. Federal Censuses. The 1920 Census contains a useful summary for the years 1850–1920 [Census 1920, vol II, 695 & 897.] The figures for number of Swedes emigrating from Sweden are based on the official Swedish emigration statistics as reported in Barton 1994, 343–45.

Swedish-born parent.[6] The second generation was first recorded by the Census in 1890, and in that year some 250,000 persons in the U.S. were classified as second-generation Swedish Americans. During the next decades, this figured increased quickly. In 1900 the second generation stood at 500,000, and by 1910 the second generation had passed the first and numbered 700,000. In 1920, the figure was 824,000.

The rural and agricultural profile of Swedish immigration of the first decades gradually changed; by the turn of the century, a majority of Swedish Americans were urbanites, and a part of the rapidly growing American industrial economy. This also reflected a development from a migration of families during the first decades of emigration to a movement dominated by single young men and women after the turn of the century.

Return migration was also a part of the Swedish migratory patterns, and approximately one fifth of the emigrants returned to their homeland. Re-migration was especially strong towards the end of the emigration era, and was more common among men, urbanites, and persons active in the American industrial sector.

The Settlements in America

As the result of immigration, the population group in the U.S. of Swedish extraction was thus well over one million during the first decades of the twentieth century.[7] It was not, however, evenly distributed throughout the country. The early phase of Swedish immigration established the Midwestern states as a prime receiving area. The agricultural areas in western Illinois, Iowa, Minnesota, and western Wisconsin formed the nucleus of the first Swedish settlements. Migration chains were quickly established between many places in the Midwest and in Sweden, encouraging and sustaining further movement across the Atlantic.[8] After the Civil War, the Swedish settlements spread farther west to Kansas and Nebraska, and in 1870 almost 75 percent of the Swedish immigrants in the United States were found in Ilinois, Minnesota, Kansas, Wisconsin, and Nebraska. Ten years later 74 percent of the Swedish immigrants still resided in the Midwest.[9]

By 1910, the position of the Midwest as a place of residence for the Swed-

---

[6] This definition is partly a function of the way the Federal Census is organized. The figure thus includes children born to two Swedish parents in the U.S. and those born to only one Swedish-born parent.

[7] This section is based on Nelson 1943, Runblom & Norman 1976, and Norman & Runblom 1988a.

[8] For the role of migration chains, see Norman 1974, Ostergren 1988.

[9] Census 1870, vol I, 342, Census 1880, vol I, 495.

ish immigrants and their children was still strong, but had weakened.[10] 54 percent of the Swedish immigrants and their children now lived in these states, with Minnesota and Illinois dominating. 15 percent lived in the East, where the immigrants were drawn to industrial areas in New England. New York City and Worcester, Massachusetts, were two leading destinations. A sizeable Swedish-American community had also been established on the West Coast, and in 1910 almost 10 percent of all Swedish Americas lived there. There, the states of Washington and California had the largest Swedish-American communities. In Washington, a heavy concentration of Swedish Americans grew up in the Seattle-Tacoma area.

Minnesota became the most Swedish of all states, with the Swedish Americans constituting more than 12 percent of Minnesota's population in 1910. In some areas, such as Chisago or Isanti counties on the Minnesota countryside north and northwest of Minneapolis, Swedish Americas made up close to 70 percent of the population. If Minnesota became the most Swedish state in the union, Chicago was the Swedish-American capital. In 1910, more than 100,000 Swedish Americans resided in Chicago, which meant that about 10 percent of all Swedish Americans lived there. At the turn of the century, Chicago was also the second largest Swedish city in the world; only Stockholm counted more Swedish inhabitants than Chicago.[11]

The Swedish-American Community

The preceding discussion has provided figures from the U.S. censuses about the size of the Swedish immigrant group in the United States from several points of view. However, it does not necessarily follow that the figures also measure the magnitude of the Swedish-American community. The mere fact that a person was born in Sweden or to parents of Swedish descent does not automatically mean that he or she was a member of the Swedish-American ethnic group. It is clear that many Swedish immigrants as well as their children and grandchildren did not associate with or become a part of the Swedish-American community, which, as Sture Lindmark has pointed out, was "a collective description of the cultural and religious heritage which the Swedish immigrants brought with them and perpetuated in America,"[12] primarily through institutions, such as churches, organizations, associations, and clubs which served the varied needs of its members.

One of this study's contentions is that ethnicity and expressions of ethnic

---

[10] For the following paragraphs, see Census 1910, vol I, 834–39, 927–34.
[11] Census 1910, vol II, 998 & 1002; Anderson & Blanck 1991b, 1–2.
[12] Lindmark 1971, 37.

sentiments vary in different historical contexts. Thus, as has already been discussed in chapter one, different individuals can express their ethnicity to different degrees, or as McKay and Lewins have argued, from a rather weak "awareness" to a more developed "consciousness."[13]

The Census figures record the genealogical characteristics of individuals, figures which do not necessarily translate into feelings of either ethnic awareness or consciousness. In this context, the different organizations formed by Swedish immigrants from the middle of the nineteenth century and on will instead be used to gauge the size of the community. By focusing on organizations and their members, we can establish a clearer element of identification with a Swedish-American ethnic organization and interaction with other members on the part of the individual. This, in turn, can be seen as an identification with the ethnic group and its ethnic identity, and will provide an alternative to the census measurements of the Swedish-American community.

Swedish-American Organizations

Swedish immigrants and their descendants founded a great number of organizations, such as churches, associations, clubs, and cultural societies of different kinds in the United States, and together they formed an intricate pattern of institutions that by the turn of the century spanned the entire American continent. It is difficult to establish how many organizations that have existed, and various estimates are offered. In 1898, the journalist C.F. Peterson believed that about 1,000 secular organizations existed in that year, a figure which Ernst Skarstedt, a keen observer of the Swedish-American scene concurred with in 1917.[14] In 1938, it was estimated that about 3,500 Swedish-American organizations had existed up until that time.[15]

The largest organizations were the various religious denominations founded by Swedish immigrants in the United States.[16] These churches had their roots in both the religious experience of the homeland and the United States: the Augustana Synod was founded by ministers from the Church of Sweden, the Mission Covenant had its Swedish parallel in Svenska Missionsförbundet, and the Evangelical Free Church developed from the Covenant Church. Other "American" denominations also attracted Swedish immigrants as members. In some cases, as with the Baptists, Methodists, Adventists, and the Salvation

---

[13] McKay & Lewins 1978, 413–22

[14] Peterson 1898, 412, Skarstedt 1917, 133.

[15] Benson & Hedin 1938, 142.

[16] For general discussions of Swedish-American religion see Stephenson 1932, Olsson 1982, and Granquist 1994. The U.S. Census Bureau's special reports on U.S. churches [Religious Bodies 1906, 1926] provide data about the number of members in the various Swedish-language congregations of the different denominations.

Army, separate Swedish-language conferences were organized as part of the American mother institution, whereas still others, such as the Congregationalists, Mormons, and Presbyterians, organized Swedish-language services in the American congregations with some regularity.

As already noted, the Augustana Synod was by far the single largest Swedish-American organization. In the 1910s it was almost nine times as large as the Mission Covenant Church which came in second place. In 1915, the Augustana Synod had 274,000 members and the Mission Covenant Church about 30,000. The Methodists counted 20,000, and the other denominations all fell below that figure.[17] The total membership in the Swedish-American denominations has been estimated to 365,000 at the end of the immigration era,[18] which means that roughly a quarter of the Swedish Americans of the first and second generations were members of a Swedish-American church at that time. The larger Swedish-American denominations did not only serve the religious needs of their members, but also founded educational and benevolent institutions, such as colleges, academies, hospitals, orphanages, old people's homes, etc.

The secular organizations attracted fewer members. The statistics are not as easily available as for the churches, but the largest organizations included the mutual-aid societies, which began to be established towards the end of the nineteenth century. The largest of them in the 1920s were the Vasa Order (approximately 50,000 members), the Svithiod Order (approximately 15,000 members), the Viking Order (approximately 15,000 members), and the Scandinavian Fraternity of America (approximately 40,000 members), all of which became national organizations with substantial financial resources. In addition there were numerous smaller organizations and clubs scattered throughout Swedish America, with a wide array of undertakings. Some examples include organizations for individuals from a particular province in Sweden, whereas others focused on musical, theatrical, educational, or political activities.[19] A small, but vocal Swedish-American labor movement also developed, mainly in the urban areas.[20] Ulf Beijbom has estimated that at the close of Swedish mass immigration in the mid-1920s, the total membership in the secular organizations, both mutual-aid societies and social clubs, stood at 115,000, which represented not quite ten percent of the first and second generation Swedish Americans.[21]

A very important dimension of the Swedish-American community was the

[17] For these statistics see Referat 1921, Religious Bodies 1926, 1291 and Lindmark 1971, 243.
[18] Beijbom 1990b, 63.
[19] Beijbom 1990b, is the best overview of the history of the secular organizations.
[20] Nordahl 1994, 48–56.
[21] Beijbom 1990b, 63.

Swedish-language press. The beginnings of a Swedish-American press had already been laid in the 1850s, and it has been estimated that between 600 and 1,000 Swedish language newspapers were published. The Swedish-American press was the second largest foreign-language press in the United States. In 1910, for example, the German language press dominated greatly, with an estimated three million plus copies of German language newspapers and periodicals published. In second place came the Swedes with a total of over 650,000 copies.[22]

It can thus be estimated that the Swedish-American organizations counted close to half a million Swedish Americans among their membership ranks in the 1920s, or about a third of all Swedish Americans recorded in the census. Allowing for individuals with membership in several organizations, the actual figure might be somewhat lower. This figure constitutes a much more narrow definition of the Swedish-American community than the Census figures provide, but it provides us with an indication of how many Swedish Americans showed a high enough degree of ethnic identification to join a Swedish-American organization. Using the circulation figures for the Swedish-American press in 1910, we find that the circulation statistics correspond to close to half of the first and second generation Swedish Americans in that year. Following the reasoning of McKay and Lewins from chapter one, this does not necessarily mean that the ethnic identification is higher, since reading a Swedish-language newspaper suggests a lower degree of interaction with other Swedish Americans than belonging to a Swedish-American organization.

The different organizations catered to the different needs of its membership—be they religion, sick insurance, or the affection for a particular province in Sweden. However, they also eventually transcended these specific functions and came to serve as places where one could meet fellow countrypersons, speak the Swedish language, and partake in the various social activities that were connected with the organization. This was particularly true with the churches and mutual-aid societies. In Breton's sense they allowed the Swedish-American community to develop towards institutional completeness, and can thus be said to have been the bearers of a Swedish-American ethnicity.

[22] Williams 1991, 29–34.

The Augustana Synod—A Brief Presentation

The Augustana Synod[23] was founded in June 1860, but traced its origin back to the beginnings of Swedish immigration during the previous decade.[24] In 1849, the Swedish minister Lars Paul Esbjörn led a group of emigrants to the prairies of western Illinois, where they established a Lutheran congregation in Andover, Illinois in 1850. During the following years, Esbjörn was followed by several other Swedish ministers, including Erland Carlsson, Tuve Nilsson Hasselquist, Erik Norelius (who received his theological training in the U.S.), and Jonas Swensson, all of whom also brought groups of emigrants with them to the New World and founded congregations where they settled in America. During the 1850s, immigration from Sweden continued, and more congregations sprang up. When the Augustana Synod was formed in 1860, it included thirty-six Swedish and thirteen Norwegian Lutheran congregations, with some 4,900 communicant members.[25]

Prior to the establishment of the Augustana Synod, the Swedish Lutherans maintained different kinds of relationships with other American denominations, both Lutheran and non-Lutheran. Both Lars Paul Esbjörn and Tuve Nilsson Hasselquist were supported in their work among the Swedish immigrants by the American Home Missionary Society, a Congregationalist association, and were employed as missionaries among their fellow Swedes in Illinois during the 1850s. In addition, the Swedish Missionary Society, an interconfessional mission group, had given Esbjörn some travel support.[26] The Swedish Lutheran congregations were from 1851 also affiliated with the Synod of Northern Illinois, which was a district synod of the General Synod, a larger American Lutheran body organized in 1820.[27]

Several reasons for the organization of the Augustana Synod have been advanced, including confessional differences, personality problems, and issues of nationality.[28] The most prominent of these seems to have been the confessional differences between the Swedes and a group of Norwegians, and the rest of the Synod of Northern Illinois, which came to the fore toward the end of the 1850s. The discussion centered on, among other things, the interpretation of the Augsburg Confession, from whose Latin form, *Confessio Augus-*

---

[23] The Synod's name varied over time. In the official minutes, it is referred to as the Scandinavian Evangelical Lutheran Augustana Synod 1860–1894, from 1895–1900 as the Evangelical Lutheran Augustana Synod, and from 1901 as the Augustana Synod. I will, however, use the name Augustana Synod throughout the entire period.

[24] There is an extensive literature on the history of the Augustana Synod. For good overviews that also serve as the basis for the following, see Arden 1963, Stephenson 1932, Söderström 1973.

[25] Referat 1860, 26–27.

[26] Söderström 1973, 25–30.

[27] Arden 1963, 44–58, Stephenson 1932, 178–95, Söderström 1973, 47–55.

[28] For the following see Arden 1963, 51–58, Stephenson 1932, 178–95, Söderström 1973, 61–66.

tana, the name Augustana was chosen. Hugo Söderström has also argued that in addition to the confessional differences, the issue of nationality was an important factor for the establishment of the Augustana Synod.[29] Although the early leadership of the Synod downplayed the issue of nationalism and expressed hopes that Americans with the correct confessional viewpoint would join the Synod as well,[30] this did not come to pass and the Synod did remain a distinct ethnic institution.

The cooperation with the Norwegians lasted until 1870, when the latter withdrew to form their own denomination. Arden argues that the reasons for the separation had to do with the much more divided and competitive religious scene among the Norwegians in America, as well as with the fact that the Norwegian congregations remained a minority within the Synod.[31] Still, issues of nationality also played a role, and in 1869 August Wenaas, the Norwegian professor in the Seminary, wrote in *Den Norske Lutheraner* that the Swedes "cannot fully understand our peculiar Norwegian character and our ecclesiastical and national traditions."[32] The withdrawal of the Norwegians from the Augustana Synod seems to conform with a general pattern of interaction between the Scandinavian groups in America. Although little systematic work has been done on the issue, it is clear that pan-Scandinavian cooperation, such as joint organizations, were not uncommon during the early phases of Scandinavian immigration to the U.S. Eventually, however, many of these organizations were dissolved and reorganized on purely national grounds.[33] One reason for this, Harald Runblom has argued, was the different development and character of nationalism in the Scandinavian countries themselves, which also affected the Scandinavian groups in America. For example, Norwegian immigrants to the U.S. in the mid-to-late nineteenth century had been exposed to the growth of the Norwegian nationalism of the nineteenth century prior to leaving Norway, a nationalism which was much stronger and far-reaching than that which their fellow Swedish immigrants experienced.[34]

The early leadership in the Augustana Synod was a part of a low-church revival movement that affected Sweden in the mid-nineteenth century and that was one dimension of a re-alignment of Swedish society in general and religion in particular during the nineteenth century.[35] Complex in its nature, this

---

[29] Söderström 1973, 72–76.

[30] *Hemlandet*, 22 August 1860. See also Blanck 1983, 12–16 for a further discussion of this point.

[31] Arden 1963, 135–42.

[32] Quoted in Arden 1963, 138. Cf. also Söderström 1973, 99–100.

[33] Jenswold 1985.

[34] Norman & Runblom 1988a, 270–71.

[35] This paragraph is based on Gustafsson 1966, chapter 8. Cf. also Sanders 1995, chapters 1 and 2 for a recent discussion of the revival and Stephenson 1932, chapters 2, 3 and 10. Söderström 1973, 15–21 discusses the precise position of the early Augustana leaders in the revival.

movement represented a Swedish religious dissent, which emphasized the role of the individual as opposed to church hierarchy and which was critical of both the Church of Sweden and its status as a state church. The movement was, in the words of Hanne Sanders, a way of questioning the established society, of "breaking the church's monopoly of interpretation...and of creating its own alternatives."[36] During the nineteenth century, several new religious bodies were also established in Sweden, both inside and outside the Church of Sweden. Evangeliska Fosterlandsstiftelsen (The National Evangelic Foundation) founded in 1856 and with which the Augustana Synod shared many traits, worked to create a revivalistically inspired institution within the Church of Sweden.[37] The establishment of Svenska Missionsförbundet in 1878 is an example of how the low-church revival resulted in the creation of a denomination outside the Church of Sweden.

This Swedish religious background shaped the way the Augustana Synod developed.[38] For example, the suspicion of central ecclesiastical authority in the Swedish revival can be seen as one of the reasons for the relatively strong position of individual congregations in the Augustana Synod. Another example is the refusal of the Synod to establish the office of bishop, as well as the fact that the head of the denomination was always called president. Moreover, the religious heterogeneity which characterized the American scene as a whole left the Augustana Synod in a much more vulnerable situation than was the case for the Swedish State church, which benefited from compulsory membership. After less than three years in America, Lars Paul Esbjörn expressed concerns over American religious pluralism in a report to Svenska Missonssällskapet, the Swedish mission group from which he had received financial support prior to his emigration, as there were many religious groups competing for the souls of the Swedish immigrants, and he warned those in Sweden who advocated religious freedom there.[39]

The Augustana Synod grew very rapidly during its first four decades. The membership increased from some 3,700 in 1860 to ten times that number, 33,000, a decade later. During the following two decades the membership doubled twice to 75,000 in 1880 and 146,000 in 1890. Although the Synod kept growing during the following decades as well, the pace was somewhat slower. In 1900 there were 210,000 members, in 1910 261,000 and in 1920 the Synod counted 291,000 members.[40] The number of congregations grew equally fast, from 36 in 1860 to 1,250 in 1920, and various congregations were organized into conferences. The Synod also expanded geographically

---

[36] Sanders 1992, 193.
[37] Andrén 1971, 116.
[38] For the following, see Erling 1992, 34–36.
[39] Runeby 1969, 263, 273–74.
[40] See the statistical sections in Referat 1871, 1881, 1891, 1901, 1911, and 1921.

beyond its Midwestern origins; in 1870 the New York Conference was established for the East Coast congregations and in the 1890s two new West Coast conferences were established.[41]

The nucleus of the Augustana Synod was the individual congregations, which were present throughout both rural and urban Swedish America in the form of the church building and its spire. Typically, a congregation would be founded in an area with a large Swedish population, and after some time the congregation would decide to apply for membership in the Augustana Synod. Especially during the first several decades, the individual congregations retained a great deal of independence from both the conferences and the Synod as a whole. In this way, it is possible to see parallels between the synod during its first several decades and the Swedish low church revival, such as Svenska Missionsförbundet, without bishops and with a strong emphasis on congregational independence, something which George Stephenson has called the "decentralizing tendencies"[42] present in the Synod until 1894. In that year a new constitution was adopted, balancing the relationship between the congregations, the conferences, and the Synod. It strengthened the position of central authority the Synod, while still granting considerable independence to the congregations. This arrangement represented what one historian of the Augustana Synod called "a Lutheran middle way between an ecclesiastical hierarchy on the one hand and congregationalism on the other."[43] The lack of synodical authority also meant that control over individual congregations became much more difficult than in Sweden, as is seen for example during the schism with the Mission Covenant Church in the 1870s and 1880s.

In addition to the local congregations, a number of other institutions were formed which all contributed to the growth of the Augustana Synod. The Synod and its conferences operated over a dozen of educational institutions—colleges, academies and a theological seminary. Of these, Augustana College was in many ways the central institution, as it was the oldest of the colleges and also owned by the Synod as a whole, unlike the other schools which were operated by one of the eleven regional conferences into which the Augustana Synod was divided. Moreover, the Synod's only seminary was located at Augustana, which meant that all the ordained ministers in the Augustana Synod had to attend school in Rock Island.

Apart from educational institutions, the Synod operated a great number of what were officially called "our benevolent institutions," including orphanages, hospitals, deaconess institutes, and homes for the aged. With the exception of the Immanuel Deaconess Institute in Omaha, Nebraska, these institu-

---

[41] Minnesskrift 1910, 480.
[42] Stephenson 1932, ch. 22.
[43] Olson 1956, 48. Cf also Mattson 1941, 267–68.

tions were regional in character and support, and were owned and controlled by the different conferences. In 1917, the Synod's annual report included twenty-eight benevolent institutions, including nine orphanages, five hospitals, two deaconess institutes, eight homes for the aged, two immigrant homes, one home for invalids and one home for women.[44]

The Augustana Synod also had an extensive publishing program.[45] One of the largest and most influential Swedish-American newspapers, *Hemlandet*, was started by the Augustana Synod president T.N. Hasselquist in 1854, and although it was sold in 1872, it remained closely associated with the Synod. Over the years, the Augustana Synod also published at least twenty other magazines, newspapers, journals of religious and cultural-literary character, including the Synod's official organ *Augustana*, as well as such literary and cultural publications as the annual calender *Prärieblomman* and the monthly magazine *Ungdomsvännen*. A great number of books were also published by the Synod's publishing house, the Augustana Book Concern (A.B.C.) Between 1891 and 1920, 643 Swedish-language titles were published by the A.B.C., and between 1911–1915 alone, a total of 840,000 copies appeared of the Swedish-language imprints. It was not until after World War I that the English-language editions overshadowed the Swedish at the Augustana Book Concern.

Augustana in Swedish America

It is difficult to exactly measure the influence of the Augustana Synod in Swedish America, but table 1 shows the relationship between the size of the Augustana Synod and the persons living in the United States of Swedish extraction between 1860–1920. The Synod statistics do not state the ethnic background of its members, but it can be safely assumed that the vast majority of the Augustana members until at least 1920 were of Swedish background, and the figures can thus be seen as one indication of the Synod's relative position in the Swedish-American community. For the period 1860–1880, the percentage is calculated on Swedish-born individuals, and between 1890–1920 the figure includes those born in Sweden and those born in the United States of at least one Swedish parent.

[44] Referat 1917, 284–89. Cf also Minnesskrift 1910, 230–90.
[45] This section is based on Hasselmo 1974, 63–72, Minnesskrift 1910, 293–318 and 437–74, and Olson 1910.

Table 1. *Augustana Synod Membership as Percentage of the Population of Swedish Extraction.*

1860	1870	1880	1890	1900	1910	1920
20.1	34.2	38.4	19.9	19.4	19.6	20.1

Sources: U.S. Censuses, Augustana Synod Statistics

As can be seen in table 1, the synod's dominance was probably greatest during the decades prior to the turn of the century, particularly during the 1870s and 1880s, when the Synod's membership corresponded to a more than a third of the Swedish-born population. The inclusion of the American-born Swedish Americans lowers the share to about a fifth, but this is still much higher than for any other Swedish-American group.

It should, however, also be noted that Augustana's influence in Swedish America cannot be measured only through its membership figures. A fairly large number of Swedish Americans who did not belong to the denomination still used its services at different times, and can thus be said to have been a part of the Synod's field of influence, although to a lesser extent than the actual members. It was quite common for non-members to be married, buried, or have their children baptized in an Augustana congregation, a tradition which many of the immigrants most likely brought with them from Sweden. The sources are at the best uneven in their information about these activities, but in 1920 there were roughly as many non-members as members who sought out Augustana congregations for these ceremonies.[46] No information is available for how many non-members might have been affected by other Augustana Synod activities, but the figures do suggest that the Augustana influence probably extended beyond the limits of its membership, and it is interesting to note that Conrad Bergendoff has suggested that as many as half of the Swedish immigrants were included within its "sphere of influence."[47]

Another way of measuring the Synod's relative importance in Swedish America is to compare its membership figures with those of other Swedish-American organizations. As noted above, not quite 40 percent of all persons of Swedish extraction in the United States in 1920 belonged to one of the many Swedish-American organizations at that time. Of that group of close to half a million individuals, the Augustana Synod membership made up close to 300,000 persons, or 60 percent. Allowing for the fact that some persons may have belonged to other Swedish-American groups in addition to the Augustana Synod, the figure still clearly illustrates the dominance of the Synod

[46] Augustana Synod Statistics, Referat 1921.
[47] Bergendoff 1973, 238.

among those Swedish Americans who chose to identify with one of the many Swedish-American organizations.

The position of the Augustana Synod in Swedish America varied in urban and rural areas. The Synod had many strongholds in rural Swedish America, where large parts of heavily Swedish-American communities belonged to the Augustana Synod. In an analysis of a rural Swedish settlement in Frankfort Township, Montgomery County in southwestern Iowa, Ann Legreid shows that in 1895 83 percent of the Swedish-born heads of household were members of the local Augustana congregation, whereas 14 percent belonged to the local Covenant congregation.[48] Almost the entire Swedish population in the area thus professed membership in a Swedish-American denomination in this area in rural southwestern Iowa, with a clear dominance for the Augustana congregation. Similarly, Robert Ostergren has shown that in the heavily Swedish settled Cambridge West township in rural Isanti County, Minnesota, some 70 percent of the households claimed membership in the (Augustana) Cambridge Lutheran Church.[49]

The situation was much different in the urban areas, where a smaller fraction of the Swedish Americans tended to belong to a church of any denomination, and where the Augustana Synod thus had a much weaker position. Anita Olson's analysis of religious patterns among Swedish Americans in the largest Swedish-American urban settlement, Chicago, shows that in 1900 some 11 percent of the Swedish-born population in Chicago were members of an Augustana congregation and that roughly a quarter of the Chicago Swedes belonged to any Swedish-American denomination, thus leaving three fourths of the group outside of organized Swedish-American religious life.[50]

It is also evident that the Synod had a geographic profile rooted in the Midwest. In 1910, six Midwestern states (Minnesota, Illinois, Iowa, Michigan, Nebraska, and Kansas) represented 67 percent of the Augustana Synod membership, while the same six states only encompassed 53 percent of the first and second generation Swedish Americans recorded in the U.S. census that year.[51] Minnesota and Illinois alone made up close to half of the 1910 Augustana membership (47 percent), while 37 percent of all Swedish Americans lived in these two states. Augustana's position on the East and West coasts was weaker: 12 percent of all Swedish Americans lived in the two major east coast states of New York and Massachusetts in 1910, but only seven percent of the Augustana Synod members lived here, and while eight percent of the Swedish

[48] Legreid 1993, 78.

[49] Ostergren 1988, 221–22.

[50] Olson 1990, 306. It should, however, be noted that these figures do not include non-members who still chose to get married or baptize their children in a Swedish-American church.

[51] The following figures are based on 1910 Augustana Synod Statistics [Referat 1911], and Census 1910, vol I, 834–39, 927–34.

Americans lived in California and Washington, only three percent of the Augustana membership was found in these western states.

The geographic profile of the Augustana Synod can at least partly be explained in generational terms. Those states with the largest share of Augustana Synod members were also those states which experienced early Swedish immigration. Illinois, Minnesota, Iowa, Kansas, and Nebraska belonged to a core group of early Swedish settlements from the 1850s and on. In 1880, for example, the Illinois, Minnesota, and Iowa conferences of the Synod made up 80 percent of its membership.[52] Although Swedish immigration to these Midwestern core areas continued all throughout the immigration era—especially to urban areas such as Chicago and Minneapolis-St. Paul[53]—a gradually larger part of the immigration after the turn of the century went to urban destinations on the east and west coasts, where the Augustana Synod was weaker.

Its relative weakness in these areas was to a large extent a function of the Synod's inability to attract these newer immigrants as members. The post-1900 Swedish immigrants were different from their compatriots of the early decades of Swedish immigration, as the Sweden they left in the first decades of the twentieth century was also quite different in terms of social and economic development than the Sweden of half a decade earlier. The newer immigrants were often younger and single and more urban and industrial in their Swedish background and more urban-oriented in their choice of American destinations than those arriving before 1900.[54] Apparently these immigrants were less likely to be attracted to the Augustana Synod, and Bergendoff notes that the Synod began having problems in attracting Swedish immigrants arriving in the 1880s and 1890s and characterizes many groups that came after World War I as openly hostile to the Augustana Synod. To Bergendoff, the "height of the Synod's activities among Swedish immigrants was reached around 1910." [55]

The Synod leadership was also aware of this problem, and it was discussed frequently after the turn of the century. In March 1902, the dilemma was addressed in the official Synod organ *Augustana* in an article with the appropriate title, "The mission of our church with regard to the scores of countrymen, especially in the larger cities, who remain outside her." The author points out that the immigrants of recent times came from a Sweden in which many people showed indifference to religion and who therefore chose to remain outside the church. The article states that this was a radically different situation from the early years of the Augustana Synod, when the immigrants in-

[52] Augustana Synod Statistics, Referat 1881.
[53] Cf. Runblom 1991 for a interesting analysis of the simultaneous presence of several waves of immigrants and their descendants in Chicago's Swedish-American community.
[54] Carlsson 1976, 125–48.
[55] Bergendoff 1973, 238.

46

fluenced by the pietism associated with the revival were "true Lutherans" and actively sought out the Lutheran church.[56] A year later, pastor C. W. Andeer addressed the same question, when he encouraged the Synod to try to attract as many of the 45,000 new Swedish immigrants as possible that year. However, he realized that this would be a difficult task, since "they have another mindset than those who founded Swedish America" affected as they were by political, social, and religious struggles in Sweden and "contaminated" by socialism.[57] In 1912, *Augustana* attributed the problem to religious indifference. A couple of decades earlier, the paper noted, the immigrants had "deep religious needs" and founded churches in America, whereas at the present time the Swedish immigrant was indifferent or even hostile towards religion.[58] A comment from 1914 also emphasized the difference between rural and urban areas; most Swedes were settling in urban areas at the time and as these Swedes were of "a completely different mind-set" they were also the most difficult to recruit as Synod members.[59]

As a consequence of this shift, by the turn of the century the Augustana Synod seems to have been on its way to becoming an institution dominated by an immigrant generation from the early decades of the immigration era, and their children. It is difficult to make a generational analysis of the Synod membership since the Synod statistics provide no such information. However, those states with the highest membership shares in the Synod were also those states where the second (American-born) generation of Swedish Americans dominated. In 1910, the second generation made up 55 percent of all Swedish Americans in the Midwest, the source of strength for the Synod. On both the East and West Coasts the first generation dominated (55 and 57 percent respectively). The picture is even clearer when one examines the data for individual states. In such strong Augustana states as Iowa, Nebraska, and Kansas the second generation dominated, making up over 60 percent of the Swedish Americans, while the situation was the reversed in states dominated by first generation immigrants such as Massachusetts, New York, Washington, and California, where the Synod was weak.[60]

To summarize, the Augustana Synod was thus the largest, and most dominant of the organizations in Swedish America. The Synod based its membership on a group of core states in the Midwest, where the original Augustana congregations and other institutions were established during the decades after 1850. It continued to draw its strength from these areas, even when the first

---

[56] "Vår kyrkas kallelse med afseende på de skaror landsmän som, särskilt i de större städerna, stå utanför henne," *Augustana*, 13 March, 1902.

[57] C. W. Andeer, "Årets stora folkvandring," *Augustana*, 16 July 1903.

[58] *Augustana*, 16 May 1912.

[59] *Augustana*, 13 August 1914. Cf. also *Augustana*, 2 August 1918 for similar attitudes.

[60] Census 1910, vol I, 834–39, 927–34.

generation was fading from the scene and being replaced by the second (American-born) generation of Swedish Americans, and was less successful in attracting members from later waves of Swedish immigrants.

Augustana and Swedish America

In discussing the various facets of the Swedish-American community, Arnold Barton has pointed to four major components in organized Swedish America: groups that represented different social categories of Swedish Americans as well as differences in their attitudes about the nature and identity of the Swedish-American group.[61] According to Barton, the Augustana Synod was the leading of these, and from it emerged Swedish America's "dominant ethnic ideology."[62] The second group consisted of other Swedish-American religious groups, notably the Mission Covenant Church, but also Swedish Methodists, Baptists, Adventists, and Mormons. Secular groups, or "freethinkers" as Barton also calls them, made up the third segment. Included here were, for example, several newspapers and other, often urban-based organizations, such as the Swedish-American orders and lodges. Although very small numerically, the politically radical Swedish-American groups, often Socialist in nature, made up the fourth part of Swedish-American opinion. These groups competed for influence within the Swedish-American community and were frequently in conflict with each other. The strong dichotomy that existed especially between the religious and secular organizations has often been underscored.[63]

It should, however, also be noted that the strife within Swedish-American religion could also be keen. For the Augustana Synod, the relationship with the Swedish Evangelical Mission Covenant Church became especially important. The Mission Covenant Church was formally established in 1885, although several organizations had preceded it from the late 1860s. Like the Augustana Synod, the Mission Covenant Church had its roots in the nineteenth-century Swedish religious revival movement, and maintained a close relationship with Svenska Missionsförbundet, established in 1878, and it seems likely that many members of the Mission Covenant Church had been associated with Svenska Missionsförbundet prior to their emigration. In Sweden, the early Augustana leaders had maintained close contact with persons connected with what would become Svenska Missionsförbundet, and its leader

---

[61] Barton 1994, 332–34.
[62] Barton 1994, 333.
[63] Beijbom 1990b, 48–49. Cf. Bodnar 1985, 142 for the same point among other ethnic groups.

Paul Peter Waldenström had even been offered a professorship at the Augustana Seminary in 1862.[64]

Still, when controversy broke out in Sweden over Waldenström's teaching on the atonement in 1872, a parallel conflict developed in America between the sympathisers of Waldenström and the Augustana Synod.[65] In 1874, the Synod minutes mention the "firestorm" that the teachings of the Covenant movement had set off among the Augustana Lutherans,[66] and an Augustana pastor from Jamestown, N.Y. spoke of the Mission Covenant sympathizers as "worse than the grasshoppers in Minnesota and Kansas" as they "buzz, bite, eat, and gnaw wherever they advance."[67] Thus, Augustana and the Covenant grew apart, and Philip Anderson speaks of their conflict as a religious "schism," whereas G. Everett Arden talks about "the theological crisis."[68]

Like certain high church groups in Sweden, the Augustana Synod also showed hostility to many of the secular societies, or "secret societies" as they were called, which seem to have included a variety of groups, ranging from the Free Masons to temperance organizations. Hugo Söderström has suggested that no fewer than 258 members were excommunicated in 1890 for being members of "secret societies,"[69] and in 1892 Synod President Swärd complained about the great number of associations that existed in the cities, which had become an "anti-church movement" and hindered the Synod's work.[70] In addition, the Synod objected to many cultural expressions associated with the secular groups, such as dancing and theater throughout the period of investigation.[71] The small Socialist groups also seem to have maintained a distance not only from the religious community, but also from other secular groups.[72]

The Augustana Synod clearly sought to establish itself as the dominant Swedish-American organization. In 1910 Synod president Erik Norelius reflected on the first half decade of the Synod's life. Although he noted the existence of other Swedish-American denominations, Norelius underscored the great significance of the Augustana Synod in Swedish America, claiming that it better than any other denomination had succeeded in establishing educational and benevolent institutions and a publishing house. The schools, for example, had been especially important for the creation of a Swedish literary culture in America, and the Synod as a whole, Norelius claimed, was thus "the

[64] Olsson 1963, 108–09.
[65] Olsson 1962, 175–303 provides an insightful analysis of this process. Cf. also Anderson 1994, 6–11.
[66] Referat 1874, 14.
[67] Quoted in Ander 1931, 166–67.
[68] Anderson 1994, 8, Arden 1963, chapter 9.
[69] Söderström 1973, 149. Cf. Erling 1996, 64–65.
[70] Referat 1892, 19–20, Stephenson 1932, 318.
[71] Cf chapter three.
[72] Barton 1994, 334.

only force among Swedish immigrants in America which has preserved the faith of our fathers [and] the Swedish culture and language which has sprung from it."[73]

The distance between the Augustana Synod and other groups in Swedish America was clearly expressed during the celebrations of the fiftieth anniversary of both the Synod and of Augustana College and Theological Seminary in 1910. During the week-long celebrations, many greetings were received from both Sweden and the United States.[74] The American greetings came from other colleges and academies in the Augustana Synod, several colleges and universities in Illinois and elsewhere in the Midwest, other American Lutheran seminaries, several other American Lutheran denominations (including three Norwegian-American Synods and the Finnish-American Suomi Synod) as well as a number of individuals, such as President Taft. It is striking that, with the exception of the Covenant North Park College in Chicago, no other Swedish-American institutions or organizations were included among those sending congratulatory messages. Thus, to the Augustana Synod, contacts with other Lutheran institutions, including other Scandinavian-American groups and other American institutions of higher learning, played a more important role than did contacts with other Swedish-American organizations outside the Augustana Synod.

The cultural differences between the various factions in the Swedish-American community have not yet been systematically studied, but some examples will illustrate these variations. Swedish-American cultural expressions, as they were formulated by David Nyvall of the Mission Covenant Church, have been discussed by Scott Erickson,[75] and analyses of the often acrimonious newspaper debates by Ulf Beijbom and Anna Williams over such crucial issues as assimilation, language retention, and political preferences further point to the strong diversity of opinion within the community, especially between religious and secular groups.[76] As will be shown in chapter four, a specific cultural and literary profile also emerged within the Augustana Synod which at times was quite distinct from other factions of the Swedish-American community.

One example of the differences within the Swedish-American community is the discussion about a suitable Swedish candidate for a statue in Chicago's Lincoln Park in the 1880s.[77] As Eric Johannesson has shown, Johan Enander proposed erecting a statue of King Gustavus Adolphus in 1882, plans which

[73] Referat 1910, 32–33. Quotation from p. 32.
[74] Minnen 1911, 101–41, 234–58.
[75] Erickson 1996, 74–131.
[76] For the situation in Chicago, see Beijbom 1971, 288–332 and Williams 1991, 96 & 107. Nyberg 1977 discusses the situation in Minnesota.
[77] For the following see Johannesson 1991a, 269–75.

50

created strong differences of opinion between the city's religious (primarily Augustana) and secular Swedish groups. The secular and liberal leaning Swedish Americans in Chicago opposed the idea, as Gustavus Adolphus was seen as too closely associated with religion. In addition, it was argued, it was impossible to raise a statue of a king in the American republic. In 1886, the project was once more brought up, but this time the person chosen was Linnaeus, the eighteenth-century Swedish botanist, and after a five-year fund-raising campaign headed by Enander, the statue was finally unveiled in May 1891 in Chicago's Lincoln Park, with several thousand Swedish Americans present. As Johannesson notes, Linnaeus became a compromise candidate, behind whom both the secular and religious factions of the Swedish-American community could unite. Lars Wendelius' study of cultural life among Swedish-Americans in Rockford, Illinois, also shows the differences in cultural outlook between the religious groups on the one hand, and the temperance and radical organizations in the city on the other.[78] Finally, the special nature of the cultural expressions among Swedish-American radicals in Chicago, and their connections to similar secular and culturally radical patterns in the labor movement in Sweden, has been analysed by Per Nordahl.[79]

One should also, however, recognize the commonality of interests between the various factions in the Swedish-American community. At times, and especially after the turn of the century, opposing sides of the community could come together for joint manifestations when it provided the community with an opportunity to show its strength to the surrounding American society. Two such Swedish-American examples are the celebrations of the 250th anniversary of the New Sweden Colony in Minneapolis in 1888 and the "Swedish Day" during the Columbian Exposition in Chicago in 1893.[80] Anna Williams has also pointed to a convergence of opinions within Swedish America after the turn of the century, concluding that the "antagonism" between the religious and secular groups of the 1870s and 1880s had been overcome. Instead, the earlier antagonists (excepting the Socialists) could now unite behind an ethnic identity, in which the Augustana Synod and its "ideology" played a leading role.[81] There are also parallels between Scott Erickson's description of David Nyvall's views of what it meant to be Swedish-American, with its focus on the development of a distinct Swedish-American identity, based on a dual Swedish and American heritage,[82] and what we shall see developed within the Augustana Synod.

---

[78] Wendelius 1990, 32–55.
[79] Nordahl 1994, 114–55.
[80] For the 1888 celebration see Blanck 1988, and for the 1893 celebration see Blanck 1991.
[81] Williams 1991, 167.
[82] Erickson 1996, 124–31.

Augustana and Sweden

The relationship between the Augustana Synod and Sweden varied over time. During the early phase of the emigration era, some homeland Swedes often looked with skepticism at the growing Swedish-American community on the other side of the Atlantic, portraying the emigrants, in Arnold Barton's words, "as vain seekers after purely material advantages, gullible dreamers, 'deserters,' and even violators of God's Sixth Commandment." This was a sentiment especially noticeable in conservative intellectual and religious circles in the country.[83] Following this general pattern, contacts between the Augustana Synod and the Church of Sweden were not particularly close up until *circa* 1890, and the Church of Sweden seems to have regarded the Synod with some suspicion. This attitude can be traced as far back as the emigration of Lars Paul Esbjörn, when Archbishop af Wingård expressed his "displeasure" with the migration of Esbjörn and his group.[84] The Church of Sweden had also at times suggested that the Episcopal church in the United States would be the logical church for the Swedish emigrants to belong to, a judgement which of course resulted in negative reactions in the Augustana Synod.[85]

By the turn of the century, however, this relationship was improving. For example, in the early 1890s, when the faculty of the Augustana Theological Seminary wrote to the Swedish bishops to ascertain how they viewed the Augustana Synod, six wrote back saying that they saw the Synod as the "daughter church" in America of the Church of Sweden.[86]

Moreover, in 1893 when the 300th anniversary of the Uppsala meeting of 1593 at which the Swedish Reformation was codified, Knut Henning Gezelius von Schéele, professor of theology at Uppsala University from 1879 and bishop of Visby from 1885, became the first Swedish bishop to come to Swedish America in general and the Augustana Synod in particular, a visit which can be seen as a turning point in the relationship between at least the Augustana Synod and official Sweden.[87] Von Schéele participated in a major celebration in Rock Island in June 1893 as the official representative of the Church of Sweden, where such leading figures in the Augustana Synod as Erik Norelius and P.J. Swärd welcomed him and noted with great pleasure that his visit marked the first recognition from the Church of Sweden that the Augustana Synod had received since its beginning in 1860.[88] It is "quite re-

---

[83] Barton 1993, 89–90. Quotation from p. 90.

[84] Runeby 1969, 265; Letter from af Wingård to Esbjörn, 8 March 1849, printed in Westin 1932, 37–38.

[85] Stephenson 1932, 214–18, 223–39, Erling 1992, 46–48.

[86] *Augustana*, 14 April 1892.

[87] Barton 1994, 96–97.

[88] *Augustana*, 14 June 1893.

markable" to greet a Swedish bishop as an official visitor, wrote *Augustana*, given the fact that the Church of Sweden has paid "very little attention" to the Synod and its important work among the Swedes in America,[89] and at the Jubilee celebrations in Rock Island, Synod President Erik Norelius said that the Synod thought "it took very long" before "the mother church turned her eyes upon the daughter church."[90]

Von Schéele returned to America twice; in 1901 when he visited several of the Swedish-American colleges, and was greeted as an old friend by the Augustana Synod, and in 1910 when the Augustana Synod and Augustana College celebrated their fiftieth anniversary on a grand scale in Rock Island. *Augustana* commented that his visit in 1901 showed that the Swedes in America were better appreciated in Sweden now than during the past five decades, attributing a major role to von Schéele for this.[91]

Von Schéele was obviously impressed by the intellectual and religious life he found during his visits to Swedish America. For example, in his account of his journey in 1893 he gave high praise to the Augustana Synod as the church that was preserving the old Swedish faith in America.[92] He noted that the graduating class at Augustana College in 1893 was of the same academic standard as those at comparable schools in Sweden, and was especially pleased by the fact that many students in Gotland (his home province) would have a hard time measuring up to the level of expertise exhibited at Augustana College in Swedish language and literature "by boys and girls born and raised in America."[93] Von Schéele's positive assessment of Augustana is also shown by his interest in admitting many returning Augustana pastors to the diocese of Visby, more than any other contemporary Swedish bishop.[94] In total six pastors were admitted to Visby diocese, which Sten Carlsson calls "remarkable" since not one out of the 58 returning Augustana pastors identified by Carlsson was born on Gotland.[95]

Following von Schéele's first visit to America, official Sweden began to bestow orders and medals to prominent Swedish Americans. Up until 1910 about a dozen medals were bestowed, and the recipients were almost exclusively connected with the Augustana Synod. It is clear that Bishop von Schéele played an important role in proposing the candidates for the medals to the Swedish government.[96]

[89] *Augustana*, 25 May 1893.
[90] *Augustana*, 10 June 1893.
[91] *Augustana*, 5 December 1901.
[92] von Schéele 1894, 3–6.
[93] von Schéele 1894, 151–52. Quotation from p. 152. Cf. also von Schéele's very positive speech at the celebrations in Rock Island in *Augustana*, 22 June 1893.
[94] Carlsson 1984, 241.
[95] Carlsson 1984, 245.
[96] Blanck 1995, 275–79.

Contacts between Sweden and the Augustana Synod in general and Augustana College in particular became substantially strengthened after the turn of the century. One illustration of this was a campaign to raise money for Augustana in Sweden in which the fourth (and first American-born) president of Augustana College, Gustav Andreen, played an important role. Andreen was born in Baileytown, Indiana in 1864,[97] the son of Swedish-born Andreas Andreen, one of the first ministers in the Augustana Synod.[98] It was only natural that Gustav would attend Augustana College, and he graduated in 1881.[99] Following his graduation, he taught for two years at Augustana, and later, between 1886–1893, at Bethany College in Lindsborg, Kansas. In 1893 he attended Yale University, earning a Bachelor's degree in 1894 and a Ph.D. in Germanic Languages in 1898. An offer of a position as instructor in Scandinavian Languages at Yale required that Andreen spend two years in Scandinavia,[100] and in the summer of 1898 the Andreen family sailed for Sweden. Andreen spent two years in Scandinavia, mainly at Uppsala University but also at Christiania and Copenhagen. At Uppsala he spent most of his time studying in the Department of Scandinavian Languages with professor Adolf Noreen and was a an active member of the Noreen's seminar in Nordic Languages.[101] It was also during Andreen's time at Uppsala University that he presented a lecture about the Swedish language in America,[102] which was also published in Sweden in 1900.[103]

During his years in Sweden, Andreen managed to establish a number of important contacts for Augustana College, as he met a number of prominent Swedes, primarily in the universities. He also conceived of a plan to raise money for Augustana College in Sweden, and the so-called Augustana Plan was launched with his Swedish academic contacts playing important roles in enlisting support in the Swedish academic, cultural and political establishment for the plan.[104] The plan was officially announced in 1901 in a "petition to the Swedish public," and a campaign was launched in Sweden to raise 100,000 Swedish crowns.[105] The money would be used for a professorship at Augus-

---

[97] Bergendoff 1980, 74.

[98] Bergendoff 1980, 14–15.

[99] Albrecht 1950, 23–25, Catalog 1880–1881.

[100] ACL, GAP, Yale University to Andreen, 31 May 1898.

[101] Wilstadius 1961, 163 states that Andreen was in Uppsala to "study Scandinavian Languages." See also a letter from Andreen to Adolf Noreen, from September 1899, where Andreen speaks fondly of the seminar and the pleasant informal get-togethers after the seminar. [UUB, ANC, Letter from Andreen to Noreen, 18 September 1899.]

[102] Letter from Andreen to "a friend" in Rock Island, 6 June 1900, reprinted in "Stor och glädjande nyhet," *Augustana*, 2 August 1900.

[103] Andreen 1900.

[104] UUB, ANC, Letter from Andreen to Noreen, 8 July 1903 and ACL, GAP, Letter from Andreen to Schück, Rock Island, 27 January 1910.

[105] For the following, see "Till den svenska allmänheten," (1901) in ACL, GAP.

tana College, which the petition claimed, had an "immeasurable influence on the Swedish-American people," and was said to be the "main center for the preservation of Swedishness" in America. It was signed by a number of leading Swedish academics, authors, church people, and politicians, including professors Harald Hjärne, Adolf Noreen, authors Selma Lagerlöf and Verner von Heidenstam, Bishop von Schéele, Archbishop Ekman, and Prime Minister Erik Gustaf Boström.

The campaign went on for several years, and Andreen returned to Sweden in 1903 to lecture about Augustana and further promote the plan, at which time he was also received by King Oscar II, who agreed to lend his name to the professorship.[106] The campaign eventually raised 100,000 crowns in Sweden, a sum which was matched by funds from the United States, so that by the fiftieth anniversary of the college in 1910, it was announced that a total of more than $250,000 had been collected.[107]

It is thus possible during the years after the turn of the century to discern a new interest in and understanding for Swedish America in general and Augustana in particular in circles of Swedish society which until then had had little contact with the emigrants and their descendants in the United States. Augustana's professor of Swedish from 1901, Jules Mauritzson, followed in Andreen's footsteps at Uppsala University in 1902, studying both literature and Scandinavian languages. He observed that there was a great interest in what the Swedish Americans were doing culturally, and that some of the Uppsala academics were pleasantly surprised to learn about the academic life at Augustana College.[108] As mentioned above, the fiftieth anniversary celebration of the Synod, the college, and the seminary also attracted numerous Swedish visitors and congratulatory messages. The Swedish delegation included Bishop von Schéele, now on his third visit to Swedish America, as well as Henrik Schück, professor of literature and *rector magnificus* of Uppsala University. Greetings were conveyed from various quarters in Swedish society, including religious, governmental, and educational institutions, as well as from individuals such as the author Selma Lagerlöf and Uppsala University professor Adolf Noreen.[109] Both von Schéele and Schück spoke in very positive terms of the Augustana Synod and of the college and seminary, Schück calling the college "that place where Sweden and America join together, Augustana Conciliatrix, a patriotic institution of higher learning for the Swedish American's both homelands: that large, new, and energetic

[106] *Augustana,* 19 and 26 March 1903; *Vårt Land,* 23 March 1903; *Aftonbladet,* 23 March 1903; UUB, ANC, Letter from Andreen to Noreen, 28 January 1903.

[107] Referat 1910, 64–65.

[108] "Bref från Sverige," *Augustana,* 6 November 1902.

[109] Minnen 1911, 112–41.

country which has become his, and that old home where his forefathers rest, but over which the sun of memories always will shine."[110]

Finally, a definite shift in attitudes from the Church of Sweden vis-a-vis the Augustana Synod can also be noted at this time. In 1912 a brochure was published by the Rev. Per Pehrsson from Göteborg, called *Råd och anvisningar till utvandrare* (Advice and Instructions to Emigrants).[111] Prospective emigrants were here actively encouraged to seek out and join an Augustana congregation upon arrival in America, and the brochure includes a listing of addresses to Augustana churches throughout America.

Conclusion

The Augustana Synod was by far the single largest Swedish-American organization. Organized in 1860 in the Midwest, by the turn of the century the individual congregations which made up the Synod spanned the entire North American continent. In addition, a number of other institutions were connected with Augustana, such as schools, benevolent organizations, and a publishing house. Throughout the period of investigation, the Augustana Synod seems to have attracted at least 20 percent of the entire Swedish-American population, and at least half of those Swedish Americans who were a part of the Swedish-American ethnic institutions. The Synod played a major part in building the institutional completeness of the Swedish-American community, through its varied and extensive activities. There were other Swedish-American organizations as well, meaning that a number of Swedish-American ethnic institutions existed that both competed with and complemented each other, but the Augustana Synod was the largest and most developed of these organizations, and became the dominant ethnic institution in Swedish America.

During the years prior to World War I, when the Swedish-American community in different respects stood at its apex, the Augustana sphere was well developed with established institutions and a substantial population. However, it was also unquestionably rooted in the early phase of the Swedish immigration to America, and the institution remained shaped by this heritage, geographically, generationally, and socially.[112] This "traditional" character of the Synod is not least illustrated by the fact that Augustana seems to have had difficulties attracting the large number of Swedish immigrants who landed in the U.S. after the turn of the century, and who clearly had a greater urban-industrial background than their compatriots of the previous decades.[113] It is against

[110] Minnen 1911, 115.
[111] Pehrsson 1912.
[112] Cf. Arden 1963, 15–16.
[113] Norman & Runblom 1988a, 76–79, 89–90.

the background of this nature and character of the Augustana Synod that the analysis of the ethnic consciousness that developed within the Synod has to be made.

The years around the turn of the century seem to have been of great importance for the Synod, with a number of changes. The new constitution of 1894 curbed the earlier decentralizing tendencies, giving more authority to the Synod's central leadership. Moreover, as the Synod experienced growing difficulties in attracting recent Swedish immigrants as members, it was thus becoming more dominated by American-born Swedish Americans. By this time, there was also a change in the relationship between Sweden and the Augustana Synod, and beginning with Bishop von Schéele's visit to Rock Island in 1891, in many ways both the Synod and the college received almost an official sanction from Sweden as the Swedish cultural and religious outpost in America. The history of the Augustana Synod between 1860 and 1917 can thus be divided into two phases: the first extending from 1860 to *circa* 1890, and the second from *circa* 1890 to 1917. Further support for this periodization will be given in the following chapters.

An "Augustana sphere" thus existed within Swedish America, in which a particular form of a Swedish-American identity was created. Other versions of a Swedish-American identity emerged within other sections of the diverse Swedish-American community. It is, however, clear that the Augustana Synod represented the leading cultural force in the community, and, as we will see in the following chapters, in its struggle for cultural hegemony in Swedish America, the Synod sought to establish its version of a Swedish-American identity as the predominant one.

Chapter Three

Introduction

To many immigrant groups in the United States, it was of great importance to exercise some degree of control over their education and socialization as well as that of their children. Although many immigrants embraced the American system of public education, there were notable exceptions, with some that sought to provide their own educational opportunities for their children. As Mark Stolarik has underscored, education in the U.S. has never been uniform in its practice, and "private, parochial, and public schools have existed side-by-side since the early nineteenth century and have all vied for support from different constituencies."[1] Even so, the majority of the scholarly work in American educational history has focused on public education, and relatively little attention has been devoted to schools that provided an alternative to American public education.[2]

The immigrants' need to maintain and affirm religious traditions was one of the most important reasons for the creation of private schools, as the separation between state and church excluded religious instruction from the curricula of American public schools. This was particularly true for Catholic immigrant groups; thus a system of Catholic elementary, secondary, and post-secondary education was established in the United States. Similar tendencies can also be found among Lutheran groups, in particular among German Lutherans, as well as Swedes, Norwegians, and Danes. Separate schools also existed among different Orthodox groups, and among the Jews.[3]

Another reason identified by several scholars for the ethnic schools was the maintenance of ethnic traditions in the new land. Often, these ethnic traditions were linked to a religious heritage, but preserving the language and more general ancestral patterns was also important to ethnic educators.[4] In some cases these schools became important *foci* for attempts to provide answers to the question of how the immigrants and their children could best combine their

---

[1] Stolarik 1995, 18.
[2] Seller 1981, 5.
[3] Bodnar 1985, 189–197. See also Anderson et al. 1995, Beck 1939, Cremin 1984, 383–85, Olneck & Lazerson 1980, Weiss 1982.
[4] Bodnar 1985, 196. See also Christianson 1995.

ethnic backgrounds with the demands of the new land. Educational historian Timothy Smith has pointed to the role these schools played in the search for a definition of "national identity" that was able to combine "a sense of duty to their homeland ... and still not contradict their new allegiance to America."[5]

This chapter focuses on the role of Augustana College—the leading school in the Augustana Synod—in creating a Swedish-American identity. The major questions that will be addressed include how the college and its curriculum developed from 1860 and its role in the creation of a Swedish-American identity. The first part of the chapter will trace the institutional developments at Augustana College. Following a brief history of the institution, we will look at the general educational development at the college by examining how the curriculum at Augustana developed, and what was taught at the school. Furthermore, the question of how the Augustana Synod viewed education will be addressed. What was the purpose of the school? To what extent was it influenced by Swedish and American educational ideas? In this context the role of religion will also be addressed, which, given the fact that the school was operated by a denomination, played an important role in the college's life. To what degree did religion shape the Augustana curriculum? Finally, the role of the subject of Swedish in the Augustana curriculum will be analysed.

The second part of the chapter deals specifically with the role and contents of Swedish in the Augustana curriculum. How did the subject develop? What was the nature of the Swedish curriculum? As the Swedish dimension at the college was not restricted to formal instruction, it will also be important to examine Swedish-related activities at Augustana College that took place outside the classroom, and so a number of student organizations on campus will be scrutinized. Thus a number of public celebrations in conjunction with jubilees or visits by different persons with Swedish or Swedish-American focus will provide further evidence of the emerging Swedish-American identity at the college.

The Making of a Swedish-American Education

Charley Washington—A Student at Augustana College

Sometime in the 1910s, the writer and editor at the Augustana Book Concern E.W. Olson published a play called *Charley Washington. En studentkomedi* (Charley Washington. A Student Comedy).[6] The play is set at Augustana Col-

---

[5] Smith 1969, 525.
[6] The following paragraphs are based on Charley Washington 1917.

lege in the 1910s, and deals with the student Karl Törngren (or Charley Turn-green), who arrives on campus from his parents' farm in Wausa, Nebraska, to study at Augustana and, as he puts it, "become educated."[7] Charley appears on campus dressed in country style in a heavy wool coat and long wool scarf and speaking in heavy Swedish dialect, at times mixed up with some English.

He does not quite seem to know what he wants to study, just that he wants a good education at Augustana. He also decides that now that he is entering a new phase of his life, he needs a new name, "a student name."[8] The registrar, professor Ultimus (who is obviously based on Augustana's professor of Swedish at the time, Jules Göthe Ultimus Mauritzson) suggests several names, ranging from the Swedish Oxenstjerna [sic!] to the English Shakespeare, but Charley finally settles on Washington as a good name. (He objects to Shakespeare as he thinks that name sounds too much like a pitchfork.) Washington, however, Charley notes, does not only indicate his allegiance to America, but he also identifies elements of both his hometown Wausa and the Swedish king (Gustav) Vasa in the new name.

Seven years later, in the third act of the play, we meet Charley again. He has now completed his studies at Augustana, speaks eloquently in correct standard Swedish, and his uncouth country manners are gone. As he calls on the house of young Miss Fifi Eklut,[9] the daughter of a rather strict widow of an Augustana professor and also the young woman whom he proposes to marry, he quotes Bellman to Mrs. Eklut and bursts out in "Studentsången"—a traditional song among university students in Sweden. Charley has come a long way from his Nebraska farm, and has indeed become an educated man.

Professor Ultimus also calls on the Ekluts to give Charley the good news that the college's faculty has just decided to offer him a position at the school, to teach science and Swedish, something which finally convinces Mrs. Eklut that he is worthy of her daughter. She consents to the marriage and as the curtain falls in the final scene of the play, the happy young couple is engaged to be married.

It is probably fair to say that *Charley Washington* never became a theatrical success, and it is uncertain whether it was ever staged. The play is instead more interesting from the point of view of the education of Charley Washington: how a young Swedish-American farmer's son leaves his home in rural Nebraska to travel several hundred miles east to Rock Island, Illinois, to receive a solid education at the leading Swedish-American institution of higher learning. It illustrates one dimension of the educational process at a

[7] Charley Washington 1917, 5.
[8] Charley Washington 1917, 4.
[9] The Swedish expression *gå igenom ekluten* (to mature through hard times) was often used to refer to the immigrants' first difficult years in America.

school like Augustana College, namely how an uneducated young Swedish American, with little knowledge of Swedish high culture and who spoke in a dialect mixed with English, is taught to speak standard Swedish and learns enough about the cultural history of Sweden so that he can both quote the eighteenth century poet Carl Michael Bellman and sing "Studentsången."

The fact that Charley Washington, the son of a Swedish immigrant farmer, also receives a job as a teacher at the conclusion of his studies is also a good example of the kind of social mobility into the middle classes as ministers, teachers, doctors, and lawyers that many graduates of an institution like Augustana experienced. Moreover, it is also significant that Charley becomes a teacher at Augustana College and thus remains within the Swedish-American cultural sphere, and will, in his turn, be able to teach other young Swedish Americans, from farms and cities, to speak proper Swedish and to become familiar with Swedish literature, history, and culture.

The play thus highlights some of the general themes in this chapter on Swedish-American education at Augustana College. Before we can continue this analysis in greater detail, it is necessary to provide a short overview of education in general in the Augustana Synod and a brief overview of the history of Augustana College and Theological Seminary.

Education in the Augustana Synod

Fourteen colleges and academies were established in the Augustana Synod.[10] The first was Augustana College and Theological Seminary created simultaneously with the Synod in 1860, followed by Gustavus Adolphus College in Minnesota which can trace its history to 1862. These two schools remained alone on the scene for about two decades, when beginning in the 1880s a period of what one historian of Swedish America has called a period of "college mania" set in.[11] During the two following decades no fewer than seven academies or colleges were started, namely what became Bethany College in Lindsborg, Kansas; Luther College, in Wahoo, Nebraska; and Upsala College, eventually located in East Orange, N.J., all of which survived well into the twentieth century. Other schools fared less well. Lund Academy in Melby, Minnesota and Martin Luther College in Chicago lasted only two to three years, whereas the two Minnesota academies, Hope in Moorhead and Emanuel in Minneapolis, were in operation for half a decade. During the first decade of the twentieth century, five more schools connected with the Augustana Synod were started, three in Minnesota, one in Texas, and one in Idaho.

---

[10] Person 1941, appendix, provides a listing of all Swedish-American academies and colleges.

[11] Stephenson 1932, 335.

By the mid-1930s, all of these had closed. Of the total of fourteen schools supported by the Augustana Synod, only five lasted beyond the Depression.[12]

Of all these schools, only four, Augustana, Gustavus Adolphus, Bethany, and Upsala, developed into full four-year colleges, granting baccalaureate degrees. The others were academies granting secondary school degrees, mainly serving as feeder schools to the four colleges or to non-Swedish-American institutions of higher learning. In 1910 it was estimated that over 22,000 persons had matriculated in an Augustana Synod school and that over 5,000 had been graduated from one of them, with three dominating: Augustana, Gustavus Adolphus, and Bethany. However, one must remember that these figures include all divisions of the schools, both the more strictly academic programs, as well as the very popular commercial departments teaching stenography and other secretarial skills primarily to students in the immediate vicinity of the colleges. Also, in 1910 official statistics listed more than 5,000 students as having been enlisted in the collegiate departments in the three largest colleges, whereas only 900 students were noted as having a collegiate degree.[13]

In addition to the academies and colleges, attempts were made to create a system of parochial schools that would supplement the subjects taught in the elementary public schools with instruction in Swedish and religion.[14] Still, a full Swedish Lutheran parochial school system never really developed, and by and large Augustana Swedes were supporters of the American public school system. As early as 1873, the Augustana Synod approved of sending students to the public schools, as long as they were characterized by "Christian morality" and proper instruction in Christianity was given either in the homes or through the church.[15] This meant that after 1890 or so a system of so-called "Swede Schools" emerged, which were conducted for several weeks in the summers by individual congregations, and in which students from the Augustana Seminary or one of the colleges would teach religion and Swedish language and literature. The enrollment figures for these schools ranged from

---

[12] A number of historical accounts of the schools exist. For Augustana College see Bergendoff 1969, regarding Gustavus Adolphus College see Lund 1963, Bethany College see Lindquist 1975, Upsala College see Beck 1907, Luther Academy see Hill 1906, North Star College, see Strand 1910, Northwestern College see Moody 1908, Minnesota College see Nelson 1911. Minnesskrift 1910, 155–229 provides a contemporary account of the Augustana Synod schools in 1910.

[13] Minnesskrift 1910, 483–84. These figures should be used with great care. It was, for example, not unusual to exaggerate the size of enrollment in order to enhance the school's prestige. The figure of 5,300 students at Bethany College, e.g., seems very high, and it could well have included many members of the Handel Oratorio Chorus at the school. [Personal communication from Bruce Karstadt, Minneapolis, March, 1992.]

[14] Cf. the positive comments about starting a separate teachers training school at Augustana College in 1891. [Referat 1891, 41–42.]

[15] Referat 1873, 17.

12,000 in 1889 to 22,000 in 1903, but was down to 10,000 in 1918.[16] It is interesting to note that even when attempts were made in the late 1880s to restrict the foreign language schools in several states in the Midwest,[17] the Synod still expressed support of the public schools, even though it vigorously argued that the U.S. constitution did not ban religious instruction in private schools.[18]

Thus in the Augustana Synod, most of the efforts were directed towards the establishment of institutions of higher learning, such as colleges, academies, and seminaries, although some but not very successful attempts were made to create a Lutheran parochial school system. Obviously the religious element played an important role in these schools—indeed the training of ministers was one of the main reasons behind the establishment of what became Augustana College and Theological Seminary. A system of academies and colleges developed soon, however, that would not only prepare the prospective seminarians for their theological studies, but also sought to provide students with a basic academic training that would enable them to pursue other careers.

In addition to providing the theological and general academic training for Swedish-Americans, the institutions of higher learning in the Augustana Synod were also important in maintaining what was perceived as a sense of Swedish distinctiveness in America. As we shall see, this dimension was an important part of the educational program in the Augustana Synod, and the latter part of this chapter will be devoted to an examination of how a sense of Swedish-American ethnic identity emerged at the central institution of higher learning in the Augustana Synod, Augustana College.

Augustana College and Theological Seminary

When the Augustana Synod was formed in 1860, one of the first items on the agenda in the newly founded denomination was establishing its own educational institution to train minsters and teachers. During their affiliation with the Synod of Northern Illinois, the Swedish Lutheran immigrants had attended that synod's school, Illinois State University in Springfield, Illinois, where Lars Paul Esbjörn had served as professor for a group of both Swedish and Norwegian students. Following the break with the Synod of Northern Illinois and the establishment of the Augustana Synod, a new solution to the Synod's educational needs had to be found, and thus "the Augustana Seminary" as it

---

[16] Nordgren 1935, 276. In 1906, a formal curriculum for these schools was adopted. [Referat 1906, 147–48.] The proposal was presented in 1902. [Referat 1902, 103–17.] Cf. also Arden 1963, 106–07.

[17] Ulrich 1980.

[18] Referat 1890, 22–23.

was originally known was established, consisting of a theological and preparatory department.[19]

The new school struggled during its first years.[20] The initial location was the basement of the Immanuel Lutheran Church on Chicago's Near North Side, a setting which was considered temporary from the beginning. Following a search for a more suitable site, synod and college officials accepted an offer for land by the Illinois Central Railroad, and in 1863 the school was relocated to Paxton, Illinois, a small rural community a hundred miles south of Chicago.

The location in Paxton never proved a success, primarily because it was too far away from the streams of Swedish immigrants in the 1860s and 1870s, who tended to settle farther west in Illinois and Iowa and farther north in Minnesota. Thus, a search for a new location was conducted and eventually the school bought a plot of land in Rock Island in western Illinois, close to such early Swedish settlements as Andover, Moline, and Galesburg, all dating back to the 1840s and 1850s. On September 22, 1875 the school opened its doors in Rock Island, which has been the permanent location for the institution ever since.

Following the move to Rock Island in 1875, the college grew. In 1877, the first collegiate class was graduated and during the next decade, the curriculum for students in the college included a gradually growing number of courses in the humanities and the natural sciences. (The curriculum will be discussed in greater detail later in this chapter.) The completion of a new main building in 1889, then known as Memorial Hall, now as Old Main and of Denkmann Hall in 1911, symbolized the physical growth of an expanding institution.

Student enrollments stood at the 15–20 during the pioneer years in Chicago and between 50–70 in Paxton. Following the move to Rock Island, growth quickened; in 1880 there were 136 students at the institution, and in 1890 286. In 1900 the figure stood at 602, ten years later somewhat lower at 555, and in 1920 at 944.[21]

The institution was incorporated in the State of Illinois in 1863, from that time consisting of a college and seminary.[22] In 1870 a new constitution was adopted for the school.[23] It now became formally known as "Augustana College and Theological Seminary," and its constitution identified three departments: a preparatory, a collegiate, and a theological.[24] The preparatory department was to be of "a practical nature," preparing students for "various

[19] Referat 1860, 5 and 24–25.

[20] For the following overview, see Bergendoff 1969.

[21] For enrollment figures, see Minnesskrift 1910, 485, Catalog 1910–11, 144, and Catalog 1920–21, 191.

[22] Referat 1864, 11. The Synod minutes refer to the "college" for the first time in 1865. [Referat 1865, 25.]

[23] Referat 1870, 33.

[24] The constitution is found in Referat 1869, 35–38.

branches of business" as well as for collegiate study; in the 1883–84 catalog it was described as "corresponding to a common American academy or high school."[25] From 1898 the preparatory department was referred to as the academic department or the academy, while the old preparatory department by 1902 provided training for students seeking admission into the Academy.[26]

The collegiate department was organized into four classes, "corresponding to four years and similar to the course of the American Colleges generally," which lead to the degree of Bachelor of Arts. The theological department's goal was to prepare students for the ministry in the Augustana Synod, initially including two years of study, but which over the years was expanded to three.[27]

These three units made up the institution until the late 1880s when a number of other programs were added to the curriculum, often in the form of separate "schools." In 1887, the school's Board of Directors reported to the synod that courses in music and book-keeping had been introduced at Augustana, as a need for them existed, and the Synod decided that a "conservatory of music" and a "commercial department" be started.[28] The conservatory and the commercial departments got underway in 1888,[29] and especially the latter attracted numerous students, many from the local area and of non-Swedish background. A Normal Department was also started in 1891, which trained teachers for parochial and public schools.[30] A school of art was established in 1895,[31] which eventually became an art department within the college. Some of these programs became quite successful in terms of enrollments. In 1910 688 persons had graduated from the Augustana commercial department compared to 468 from the college itself. The situation was similar at Gustavus Adolphus and Bethany Colleges.[32]

The Development of the Curriculum

We will now examine in greater detail the curricular development at Augustana College, first looking at how the general curriculum developed. What kinds of courses were offered at the school and how did various tracks of study develop? How strongly influenced was the school by educational traditions in Sweden, and what role did American educational practices play?

[25] Catalog 1883–84, 36, Bergendoff 1969, 56.
[26] Catalog 1902–03, 11.
[27] Referat, 1869, 35–36. Quotation from p. 35.
[28] Referat 1887, 30.
[29] Bergendoff 1969, 70–71.
[30] Referat 1890, 25 and Referat 1891, 41. Cf. also Catalog 1892–93, 7.
[31] Bergendoff 1969, 100.
[32] Minnesskrift 1910, 483.

Given the fact that Augustana College was a denominational institution, the second section will address the significance of religion at the college. An examination of the role played by and the position of Swedish in the school's curriculum will also be important, as it will provide a basis for an answer to the question of the role that ethnicity played at the college.

The 1860 constitution stated that the purpose of the institution was to train ministers, especially for the Augustana Synod, and to educate school teachers.[33] Article III had established two parts of the school: a preparatory department (which developed into the college) in which languages, history, geography, mathematics, and the natural sciences would be taught, and a theological department including both theoretical and practical courses. "Three or more professors, of which one should be Swedish, one Norwegian, and one English"[34] were also established, suggesting that different subjects were taught in different languages and that one teacher had to teach in more than one field.

The instruction during the early years included languages (the Scandinavian languages, English, German, Latin, and some Greek and Hebrew), history, geography, mathematics, and natural sciences,[35] but seems to have varied somewhat. In 1863, chemistry and physics are mentioned as new additions.[36] In 1865, President Hasselquist reported that fifteen students were enrolled, studying Latin, Greek, English, German, Swedish, world history, geography, philosophy, arithmetic, and algebra, as well as a number of theological subjects. The medium of instruction was one of the Scandinavian languages in seven of these subjects and English in six.[37]

As noted above, the new constitution from 1870 established a more coherent structure for the institution with the three distinct elements: the preparatory department, the college, and the seminary. Except for a general course in Christianity required of all students, the theological education offered at Augustana was concentrated to the Seminary, while the general, more advanced academic schooling was located in the college. The following analysis of the academic developments at Augustana and the role Swedish played will thus be on the college.

From an examination of the curricular developments in the college, we notice that, from the very beginning, a distinction was made between two tracks of study, the classical and the scientific. The 1875/76 catalog from the school's first year in Rock Island speaks of the classical course as the most extensive one, with special emphasis on Greek and Latin. However, the catalog noted that the scientific course (*realvetenskapliga kursen*) had recently

---

[33] The following is based on Referat 1860, 24–25. Cf. also Bergendoff 1969, 20.
[34] Referat 1860, 24.
[35] Referat 1860, 24.
[36] Referat 1863, 22.
[37] Referat 1865, 24.

been growing in strength and was placing special emphasis on mathematics and the natural sciences. The former course was said to be of special importance to ministers and scholars with a need for classical training, while the latter was suited for persons seeking positions in public life, the law, the military, and industry.[38]

This duality in the curriculum can be followed during the coming years. The 1883/84 catalog noted two courses of study, a classical and a scientific, leading to Bachelor of Arts and Bachelor of Science degrees. In both courses, all students studied Christian Science, languages (Swedish, English, German, Latin), history, mathematics, natural sciences, and philosophy. The classical track added Greek and more Latin, whereas the scientific track included more mathematics and natural sciences.[39] The following year, the catalog also noted that it was possible to graduate from the classical course without studying Swedish, and that this arrangement would be made more permanent in the coming years.[40]

At the synod meeting in 1889, the faculty of the college and seminary reported to the Synod that these changes had been achieved as there were now three tracks of study in the college: a classical course including Swedish, a classical course without Swedish, and a scientific course with both Swedish and English,[41] a system which was first mentioned in the college catalog in 1890/91. Most of the courses in the three tracks were similar, including a number of core subjects such as languages, Christianity, and scientific subjects that were required in all three tracks. In the English classical track, Swedish was substituted for more scientific subjects such as physiology, and more mathematics was included than in the Swedish-classical track. The scientific track included even more scientific subjects, such as chemistry and botany, omitting some Greek and Latin.[42]

The curricular discussions continued, resulting in the continuance of two basic tracks of study in 1895, one classical and one scientific, with the choice between Swedish and English in each. Both tracks included subjects such as Christianity, languages, philosophy, history, political economy, mathematics, and physics. The classical tracks put greater emphasis on Latin and Greek, while the scientific track included more mathematics and subjects like natural history, chemistry, botany, and German. In addition, a number of elective subjects were introduced in both tracks, for example French and more advanced mathematics.[43] In 1900/01, a further distinction was made, and the

---

[38] Catalog 1875/76, 8.
[39] Catalog 1883/84, 28–33 and 36.
[40] Catalog 1884/85, 21.
[41] Referat 1889, 45.
[42] Catalog 1890/91, 29–39.
[43] Catalog 1895/96, 26–28.

catalog mentions two classical tracks, one scientific and one mathematical-language track, in which Swedish was a required subject of study in one of the classical tracks.[44]

Beginning in 1902/03, the courses of instruction in the college were arranged in several "groups," which were intended to be "equally difficult ... and designed to promote specialization ... of the student's own choice." In addition to these groups, students also had a number of elective courses to choose from. In that year, six groups of study were listed: the classical, the modern language, the Latin-scientific, the general science, the pre-medical, and the mathematical groups.[45] The classical group was sub-divided into two, the second one called "the classical group with Swedish."[46]

Although the Augustana curriculum thus became even more diversified, there were still a number of core subjects required of all students, as the school, according to the catalog, insisted "upon certain fundamental disciplines with which it is believed that every educated man of the present day should be familiar."[47] These subjects included Christianity, English, German, history, mathematics, physics, and logic.

This curricular model with groups of subject, elective courses, and required courses continued at Augustana College throughout the two first decades of the twentieth century. In 1916/17, the number of groups was changed to ten, and at the same time, the Swedish-classical group disappeared from the curriculum.[48]

The Augustana view of education was rooted in the Swedish experience out of which its early leadership came, but was obviously also shaped by the new American context in which the school functioned. In Sweden, the church played an important role in all levels of education, and when compulsory elementary education became law in 1842, for example, the educational system was outlined by the state but by and large controlled and conducted by the church.[49] The connection between church and education was thus a natural one for the school's founders and became an integral part of the lives of the Augustana Synod schools. The American separation between church and state and the subsequent ban of religious instruction in public schools made this connection even more important for the Augustana Swedes.

In assessing the development of the Augustana curriculum, one can distinguish influences from both Swedish and American educational traditions. The

---

[44] Catalog 1900/01, 28–34.
[45] Catalog 1902/03, 17.
[46] Catalog 1902/03, 19.
[47] Catalog 1902/03, 17.
[48] Catalog 1916/17, 21.
[49] Petterson 1992 is a recent discussion of the growth of elementary education in Sweden in the nineteenth century.

Swedish influence seems to have come mainly from the secondary schools, the *läroverk*, also the word which was used when Augustana and other colleges were referred to in Swedish.[50] The significance of the Swedish schools is also noted by Fritiof Ander, who writes that up until 1890, developments at Augustana were more influenced by European practices than American and that the methods of instruction "were similar to those employed in the Swedish and German *Gymnasia*."[51]

The division of the curriculum in two basic tracks, the classical and scientific, also shows an influence from a Swedish practice. In Sweden, much of the discussion on secondary education during the nineteenth century revolved around the relationship between the "classical" and what was called "practical" subjects, which, for example, included the modern languages and the natural sciences.[52] The changing needs of a society that was undergoing major economic and social transformations also required a different kind of education. Christina Florin and Ulla Johansson have shown how the emphasis in the secondary school education gradually shifted from an older ideal of training civil servants to educating students who would make and execute decisions, in which the more "practical" subjects, such as modern languages, natural sciences, etc. were introduced as complements and alternatives. This development can be traced in several ordinances from 1849, 1856, and 1859. The 1859 ordinance established two tracks of study (*linjer*), a classical and a scientific (*klassisk* and *real*), terms which were also used in the Augustana collegiate curriculum.

It is also clear that Augustana was not conceived of as a university in the Swedish sense, although there were hopes that the college would eventually develop into such. It was, for example, possible to receive a Master's Degree from 1888, but relatively few degrees were ever awarded.[53] At the fiftieth anniversary in 1910, the visiting rector of Uppsala University, Henrik Schück, also expressed his hope that the school would develop into a university, noting that this had not happened yet.[54]

American patterns of higher education can also be discerned. Already in 1870 the new constitution of the school claimed that Augustana College was to be comparable to American colleges in general, the degree granted was an American Bachelor of Arts, and the American practice of organizing the students into the four classes (freshman, sophomore, junior, and senior) was also adopted. The role the American context played for Augustana is clearly evi-

---

[50] This term was, for example, still used in 1914, towards the end of the period of investigation. [Referat 1914, 18.]

[51] Ander 1931, 75.

[52] The following is based on Florin & Johansson 1993, 81–86.

[53] Bergendoff 1969, 102, 118.

[54] Minnen 1911, 115.

denced in the curricular reform of 1902. The division of the curriculum into a classical and scientific track of study was replaced with an elective system, where students could choose between several groups of subjects, an approach that was gaining prominence among American colleges and universities toward the end of the nineteenth century.[55] The college catalog from 1902 also clearly stated that its curriculum was "patterned after the most modern and approved models" and that the institution sought to be "in the very front rank of American institutions of learning."[56]

The Role of Religion

As noted in chapter one, religion was a powerful factor in many nineteenth-century American immigrant communities. This was also the case at Augustana College. One of the main reasons behind the founding of the institution was to educate a clergy for the Augustana Synod. In 1865 Lars Paul Esbjörn reported on the conditions in the Augustana Synod to the ministerium of the archdiocese in Uppsala. He emphasized the necessity for the Synod to establish its own educational institution by reminding his listeners of the history of the Swedish congregations in the New Sweden colony from the seventeenth century, "which little by little were absorbed by the Episcopal Church precisely because they lacked facilities for the training of their own ministers."[57] T.N. Hasselquist, Esbjörn's successor as president of the college and seminary, made a similar point in a letter to Peter Wieselgren in 1867 when he underscored that the Synod needed ministers trained in America, not in Sweden, so that they would be familiar with conditions in the New World.[58]

The theological training needed for the ministry in the Synod was provided in the Augustana Seminary, where the curriculum during the final decades of the nineteenth century gradually became longer and more comprehensive.[59] By the end of the century, the admission requirements for the Seminary had also developed to the point where an adequate academic preparation was obligatory, and this was most often interpreted to mean an undergraduate collegiate training of the nature provided by Augustana College or one of the other collegiate institutions in the Synod.[60]

The religious dimension at Augustana was, however, not limited to the seminary. From the very beginning, religion played an important role in the

---

[55] Rudolph 1962, chapter 14 provides a discussion of the introduction of the principle of elective subjects in American colleges and universities in the late nineteenth century.

[56] Catalog 1902/03, 10.

[57] Quoted in Arden 1960, 69.

[58] Printed in Westin 1932, 137.

[59] Arden 1960 provides an overview of the history of the Seminary. Chapter 5 details the development of the curriculum.

[60] Cf. Arden 1960, 192–96.

70

collegiate curriculum as well. The Synod minutes from 1872 speak of the need for a Christian education,[61] something which was reiterated throughout the years. In 1891, Edward Nelander, a minister in the Synod and president of Bethany College from 1883 to 1889, maintained that the Swedish Americans needed an education rooted in the Lutheran religion and that it was the mission of Augustana College to provide a "true, Christian education."[62] The third constitution of the college and seminary, adopted in 1893 following several years of discussion, stated in its first article that "the object of the institution" was to "impart a general classical and scientific education under Christian influences" as well as to provide theological training for the ministry.[63]

Many other examples of this attitude can be given. During the search for a new president in 1901, an editorial in *Augustana* emphasized that it was necessary to safeguard the "Christian and confessional nature" of the college.[64] In 1903 the Synod president spoke of the schools in the Augustana Synod as a place for both learning and promotion of a Christian Evangelical Lutheran world view,[65] and in 1914 the Synod president identified two dimensions of the work of the denomination's colleges, namely the inculcation of knowledge and the development of a Christian character, maintaining that only a college based on Christian principles would be able to provide both these elements.[66] These sentiments are also echoed in the general description of the institution which appeared in the college catalogs, which in 1902/03 stated that although not "sectarian," the school was still a "denominational institution" open to all "who desire a liberal education based upon the Christian religion and permeated by the Christian spirit."[67] Not even the commercial department was excluded from this, as it was considered to offer "a thorough business training under Christian influences."[68]

These religious considerations established a set of boundaries of behavior in many spheres at the school. For example, activities such as drinking alcoholic beverages or dancing were not allowed, and the 1893 constitution stated that students at the institution were not allowed to "visit billiard rooms, dances, theatres, or similar places," to drink or gamble, or to organize or belong to "any secret society."[69] These attitudes remained strong well into the twentieth

---

[61] Referat 1872, 15.

[62] *Augustana*, 12 November 1891.

[63] See Referat 1892, 50–59 for the constitution. [Quotation from p. 50.] The constitution was adopted in 1893. [Referat 1893, 42.] Cf. also Mattson 1941, 148.

[64] *Augustana*, 24 January 1901.

[65] Referat 1903, 10.

[66] Referat 1914, 18.

[67] Here quoted from Catalog 1902/03, 10.

[68] Catalog 1909/10, 13.

[69] Referat 1892, 58. Also reprinted in Mattson 1941, 161. One representative example of the struggle against alcohol is the article series "Nykterhet och reform" in *Augustana*, 17, 24 October and 1 November 1895.

century. In 1911, the Synod protested against the "introduction of dancing and theatrical performances" in the public schools, in 1912 *Augustana* warned of the negative influences of dancing and theatre, and in 1913 the paper maintained that there was no possibility that the church would be able to accept the theater, as the love of the Lord diminished as the interest in theater increased.[70]

Other examples of the religious dimension at the school include the twenty-minute daily religious services at the school's chapel as well as longer Sunday services, both of which all students were expected to attend.[71] The Augustana Foreign Missionary Society, established in 1886 to attract support for the Synod's foreign missions,[72] was another important element of the religious presence on campus, which by the turn of the century counted half the college student body as well as many faculty and others in its membership.[73]

From the more strictly educational or curricular view, the religious dimension meant that the study of Christianity was required of students at all levels and in all programs offered at the school in Rock Island and at other Augustana Synod schools as well.[74] Throughout the curricular reforms at Augustana during the following decades, with the introduction of various elective courses, Christianity remained a subject that all students were required to study, regardless of their other curricular choices.

While an Augustana education certainly emphasized the religious dimension, the schools founded by the Synod were not merely preacher schools. Although there was a great need to educate ministers, the schools also sought to provide Swedish Americans with an education for other professions, and from the very beginning, the curriculum included languages, history, geography, mathematics, and the natural sciences, as well as Christianity.[75] As Oscar N. Olson put it in a retrospective article at the 75th anniversary of the Augustana Synod in 1935, the Synod wanted an educated ministry.[76]

As will be shown later in this chapter the most common profession for an Augustana graduate was a ministerial career in the Augustana Synod. However, a growing number also pursued professional careers, especially after the turn of the century and among the American-born generation. Of all students enrolled in the college in the 1880s, for example, some 47 percent were ordained in the Augustana Synod, while only 20 percent of the college attendees between 1910–1914 followed the same career pattern. If we look at those stu-

[70] Referat 1911, 40, *Augustana*, 13 April 1911, 18 January 1912, 17 April and 8 May 1913. See also "Om dans och teaterbesök," *Ungdomsvännen*, 1906, 69.
[71] E.g. Catalog 1892/93, 45. Cf. also Bergendoff 1969, 124.
[72] Catalog 1909/10, 104.
[73] Bergendoff 1969, 123–24.
[74] Arden 1963, 94–95.
[75] Referat 1860, 24.
[76] Olson 1935, 111.

dents who followed the entire course of study and graduated from the college, 54 percent of the graduates in the 1880s went into the ministry, whereas 36 percent of the seniors 1910–1914 became Augustana ministers.[77]

This fact has also been noted by Walter Beck, an historian of Lutheran educational endeavors in America, who wrote in 1939 that the Swedish-American schools were not solely intended for "ministerial preparation" (which was much more the case among for example, German-American Lutherans), meaning that a denomination like the Augustana Synod provided its members with educational training that prepared them for "secular" careers in American society.[78]

One illustration of this attitude comes from the dedication ceremony of the new main building at Augustana College in Rock Island in 1889, when college president T.N. Hasselquist stated that religion and theology must not be isolated from the rest of human knowledge and experience, but must inform and be informed by it, and education must be the hand-maiden of this cross-fertilization.[79]

When Hasselquist's successor as president, Olof Olsson, spoke to the incoming students in 1892, he insisted that it was their mission to "bind together all Swedes in America in a Swedish-American Lutheran church." Olsson asserted that the college played a central role in this process, as it trained ministers but also educated persons for secular life. In this way a common education on a Christian basis would be provided to all students who then would be able to go out in all walks of life and thus tie together all Swedish Americans.[80] In the same way, *Augustana* argued in favor of keeping the "commercial school" as a part of the college's curriculum. A commercial school, the paper wrote, did not necessarily mean that the Synod would engage in adoration of Mammon. Instead, since earthly matters had to be taken care of, it was better if it were done on a Christian foundation and it not be left to "institutions that are irreligious or hostile to Christianity."[81]

At the installation of Gustav Andreen as president in 1901, M.C. Ranseen made a similar point, referring to Augustana as the most significant Swedish-American college, which initially had been mainly a theological institution. Now, however, the institution prepared students for "many other professions" as well, at the same time realizing that "true education" must rest on a Christian foundation. Ranseen also expressed the hope that the college eventually

[77] Augustana Student database. See pages 108–09 for explanation of the database.
[78] Beck 1939, 288.
[79] As quoted in Norelius 1900, 266–72.
[80] O. Olsson, "Välkomsthälsning till vår kunskaps- och bildningstörstande ungdom," *Augustana*, 25 August 1892.
[81] "Hvad kunna vi vänta af våra blifvande affärsmän," *Augustana*, 18 August 1892.

would develop into a university.[82] Andreen himself echoed these sentiments by saying that demands in recent years for the inclusion of more natural sciences as well as modern languages in the curriculum had been heard, and that he saw it as an important task to build a coherent curriculum, incorporating these subjects with the previous emphasis on the humanities.[83]

The teaching of natural sciences was of course a potentially explosive issue for church-related schools. At the Augustana Synod schools, however, this does not seem to have been a major problem. At Augustana College a strong program in the natural sciences was established by Joshua Lindahl, with a Ph.D. from Lund University, who taught at the school between 1878–1881 and who was followed by the geologist J.A. Udden.[84] The significance attached to the natural sciences at Augustana schools was also expressed by the Augustana College president Olof Olsson in 1898 when he talked about the many excellent courses in the natural sciences at the college, which he thought provided students who were not going into the ministry with a more useful preparation than the classic curriculum. "We have enough of ... literary people, but we often lack practical persons," Olsson concluded.[85] In the 1920s, school officials also supported the Darwinian biology taught at the college which had come under criticism from certain parts of the Synod.[86]

It is instructive to compare the view of education in the Augustana Synod with other Swedish-American denominations that had a much more difficult time dealing with the issue of both formal education as well as instruction in non-religious subjects. Within the Mission Covenant Church, e.g., the establishment of schools and the acceptance of formal education did not come as easily as in the Augustana Synod. C.A. Björk, the denomination's president when it was founded in 1885, claimed that practical experience could give as much training and necessary preparation as formal education.[87] In this he was echoing P.P. Waldenström, the leader of Svenska Missionsförbundet, who had scorned university training in his *Brukspatron Adamsson* (Squire Adamsson), where the fountain of wisdom is an un-learned woman named Mother Simple who counsels the main character to get his schooling not from Theology College, which has enrolled Strong, Cock-Sure and Wise-in-his-own-conceits, but from Father Experience in the Misery Class.[88]

This attitude made it much more difficult to gain support for the Covenant North Park College in Chicago, where its president David Nyvall struggled to

[82] *Augustana*, 31 October 1901.
[83] *Augustana*, 24 October 1901.
[84] For Lindahl, see Bergendoff 1969, 53–54, 57, and 68, for Udden 80, and 101.
[85] Referat 1898, 27.
[86] Bergendoff 1992, 3.
[87] Carlson 1945, 45.
[88] Olsson 1963, 110–12.

establish not just a preachers school but "a solid academy and college as the underpining for the seminary."[89] This fact was also noted in the Augustana Synod 75th anniversary publication from 1935, which states that the leadership in the Augustana Synod did not see "culture and learning as hindrances to spirituality, which was the case in some other religions."[90]

The Position of Swedish in the Curriculum

During the first several decades of Augustana's history, learning English and becoming American were strongly emphasized. The early leadership in the Synod and at the school believed that the Swedish language would disappear within a few decades and that the Synod needed to be ready for the day when English would be the dominant language.[91] When Lars Paul Esbjörn organized his first Sunday schools in Andover, Illinois, he used English as the language of instruction for the younger children, and in his report to the American Home Missionary Society of 1852, he stated his intention to start preaching in English to make his countrymen "more acquainted with the English language."[92] Erik Norelius, one of the most influential Augustana leaders, wrote in 1860 that "[w]e are not and will never be shut up within our own nationality" and that we "become more and more Americanized every day."[93] Years later, Erland Carlsson also told Gustav Andreen that he believed "that the Swedish language would be dead in America in twenty years, and therefore I prepared myself for the change and studied the English language."[94]

When the original constitution for the Augustana Seminary was drawn up in 1860, one of the three professorships was designated to be filled by an English-speaker. However, it proved difficult to find teachers for the institution in general, and in his annual reports to the Synod, President Hasselquist at times mentioned the fact that English-speaking teachers were needed if the school was to become successful.[95] This attitude is also reflected in the curricular developments which made Swedish an elective subject by the mid-1880s. In 1867 the Synod minutes also spoke of the institution as a school in which Swedish immigrants would be shaped by their own religious confession and where they could get the necessary education in the English language. The

[89] Olsson 1962, 514. An overview of the debate on education in the Covenant church up to 1920 is found on pp. 509–14.
[90] Olson 1935, 109.
[91] Nothstein 1945, 209–10.
[92] Nothstein 1944, 18.
[93] Erik Norelius in *The Missionary*, 24 May 1860, reprinted in Ander & Nordstrom 1942, 127.
[94] Quoted after Nothstein 1945, 210.
[95] Referat 1868, 35, Referat 1875, 44.

following year the Synod declared that no student should be allowed to leave the school without sufficient knowledge of English or Swedish.[96]

In his study of T.H. Hasselquist, the dominant figure in the Synod and president at Augustana College and Theological Seminary from 1863 until his death in 1891, Fritiof Ander also notes the tendency to emphasize English. He writes that Hasselquist "became a 'good' American in nearly every respect," and was an advocate for "Americanization"—even calling opposition to it "sinful." In Hasselquist's view, it was inevitable that the Swedish language in America would disappear, and Ander concludes that he sought to prepare the Synod "through its educational institution, for the day when the Swedish language no longer could be used."[97]

These attitudes are also reflected in the role of Swedish in the Augustana curriculum. Although Swedish was used as a language of instruction during the early years, beginning in the 1880s the number of hours and subjects taught in Swedish declined.[98] In 1884/85 almost half of the hours in the classical track were taught in Swedish, whereas the share in the scientific track was about a third.[99] The language was primarily used in Christianity classes, as well as in the Swedish, German, Latin, and Greek courses. One example of its decline was the September 1884 recommendation by the professor of Greek that English be used as the means of instruction in Greek throughout the four years of collegiate study.[100]

During the following years, the college catalogs give little specific information about the number of hours taught in the different languages. Still, the selection of textbooks for different subjects suggests that English was becoming the dominant language. Aside from the subject of Swedish, Swedish-language textbooks were partly used in Greek, Latin, and Christianity throughout the 1880s,[101] but by 1893/94 Swedish-language books were used only in Christianity and Swedish.[102] After the turn of the century, the use of Swedish disappeared in the Christianity courses as well. In 1902/03 one of the three college-level courses in Christianity was taught in Swedish, three years later the catalog stated that the course was "at present" given in Swedish, and by 1908/09 no mention is made of any Swedish-language requirements in Christianity.[103]

[96] Referat 1867, 23–24, Referat 1868, 35.
[97] Ander 1931, 229.
[98] This development can be traced from 1881/82 and on in the Augustana College catalog descriptions of the individual subjects as well as the listings of required readings.
[99] Catalog, 1884/85, 22.
[100] ACL, BdDir, Minutes, 8 September 1884.
[101] Catalog 1887/88, 34, Catalog 1889/90, 33.
[102] Catalog 1893/94, 31.
[103] Catalog 1902/03, 27, Catalog 1905/06, 25, Catalog 1908/09, 29.

As Swedish declined as the language of instruction in the college, the different curricular reforms also meant that its relative position in the curriculum receded. As shown above, from the mid-1880s it became possible to graduate from Augustana without having studied Swedish, when the classical track without Swedish was introduced. As the curriculum became even more diversified, this de-emphasis continued. It seems likely that part of the reason for establishing non-Swedish courses of study, at least in the 1880s, had to do with an increasing interest from students of non-Swedish background from the local area to study at Augustana.

The college made efforts to accommodate those students who did not wish to study Swedish. The non-Swedish track was announced in 1884/85, and made even more permanent in 1890/91. After 1895, the college catalogs do not include any information on the track of study of individual students. The general tendency in the college towards a predominance of American-born students of both Swedish and non-Swedish background during the decade before the turn of the century (see below) suggests that after 1900 the possibility of graduating without Swedish was not only due to the enrollment of "American" students, but also a reflection of the fact that many American-born students of Swedish parentage who did not speak or wish to learn Swedish attended the school.

This seeming de-emphasis on Swedish at Augustana did not go unnoticed in Swedish America. Concerns were voiced that the disappearance of Swedish was changing the nature of the school. During the early spring of 1890, a discussion took place in the pages of *Hemlandet* regarding the position of Swedish at Augustana College. A writer using the pseudonym *Skolvän* (A Friend of the School) noted that the number of hours taught in Swedish was declining and suggested that this might constitute a threat to "Swedish-American education" (*svensk-amerikansk bildning*),[104] whereas *En läroverkets vän* (A Friend of the College) wrote that recent curricular changes might lead to the suspicion that the school was changing to "a solely English institution of education ... without interest for the real needs and national feelings of our people."[105] *Hemlandet* commented that the Swedish-American colleges should pay equally large attention to teaching both English and Swedish, and a knowledge of the latter was particularly important for those students who would work "among and for the Swedish-American nationality."[106]

At the Synod meeting in 1890, the president of the Board of Directors commented on this discussion, suggesting that it was rooted in misconceptions in newspapers about the situation of Swedish at the school and the question of

[104] "Engelsk-amerikansk eller svensk-amerikansk," *Hemlandet,* 13 February 1890.
[105] "Är det välbetänkt?" *Hemlandet*, 20 March 1890.
[106] "Anspråken stiga," *Hemlandet*, 20 March 1890. George Stephenson has suggested that the author of this article was Johan Enander. [Stephenson 1932, 380.]

plans to move the college to Chicago. Now that these misunderstandings had been cleared up, it should be possible for the entire Synod to support financially the college and seminary even more.[107]

The role of Swedish was discussed again in 1892, when *Augustana* noted that some critics maintained that English played too large a role at Augustana, that Swedish was left behind, and that the college "will become solely an English institution of learning." The paper took issue with this opinion, responding that even though all instruction, except in the Swedish language and literature, was conducted in English, Swedish still remained a popular subject in the college, and anyone who attended one of the Swedish classes would understand that at Augustana it was "of the greatest importance" to educate persons who "in writing and speaking are able to use the English and Swedish languages fluently."[108]

Another sign of the decreasing use of Swedish among at least parts of the Augustana student body was the decision to conduct the daily morning prayers at the college in English. In its decision from December 1898 the Board of Directors based its reasoning on the fact that all students should attend the morning devotions, but since the school "has a large number of students who understand only the English language" the prayers should be conducted in English.[109]

This decision also generated discussion. According to George Stephenson, the 1899 Synod convention approved it after "a lengthy discussion," which included critical voices.[110] In the monthly journal *Ungdomsvännen*, which had recently been started by a group of Augustana pastors in Minnesota, Pastor C.A Hultkrans commented that not much could be done about the matter, but that the goal of making Augustana "American" as fast as possible had been reached, something which he deplored.[111] In an article in December 1899, President Olsson responded to these critics who, he stated, "had caused the present administration of the college such bitter sorrow, through the harsh attacks of some of our papers." In the article, Olsson asked "How did it go with morning prayers at Augustana College and Theological Seminary?" and answered "It went well, very well," continuing that "[f]aculty and students to a man" had been in attendance at the devotions. To Olsson, the prime concern was not the language issue, as it "was already settled." Instead, it was of the highest importance that the "love of our people to our common school" be maintained, which he hoped would not be "quenched" by what he termed "the Swedish-enthusiasts."[112]

[107] Referat 1890, 35.
[108] "Om svenska språket vid vårt läroverk," *Augustana*, 1 December 1892.
[109] ACL, BdDir, Minutes, 13 December 1898.
[110] Stephenson 1932, 381.
[111] C.A. Hultkrans, "Om vartannat," *Ungdomsvännen*, 1899, 43.
[112] Olof Olsson, "Också ett tack på tacksägelsedagen," *Augustana*, 7 December 1899.

There is also evidence from the decade after the turn of the century that some students at the college had difficulty understanding Swedish. In the fall of 1908 Marcus Skarstedt reported in his diary that, at a meeting celebrating the centennial of Lars Paul Esbjörn's birth, seminary professor C.E. Lindberg introduced the speaker Erik Norelius, saying that as Norelius would be speaking in Swedish, "some of you may not be able to understand him."[113] Skarstedt also notes that the studies in the subject of Swedish were "rather difficult" for most students, which resulted in many humorous linguistic mistakes during the Swedish classes.[114]

It is thus possible to see the developments sketched above as a process through which the position of Swedish and the school's "Swedishness" gradually declined at Augustana College from the 1880s and on, a development which would be in line with the sentiments of early leaders such as Erik Norelius and T.N. Hasselquist quoted earlier. The historian of Augustana College, Conrad Bergendoff, has also noted that "[t]hese were the years of transition" and that "English was replacing Swedish."[115]

Certainly, the nature of the institution was changing. More and more American-born students enrolled, and the curriculum became more diversified, gradually leaving the model of the Swedish *läroverk* behind and approaching that of an American college. In addition to the developments in the college noted above, other educational needs were also met, as special units for music, commerce, and art were established. In his annual report to the Synod in 1896, president Olof Olsson also noted the changing times, observing that "our time of Americanization, which is now over us in full force, brings certain difficulties in our school life," something which he thought should be kept in mind by "our mild and harsh friends."[116]

Still, although the language may not have been spoken on a daily basis as much as before, and it was no longer a compulsory subject of study, an examination of the enrollment figures in the Swedish courses suggest that, at least during the years before and after 1900, the subject held its own, attracting large number of students.

The Swedish language's continued importance at Augustana can be seen in the number of students who studied Swedish voluntarily. Between 1888/89 and 1894/95, the college catalogs noted the track of study in which individual students were enrolled. During these years a relatively small part of the Augustana student body chose a track of study without Swedish.[117] During the first two years, under the new curriculum, only two students enrolled in the

[113] SSIRC, ESC, Marcus Skarstedt diary, 25 October 1908.
[114] SSIRC, ESC, Marcus Skarstedt diary, 25 October 1908, 18 February 1909.
[115] Bergendoff 1969, 77.
[116] Referat 1896, 24.
[117] Cf. Blanck 1982, 300–01.

English-classical track. In the 1890/91 academic year, three students were noted in the English-classical track, whereas the figure for the two Swedish tracks was 48. This relationship remained stable for the next several years; in 1892/93 there were eight students in the track without Swedish and 69 in the two others, in 1893/94 the ratio was 13 to 77, and in 1894/95, the final year with statistics of this nature, it stood at nine to 75 students.[118] Thus no more than fifteen percent (and often fewer) of the students noted in the catalogs during the early 1890s were enrolled in a non-Swedish track.

Although information is lacking for the following years, it seems plausible to assume that the low interest in the track without Swedish continued during the next several years. No freshmen were enrolled in the English-classical track in 1894/95.[119] Moreover, the figures for the enrollment in the English-classical track in the preparatory department in 1894/95 was also low with only one in each of the three classes. Although the Augustana freshmen were not exclusively recruited from the preparatory department, many were—from the third class in 1894/95, 19 of the 41 students became Augustana freshmen the following year. The low figures for the English-classical track in both the freshman class and the preparatory department in 1894/95 suggest a limited recruitment pool for and interest in the non-Swedish tracks in the college during the years after 1895/96. Thus, although the possibility of graduating from Augustana without studying Swedish existed, a fairly small portion of the student body availed itself of the opportunity in the 1890s. Looked at from this perspective, the creation of the non-Swedish track of study in the college should not be necessarily be interpreted as a sign of erosion for Swedish at Augustana.

Instead, although the emphasis on English among the Augustana leadership from the college's first decades did mean that English would eventually become the dominant language at Augustana, both in the curriculum and most likely also in everyday life of the institution, the interest in Swedish at Augustana did not disappear. There is some evidence of interest in Swedish at the college in the 1870s. Looking back at his student years at Augustana 1873–76, Carl A. Swensson recalled an upsurge of interest in things Swedish during those years. Swensson and his fellow students spoke and wrote Swedish, sang Swedish songs, and were, in the author's words, "consumed, almost beyond measure, by our Swedish patriotism."[120]

If Carl A. Swensson found an interest in "Swedish patriotism" at Augustana in the 1870s, the evidence suggests that this attitude was even more prevalent

---

[118] Catalogs, 1888/89–1894/95.

[119] Catalog, 1894/95, 81–92. It should, however, be noted that not all students began their studies in the college in their freshman year. Of the 30 graduating seniors in 1897/98, 11 were not enrolled as freshmen in 1894/95, but entered mostly as sophomores, and no information is available as to which track of study they were in.

[120] Swensson 1891, 19–20.

during the decades around the turn of the century. With regard to the interest in studying Swedish, in January 1902 *Augustana* reported that the interest in Swedish courses was increasing at the college, and that in those tracks of study in which Swedish was an elective subject in the college and academy, 60 percent of the students had chosen Swedish.[121] Later the same year, the newspaper noted that close to 100 students were enrolled in the Swedish language courses, and commented that "the Swedish language lives a healthy life" in Rock Island,[122] and the following year *Augustana* wrote that the college classes in Swedish were even larger than in the previous year, something which was credited to the skills of the teachers.[123]

An article in *Augustana* from 1905 provides an illustration of the situation of Swedish in that year. The Swedish language has a "peculiar situation" at Augustana, the author states. To most students it is a foreign language, rarely used in conversations outside the classroom. Still, students at the college are expected to be able to use the language with the same ability as they speak their native language, English, after a few years at the school. Swedish is thus a very important subject, and should be practiced as much as possible, even outside the classroom, and the author also encourages Augustana students to join one of the several organizations that promoted the study of Swedish on campus.[124]

Following the curriculum reform in 1902/03 establishing the six main groups of subjects, the significance of Swedish in the curriculum was underscored, as the classical group included a separate Swedish-classical track until 1916/17. Moreover, in his second report to the Synod as college president in 1903 Gustav Andreen reported on the organization of the new curriculum, and added that "it is also our serious desire and goal that each student of Swedish background thoroughly shall study the language of his ancestors."[125]

The commitment to the study of Swedish is also reflected in the college catalogs from 1902 until 1930/31, which every year included a separate statement about the role of Swedish in the curriculum. All students "of Swedish parentage" were urged to "devote as much time as possible to the study of the beautiful language of their forefathers," not only for "sentimental" reasons, but also, the catalog claimed, since the "practical advantages of such study to the minister, the teacher, the physician, the lawyer, the business man, the cultured man in any walk of life, are too obvious to require special mention."[126]

---

[121] *Augustana*, 23 January 1902.
[122] *Augustana*, 20 November 1902.
[123] *Augustana*, 17 September 1903.
[124] *Augustana*, 26 October 1905.
[125] Referat 1903, 25.
[126] Catalog, 1902/03, 18.

Moreover, Augustana's role for the development of a specific Swedish-American identity was also emphasized. In 1891, one of the topics for the final examination in the Swedish language was "Swedish-Americanism as a factor in our country's cultural development," and from 1903/04 until 1929/30 the Augustana College catalogs also described one of the purposes and "future missions" of the school to be an "exponent of Swedish-American culture."[127] Similar ideas were also expressed by President Andreen in a speech in Stockholm in March 1903 on Swedish America and its cultural work, raising the question whether something called a "Swedish-American culture" existed. Andreen answered in the affirmative, claiming that it was indeed possible to be a Swede and an American at the same time, something one did not need to be ashamed of in either country.[128] This notion seems to have been fully developed by the fiftieth anniversary in 1910, when one of the official addresses discussed how the Swedish immigrants in the United States had "coalesced into a Swedish-American people," the identity of which had been maintained by the Augustana Synod through its educational and cultural endeavors.[129]

The special position of Swedish in the Augustana curriculum was also articulated in several ways during the years around the turn of the century. In March of 1891, C.E. Lindberg who had just assumed his duties as professor in the Seminary that academic year,[130] wrote in *Augustana* that all who loved the "Swedish name, Nordic literature and our Lutheran faith" must also love Augustana. He saw the purpose of the school as a Lutheran alternative to many of the negative and secularizing influences of American society in general, but also underscored that it provided its students with a general education and "useful knowledge of English and Swedish." Were it not for the training offered by the college and the seminary, Lindberg argued, the Swedish language would no longer be alive in America, and the influence of the "Swedish nation" in the U.S. would be far less than it is now.[131]

Similar sentiments were echoed in conjunction with the 1901 visit to Rock Island by Bishop K.H.G. von Schéele, who, as noted in chapter two, was the first Swedish bishop to visit the Augustana Synod in 1893 and returned several more times. In discussing the bishop's visit, *Augustana* commented on the contemporary state of the college's Swedishness. The paper noted that the founders of the Synod had sought to abandon their Swedishness, promoting a rapid Americanization. This had not occurred, however, and at the time "the Swedishness among the Swedish Americans is stronger and its value more

---

[127] *Augustana*, 4 June 1891, Catalog, 1903/04, 10.
[128] *Aftonbladet*, 23 March 1903.
[129] *Augustana*, 7 June 1910.
[130] Bergendoff 1980, 24.
[131] *Augustana*, 19 March 1891.

widely recognized than ever before." The Augustana Swedish Americans had learned, the paper observed, to combine Swedish culture with an American education, and that "it is not impossible to be both a Swede and an American at the same time."[132] During the same visit, Augustana geology professor J. A. Udden addressed the audience of the topic of Augustana College as "the center for Swedish-American culture."[133] The same year, a report in *Augustana* notes that the seniors in the college had sent for Swedish student caps (*studentmössor*), which they and the seminary students had begun to wear. In this respect, "things look very Swedish at Augustana College,"[134] the paper commented.

Augustana's role in the preservation of Swedishness in America was also noted and appreciated by persons outside the Synod. In 1898, the liberal journalist C.F. Peterson published *Sverige i Amerika* (Sweden in America), which in the words of Arnold Barton was "the most objective and penetrating discussion of the Swedish Americans offered by one of their number during the crucial decade of the 1890s".[135] In it he argued that to date, the Augustana Synod had been of crucial importance for the maintenance of a Swedish identity in America. "Without this ark" he wrote, "our nationality would soon have lost its distinct Swedish characteristic in the cosmopolitan whirl."[136]

An example of the combination of the Christian dimension with an emphasis on Swedishness comes from 1903. Alfred Bergin, author and long-time minister in Lindsborg, Kansas, commented that the Augustana Synod schools did not seek to compete directly with the public schools, but instead were "hearths" of Christian education, and that it was "Lutheran Christianity and Swedishness that provide the rationale for our schools." The Augustana Synod schools, he continued, "are quite necessary for our own existence as a Swedish people and [for] a Lutheran Augustana Synod."[137] Similarly, a 1906 editorial in *Augustana* spoke of the Synod colleges as excellent educational institutions providing the Swedish-American youth with a general American education without forgoing "our Christian belief" and all "the noble and beautiful" things that the Swedish Americans "possessed as an inheritance from old mother Svea."[138]

A further illustration of the discussion of the nature of the institution can be found in the Augustana *Observer*, the English-language student newspaper, which also highlights the combination of ethnicity and religion. In August

[132] *Augustana*, 21 November 1901.
[133] *Augustana* 21 November 1901.
[134] *Augustana*, 30 May 1901.
[135] Barton 1994, 120.
[136] Peterson 1898, 71–73.
[137] *Augustana*, 17 September 1903.
[138] *Augustana*, 9 August 1906.

1903, the newspaper addressed the question of "what Augustana is" and gave six main characteristics.[139] The articles emphasized that Augustana was a Christian institution, which set it apart from public schools; a denominational school, supported by the Augustana Synod; and of a co-educational nature. More importantly, the article also calls Augustana an "American" school, with English as the language of instruction, preparing students for work in American society. But, Augustana was also a Swedish-American institution, with "one of its main objects to be an exponent of a distinctly Swedish-American culture," an emphasis which accounted for its Swedish curriculum. Similar sentiments were expressed by a newly matriculated student at the college in that same year. K.G. William Dahl who after graduation became a minister in the Augustana Synod and an author within the Augustana sphere in Swedish-America, wrote in a letter back to his parents in Sweden in very positive terms about Augustana College, concluding that "I am happy to be Swedish, but I am happier to be Swedish-American, as those people have accomplished marvelous things."[140]

Summary

The role of Swedish at Augustana College thus changed during the latter part of the nineteenth century. The early leadership emphasized the need to learn English and to "Americanize." Swedish also declined as a language of instruction, morning prayers began to be held in English, and it became possible to graduate from Augustana without studying Swedish. At least two reasons for this attitude can be given. Although there was a sustained a large Swedish immigration to the U.S. during the first decades of the Synod's history, it was, of course, at this early time impossible to predict how large the Swedish-American community would eventually become and thus to what degree it would be realistic to maintain the Swedish language or Swedish cultural traditions in general. Moreover, a sense of cultural nationalism was weakly developed in mid-nineteenth century Sweden. Religion was a more important source of identity, especially to those Swedish immigrants who became members of the Augustana Synod, many of whom, as we have seen in chapter two, had their roots in the low-church revival movement, and to whom the preservation of a religious identity was more important than maintaining a sense of Swedish ethnicity. This was, as we have seen, also true at Augustana College, where religion played a central role in the curriculum and the college's life in general. As discussed in chapter two, it was also during the 1860s and 1870s that the religious rift between the Augustana Synod and what became the

---

[139] For the following, see Augustana *Observer*, August 1903.
[140] K.G. William Dahl to parents, 27 September 1903. Printed in Dahl no date.

Mission Covenant Church developed, which furthered emphasized the Synod's religious identity.

However, Swedish was always a part of the Augustana curriculum. The language was taught at the school from its beginning, and although no longer obligatory from the mid-1880s, the Swedish classes still attracted students, and the subject was a given a special position in both the curriculum and in official pronouncements by college officials. Beginning around the turn of the century, voices were heard arguing for the importance of maintaining the Swedish language and Swedish cultural traditions in general. In addition to emphasizing Augustana's Christian character, the college's role in maintaining a Swedish heritage was now also frequently mentioned. Often these two elements, the religious and the ethnic, were conflated into one, suggesting that the maintenance of the one depended on the maintenance of the other. Instead of the earlier gloomy predictions of the quick demise in America of the Swedish language and culture, leading Augustana figures now spoke about the possibilities of the Swedish language surviving for decades to come.[141] As will be shown later in this chapter, this renewed emphasis on Swedish took place during a time when a generational shift had begun at the college, so that by the turn of the century the majority of the students was second-generation Swedish Americans, that is, American-born but of Swedish background.

In looking at the role of Swedish at Augustana College during the institution's first half-century, one must distinguish between, on the one hand, what we can call a Swedish tradition at the college, that is, a concern for the contents and meaning of Augustana's Swedishness, and, on the other, the use of the Swedish language as a means of instruction or measured by the number of hours of Swedish required by Augustana students in various tracks of study. The decline in the use of the Swedish *language* did not mean that the Swedish *tradition* disappeared at Augustana. On the contrary, especially from the 1890s and on, we find the college leadership discussing and attaching significance to Augustana's "Swedishness" (*svenskhet*), which in many cases transcended the issue of the language *per se*, and instead the Swedish element at the school was now conceptualized more culturally. As we have seen, this ethnic tradition was also frequently linked to or even a part of the religious dimension of Augustana College.

Moreover, the renewed interest in Swedish expressed around the turn of the century was not limited to the study of Swedish language and culture. Clearly, an awareness had developed of Augustana College as a Swedish-American institution and of the development of a Swedish-American identity, which was seen as different from that in Sweden. The Swedish ethnic tradition at Augustana was thus also becoming a Swedish-American tradition, and one of the

---

[141] Hasselmo 1974, 44–45, Hasselmo 1978, 227.

missions of Augustana College was, as the college catalogs phrased it, to be "an exponent" of this culture. In the next section of this chapter, the specific nature and contents of this Swedish-American ethnic tradition at Augustana College will be analysed.

A Swedish-American Tradition at Augustana College

The analysis of Augustana's Swedish-American tradition will be based on an examination of the subject of Swedish in the college, as well as on the many extra-curricular Swedish-related activities at the school. The development of the teaching of the discipline at Augustana will be explored by looking at both the organization and the content of the subject. Who were the teachers? What was taught in the Swedish courses at Augustana? Which authors were studied, and what aspects of the Swedish cultural heritage were presented to the students in Rock Island? As much of the Swedish-American tradition at Augustana was played out outside of the classroom, we will also examine in some detail the many extra-curricular Swedish activities on campus, especially two of the student literary societies. What picture of Sweden and Swedish America was portrayed in them? The role played by visitors from Sweden for the college's Swedish-American tradition will also be discussed.

The Teaching of Swedish Language and Literature

As already mentioned, the Swedish language and literature were taught at Augustana from the school's very beginning. The subject of Swedish at Augustana included courses in the Swedish language as well as Swedish literature and to some degree history. Due to the scarcity of staff, a few teachers had to do instruction in several subjects at a time during the first several decades. From 1875/76 pastor C.O. Granere had the main responsibility for teaching Swedish in the college. In addition he taught several other subjects; in 1875/76, Latin and Greek in the college and church history in the seminary. From 1876/77 Granere primarily combined his instruction in Swedish with Latin, as well as some Greek. During most of these years, assistant teachers in Swedish were also hired, seemingly on a yearly basis.[142]

In October 1882, the Board of Directors extended a call to C.M.E. Esbjörn to become professor of Christianity and Swedish in the college, and Esbjörn accepted.[143] The son of Augustana's first president, Esbjörn was a graduate of

---

[142] Catalog 1874/75, 3, Catalogs 1875/76, 3, 1876/77, 5.
[143] ACL, BdDir, Minutes: 2 October 1882, 20 March 1883.

Augustana's first class in 1877, and had after his graduation prepared himself to return and teach at the college. He belonged to a group of early graduates who, with the assistance of the Synod, attended universities in both Sweden and the U.S. to prepare themselves further before joining the faculty.[144]

By the academic year 1883/84, Esbjörn had taken up his position as "professor of Christian Science and of the Swedish language and literature," a post he would hold until 1890. In that year, he announced his resignation, because he felt that "several recent actions" at the college had "adversely affected" the position of his two subjects in the curriculum. To be persuaded to stay on, Esbjörn made a number of demands, including that the number of hours previously taught in Christianity and Swedish be restored, and that Swedish "once again" be made a subject of instruction on all levels in the college and preparatory department, requests which the Board of Directors did not meet, leading to Esbjörn's resignation.[145] The "recent actions" Esbjörn referred to were most likely the introduction of the English-classical track of study, which, as we have seen, did not require all Augustana students to study Swedish and which had generated protests from other quarters as well.

Still, the Board of Directors of the college and seminary showed its continued support for instruction in Swedish, and at the Synod meeting in 1890 it was reported that Swedish (and Christianity) were subjects of "such fundamental importance" that it was necessary to split the previous joint position in the two subjects and create one professorship of Swedish and one of Christianity, a proposal which won the approval of the Synod meeting.[146]

The first person to be called as professor of Swedish was J.S. Carlson at Gustavus Adolphus College in Minnesota. When Carlson declined the call, the position was next offered to Johan Enander, who accepted.[147] Enander was one of the leading persons in Swedish America, as editor of *Hemlandet* in Chicago and as a prolific author and public speaker. His ties with the Augustana Synod were also very strong.

Enander's tenure as professor of Swedish lasted until 1893 when he returned to journalism. He does not seem to have fit in the mold of an Augustana professor; in June 1893 the Board of Directors decided "after a long and thoughtful deliberation" to ask for his resignation due to his "frivolous deportment," including charges of improper behavior with an "American woman" from Moline and "indelicate behavior" towards girls. Enander denied these charges vehemently, but left his position in the summer of 1893, for rea-

---

[144] ACL, BdDir, Minutes, 14 June 1877, Bergendoff 1969, 55. In 1879, Esbjörn was granted $ 150 by Augustana's Board of Directors for his first year of study at the University of Pennsylvania. [ACL, BdDir, Minutes, 6 June 1879.]

[145] ACL, BdDir, Minutes, 1 April 1890.

[146] Referat 1890, 39 and 42.

[147] ACL, BdDir, Minutes: 25 June, 15 July 1890.

sons that still seem somewhat unclear.[148] Still, this does not seem to have blackened Enander's name too much in Rock Island, as he was to return to the campus as a speaker on Swedish topics.

Following Enander's resignation, the Rev. Ernst Zetterstrand assumed the professorship in 1895, serving as professor of Swedish until 1901.[149] Zetterstrand seems to have had pedagogical difficulties, and a student from his time noted that he was such a bad teacher that "our class revolted against him."[150] After complaints in 1897,[151] and again in 1901, when the senior class "because of a warm zeal for the study of the Swedish language" refused to attend his courses, the Augustana Board of Directors concluded that it was in the interest of the teaching of Swedish at Augustana that Zetterstrand resign, which he also did at the end of the spring semester in 1901.[152]

Following Zetterstrand's departure, the Board considered his replacement. Four candidates were nominated, including S.M. Hill, president of Luther Academy; Prof. V.H. Heggström, at the time at the Norwegian-American Jewell Lutheran College in Jewell, Iowa, but previously also a professor at Upsala College; the Rev. J.G. Dahlberg; and the Rev. Jules Mauritzson. Five rounds of voting were required, but eventually a call went out to Jules Mauritzson, who accepted the position, and served as professor of Swedish until his death in 1930.[153]

Born in southern Sweden, Mauritzson graduated from *gymnasium* in Helsingborg in 1886 and during the next three years attended Lund University. He had emigrated in 1896 and served as an Augustana pastor in Iowa before coming to Augustana in 1901.[154] One of the conditions for the job was that Mauritzson had to spend additional time in Scandinavian universities to prepare himself for the position, and he spent the academic year 1902/03 at Uppsala and Christiana (Oslo) universities. At Uppsala he attended lectures and seminars with such leading professors as Adolf Noreen in the Department of Scandinavian Languages and Henrik Schück in the Department of Literature, and also had the opportunity to address a gathering of selected Uppsala academics on Augustana College's mission to "be a bearer of and to promote Swedish culture in America."[155] Mauritzson was also very active in Swedish-American cultural and academic circles. He was one of the founders of and

---

[148] ACL, BdDir, Minutes: 28 June 1893, 18 August 1893. SSIRC, GNS: Letters from J.A. Enander to G.N. Swan, 26 July 1893, 21 August 1893; G.N. Swan to J.A. Enander, 21 August 1893; J.A. Enander to G.N. Swan, 2 September 1893.

[149] ACL, BdDir, Minutes, 1 May 1894, Bergendoff 1980, 45.

[150] SSIRC, GNS, Letter from J. S. Carlson to G.N. Swan, 24 April 1923.

[151] ACL, BdDir, Minutes: 21 April, 2 December 1897, 29 March 1898. Referat 1897, 81–82.

[152] ACL, BdDir, Minutes, 13 March 1901.

[153] ACL, BdDir, Minutes: 14 May 1901, 9 July 1901, 4 April 1902. Referat 1901, 20–21.

[154] For the following, see Blanck 1994, vii–xv; Andreen 1931, 214–21.

[155] *Augustana*, 6 November 1902.

active member in the American academic organization for Scandinavian studies (SASS), and served as editor and contributor to several Swedish-language publications published by the Augustana Book Concern.

The way in which Swedish was established in the college clearly shows a concern for the subject, especially after 1890 when a separate department of Swedish was established. Esbjörn resigned in protest over what he perceived as a weakening of the subject, and the fact that Enander was named as the first professor of Swedish is very significant, as his appointment came at a time when the position of Swedish at Augustana was being questioned, as the discussion in *Hemlandet* referred to above shows. At the time, Enander was, in Arnold Barton's words, "unquestionably the most influential Swedish-American opinionmaker,"[156] as a journalist, public speaker, and author, and in many ways Enander was the leading Swedish-American ideologue of the Augustana Synod. The fact that he was called to run the Swedish department at Augustana in 1890 must be interpreted as a way of strengthening the subject, as well as lending a great deal of support to Enander's view of what it meant to be Swedish in America. (See chapter five for a further discussion of Enander.)

The controversy over Professor Zetterstrand seems to have revolved around issues of personalities. It should, however, be noted that both the Synod and the Augustana Board of Directors considered it enough important to have a well functioning Swedish department that they studied the matter as closely as it did, and eventually, with the interest of Swedish in mind, decided to sever Zetterstrand's connection to the college. A thorough discussion also preceded the choice of Mauritzson as the new professor. The fact that the Board demanded that Mauritzson spend further time in Scandinavian universities to qualify for the position can be seen as a further sign of the significance attached to finding a competent professor of Swedish. Finally, it should be noted that all of the Swedish professors came from within the Augustana Synod itself. Zetterstrand and Mauritzson were ordained ministers in the Synod, and Enander a leading lay-person. The selection of individuals associated with the Synod ensured that the content given to Swedish at Augustana would remain within the Synod's ideological bounds.

The Content of Swedish in the College Curriculum

Given the position of Swedish in the curriculum as well as the development of a separate department of Swedish in the college, the next issue to be looked at deals with what actually was taught in the Swedish courses. What was the image of Sweden and Swedish cultural traditions that were presented to students in the Augustana Swedish courses? An examination of the courses

[156] Barton 1994, 64.

taught dealing with Swedish literature and culture and the textbooks used will illustrate this matter.[157]

In general a diversification of the Swedish curriculum began towards the end of the nineteenth century, both in terms of topics studied and the textbooks that were used.[158] In the 1880s the college curriculum included reading and grammatical exercises during the freshman and sophomore years, with the history of Swedish literature studied during the junior and senior years.[159] Swedish literature was studied mainly through several handbooks, and although there is no comprehensive listing available for the text-books used at Augustana, until the mid-1890s a group of three general surveys of Swedish literary history seem to have been commonly used, namely Sundén's and Modin's *Svensk läsebok för elementarläroverken*, Bjursten's *Översikt över svenska språkets och litteraturens historia*, as well as Claesson's edited version of Bjursten, published as *Svenska språkets och litteraturens historia*.[160] From the mid-1880s some individual authors and literary works are mentioned in the catalogs. Two leading authors of the Romantic movement of the nineteenth century were particularly popular, the Finno-Swede Johan Ludvig Runeberg and Esaias Tegnér. Runeberg's *Fänrik Ståls sägner* and Tegnér's *Fritiofs saga* seem to have been particularly popular texts. These two authors would, as we shall see, remain central in the Augustana Swedish curriculum for several decades.[161] Other individual authors and texts studied in the 1880s include Bernhard Elis Malmström, O.P. Sturzen-Becker,[162] (both late nineteenth century authors) and the *Edda* from the golden age of medieval Icelandic literature.[163]

In 1891/92 there were some changes in the curriculum, although the basic structure remained, with instruction in reading, writing, and grammatical exercises in the lower classes and Swedish literary history in the higher.[164] In addition to general surveys of Swedish literature and the customary study of Runeberg and Tegnér, a large part of the senior year Swedish curriculum was also devoted to Old Norse literature and culture, including readings of the mythic *Edda*, lectures on *Völuspa*, *Havamal*, and the "civilization of the northmen."

[157] For the following discussion, see the Catalogs, 1870/71–1916/17.

[158] The following discussion is based on the entries in the Augustana College catalogs. The information supplied about the nature of the instruction every year is not uniform, which may account for some unevenness.

[159] Catalog 1883/84, 28–32.

[160] For the use of these textbooks, see, for example, Catalogs, 1883/84, 28–32, 1885/86, 22–23, 1893/94, 31, 1894/95, 31.

[161] See for example Catalog 1884/85, 19, Catalog 1891/92, 26–27, Catalog 1893/94, 31, Catalog 1894/95, 20, Catalog 1898/99, 23 and 34, Catalog 1901/02, 19.

[162] Catalog 1885/86, 22.

[163] Catalog 1886/87, 27–28.

[164] This paragraph is based on Catalog 1891/92, 26–29.

90

The list of textbooks used in the Swedish curriculum that year reflects this approach, as it in 1891/92 included two volumes of Runeberg's collected works, Tegnér's *Fritiofs saga*, W.E. Lindblad's *Fosterländska minnen*, a Swedish translation of the *Edda*, Snorre Sturlasson's *Konungaboken*, and Viktor Rydberg's *Fädernas gudasagor*.[165] In 1894/95 several individual works by Runeberg and Tegnér were noted, and the list of Swedish textbooks encompassed both the collected works of Tegnér and Runeberg, as well as Karl Warburg's *Svensk litteraturhistoria* and the previously used reader by Sundén and Modin.[166]

From 1895/96 the catalog lists a number of specific courses taught in both the preparatory department and the college. Apart from the linguistic courses, the curriculum offered two survey courses each covering Swedish literature and history as well as one course focusing on Old Norse literature. Among individual authors Runeberg's *Fänrik Ståls sägner* and Tegnér's *Fritiofs saga* were again singled out,[167] and in 1898/99 the catalog noted that particular attention was also devoted to Tegnér's poem "Svea."[168]

Through the curricular reform of 1902, the number of courses in the Swedish curriculum increased, and included a broader spectrum of authors. The courses in Swedish literary history now encompassed two general survey courses of Swedish literature, one course focusing on the works of Runeberg, as well as on nineteenth-century authors C.J.L. Almqvist and Viktor Rydberg, and one course called "modern literature" with "the latest of Swedish literature," including works of, among others, Strindberg, Lagerlöf, Heidenstam, Fröding, Karlfelt, and Levertin, all of whom were active during the end of the nineteenth and the beginning of the twentieth centuries. Selected works by Tegnér and the *Edda* were read in a course on composition. The two courses on Swedish history also remained in the curriculum, the first one also covering Swedish geography. In addition, courses in the Norwegian and Danish languages and selected authors were also introduced.[169] This general pattern remained in force during the following years, with some modifications. In 1905/06 the course on Almqvist, Runeberg, and Rydberg was dropped, but Runeberg was specifically mentioned in other courses.[170]

By 1910/11 the college curriculum included one grammar course, two courses each in Swedish literary and general history, a composition course with readings by Snoilsky, Rydberg, Levertin, Hallström, and Lagerlöf, as well as

---

[165] Catalog 1891/92, 52.
[166] Catalog 1894/95, 31.
[167] Catalog 1895/96, 20–21, Catalog 1896/97, 20.
[168] Catalog 1898/99, 23.
[169] Catalog 1902/03, 40–41.
[170] Catalog 1906/07, 41–42.

the modern literature course.[171] In a letter from December 1912, Mauritzson listed the reading list in Swedish that year in both the academy and the college, and the college curriculum included Warburg's *Litteraturhistoria*, Ekerman's *Läsebok till svenska litteraturhistorien*, and Carl Grimberg's *Sveriges historia 1–2*.[172] Warburg's *Litteraturhistoria* seems to have remained in the curriculum, and is noted again in 1916/17. In that same year, the modern literature course was merged with the second survey course. Again, Tegnér and Runeberg were singled out as being especially important from the earlier period, together with Atterbom, Rydberg, Strindberg, Fröding, Lagerlöf, Heidenstam, and Karlfelt as representatives of more recent literary developments.[173]

What can be said of the content of the Augustana Swedish curriculum? First, it should be noted that although a few courses dealt with Swedish history, Swedish literature was central in the teaching of Swedish at Augustana. It was by reading certain authors and their works that Augustana students became familiar with the cultural background of the country from which they or their ancestors had come. Moreover, there are clear parallels between Augustana's Swedish curriculum and that which was taught in contemporary Swedish secondary schools, or *läroverk*. Until the mid-1890s, text-books by Sundén & Modin, Bjursten, and Claesson were, as shown above, used at Augustana. These books were also frequently used in the Swedish *läroverk* during the end of the nineteenth century.[174] The introduction of Warburg's *Svensk litteraturhistoria* in the mid-1890s also follows a trend in Sweden, where it started replacing Claesson's *Svenska språket och litteraturens historia*.[175]

With regard to the contents of the curriculum, it is evident that the view of Swedish literature presented to the college students at Augustana also echoed to a large extent what was taught in Sweden in the late nineteenth century. The two most popular Swedish authors at Augustana, Runeberg and Tegnér, also played a prominent role in the curricula of Swedish secondary schools in the late nineteenth century. Karin Tarschys, Bengt Lewan, and Bengt-Göran Martinsson have all pointed to the centrality of Tegnér and Runeberg in the Swedish curriculum in the late nineteenth century,[176] and Tarschys singles out individual texts such as *Fritiofs saga* by Tegnér and *Fänrik Ståls sägner* by Runeberg as especially important.[177] Lars Brink has also pointed to the continued centrality of Tegnér and Runeberg well into the twentieth century.[178]

[171] Catalog 1911/12, 44–45.
[172] ACL, GAP, Letter from Jules Mauritzson to Gustav Andreen, December 1912.
[173] Catalog 1916/17, 48–49.
[174] Tarschys 1955, 150, 155–56 on Bjursten, and Tarschys 1955 151, 265 on Sundén-Modin.
[175] Tarschys 1955, 281.
[176] Tarschys 1955, 171–72, 276, Lewan 1972, Martinsson 1989, 156–63.
[177] Tarschys 1955, 262.
[178] Brink 1992, 250–51, 255–57.

As shown above, both these authors and specific texts such as *Fritiofs saga* and *Fänrik Ståls sägner* played an important role in the Augustana Swedish curriculum. It has even been noted that students at the college were split in two camps on whether Tegnér or Runeberg was the greatest Swedish author,[179] and in a 1904 publication of "dialogues" for Augustana Synod youth organizations by Augustana minister K.G. William Dahl, the benefits of reading are discussed, with five especially worthy authors identified: Tegnér and Runeberg from the Swedish language and Longfellow, Irving, and Shakespeare from the English.[180] Tegnér and Runeberg's popularity was not restricted to Augustana College, but were equally popular at Gustavus Adolphus College, where Lars Brink in an examination of the Swedish curriculum at that school has calls them "the most canonized authors."[181]

Tegnér and Runeberg were also well represented in the Swedish-language books which were published by the Augustana Book Concern and intended to be used in the instruction in Augustana Synod schools. The A.B.C. brought out two volumes of Swedish poetry and prose in English translation in 1906 and 1908. Tegnér and Runeberg are by far the dominant authors in both volumes of *Masterpieces from Swedish Literature*, accounting for a third and half of the total pages devoted to Swedish poetry in each volume, respectively.[182] Moreover, in 1914 *Fritiofs saga* also appeared in the A.B.C. series of Swedish literature, with vocabularies and commentaries, intended to be used in the Swedish instruction in American colleges and universities, and one year later, Runeberg's *Fänrik Ståls sägner* was published in the same series.[183] In her analysis of *Prärieblomman,* one of the leading literary periodicals and exponents of the Augustana Synod's cultural work, Birgitta Svensson also notes the role that Tegnér played for the many of the poems published in the calender.[184]

Other authors studied at Augustana were also a part of the curriculum in Sweden. This includes both names such as Sturzen-Becker and Malmström,[185] as well as Rydberg, Lagerlöf, Heidenstam, Fröding, Karlfeldt, and others who are specifically mentioned in the expanded Augustana Swedish curriculum after the turn of the century.[186]

The inclusion of August Strindberg in the Augustana curriculum may seem surprising, given his controversial status in the Swedish literary canon. Still,

---

[179] Widén 1950, 64.

[180] Andeer 1904b, 10.

[181] Brink 1988, 10.

[182] Masterpieces 1906, Masterpieces 1908.

[183] Tegnér 1914, Runeberg 1915.

[184] Svensson 1994, 147.

[185] Brink 1992, 255.

[186] Brink 1992, 249–64 discusses the position of these authors in the national Swedish curriculum.

this may be a reflection of the fact that Strindberg had begun appearing in the curricula in the Swedish secondary schools as well from the beginning of the twentieth century, although it took until 1960 before Strindberg reached the position as the leading Swedish author in the Swedish secondary schools.[187] Anna Williams has also suggested that Strindberg became more acceptable in Swedish America toward the end of his life.[188] Finally, it is unclear exactly which aspects of Strindberg's works were studied at Augustana, as no individual titles were given in the catalogs.

The Augustana Swedish curriculum thus shows an emphasis on the romantic and idealistic aspects of Swedish literature, with a focus on the nineteenth century, a tendency which was also visible in Swedish secondary schools at the same time. The textbooks by Sundén & Modin and by Bjursten place a great emphasis on Romantic and Neo-Romantic nineteenth century authors. The two leading authors, Tegnér and Runeberg, also represented the romantic and idealistic movement in Swedish literature, with emphases on Swedish and Finnish national feelings. With his background as bishop, there is also a religious dimension to Tegnér's works.[189] The individual authors studied in the Augustana Swedish curriculum after 1900 represent a wider spectrum of literary tendencies, but names such as Heidenstam, Fröding, Lagerlöf, and Karlfeldt were a part of the neo-romanticism associated with the 1890s, that emphasized both Swedish patriotism as well as an interest in provincial themes.[190]

It is also possible to discern an interest for the Viking era and its culture at Augustana. A number of works from Old Norse literature, as well as lectures on Viking civilization became particularly prominent during the early 1890s. The continued appeal of *Fritiofs saga* in the Augustana Swedish classrooms also suggests an interest in this period, as that work deals with Old Norse themes.[191] Several of the texts by Tegnér and Runeberg studied at Augustana also express national and patriotic feelings, in particular *Fänrik Ståls sägner* by Runeberg, as well as poems such as "Svea" by Tegnér and *Fritiofs saga*.[192] This interest in older periods of Swedish literary history has also been noted in the Swedish secondary school curriculum in the 1890s, which according to Karin Tarschys was expressed through the study of *Fänrik Stål* and *Fritiofs saga*, but also through a textbook like Lindblad's *Fosterländska minnen*.[193]

---

[187] Tarschys 1955, 163, Brink 1992, 258–59.

[188] Williams 1995, 216.

[189] For Tegnér see Lönnroth & Delblanc 1988a, 287–307 and for Runeberg see Lönnroth & Delblanc 1988b, 113–39.

[190] For the 1890s, see Lönnroth & Delblanc 1989, 69–113.

[191] Lönnroth & Delblanc 1988a, 295–300.

[192] For Runeberg and nationalism see Lönnroth & Delblanc 1988b, 130–35, for Tegnér and nationalism see Lönnroth & Delblanc 1988a, 287–307.

[193] Tarschys 1955, 262–65.

However, even though there were similarities between Augustana's Swedish curriculum and that in contemporary Swedish *läroverk*, the different meaning that this selection of Swedish literature took on in Swedish America must be underscored. Few of the Augustana students had any prior familiarity with Swedish literature of the kind that was taught at Augustana. The Swedish-born students had had little higher schooling prior to their emigration, and to the American-born students Sweden was, by definition, a foreign land and the Swedish literary and cultural history which was presented to students became something that literally had to be learned. The Swedish literary history at Augustana was idealized and romantic, in which national feelings and an interest in the Viking past and Old Norse literature also played an important role. *Fritiofs Saga* and *Fänrik Ståls sägner*, two of the most popular selections from Swedish literature at Augustana, were thus given a new significance in their new, Swedish-American context, as they became a part of a Swedish-American tradition at Augustana College, which, in turn, was one important element of Augustana's Swedish-American identity.

Swedish Ethnicity Outside the Curriculum

The Swedish-American tradition at Augustana was not only expressed through the college curriculum. A number of activities on the campus also provided opportunities for students and faculty to formulate and express a sense of Swedishness, as well as to reflect on its significance for the institution. A number of Swedish-related organizations existed on campus, there were meetings and celebrations of different kinds, and Swedish and Swedish-American visitors were received in Rock Island, all of which also provided important ingredients for the Swedish-American identity at the institution. In this section, some of these extracurricular Swedish activities will be examined to provide further answers to the question of what it meant to be Swedish at Augustana College. We will first look at some more general expressions, and then examine two of the literary societies on campus.

Visitors from Sweden, Elocution Contests, and Lectures

The Swedish element on campus was made visible by a number of visitors in different capacities from Sweden. These visits were often interpreted as signs of recognition of the cultural work going on among the Swedish Americans by the old country, and were important factors in strengthening the position of Swedish at the campus.[194]

The 1901 visit by Bishop von Schéele to the Augustana campus in Rock

---

[194] For a general discussion of the view of Swedish-American education among Swedish visitors, see Barton 1995.

Island became one opportunity for the college to make its Swedish-American identity visible. Von Schéele was in Rock Island to attend the reformation festivity at Augustana which was held for several days, beginning on November 17. The program included several lectures by von Schéele on both religious and Swedish topics, different addresses by representatives of the Augustana Synod, including a greeting "from the daughter church to the mother church" by Erik Norelius, talks on the development of both Augustana College and the Augustana Synod, and, as we have seen, a speech on the topic of Augustana as a center of a Swedish-American culture by professor Udden of the college's geology department. During the final evening of von Schéele's visit, there was farewell ceremony in Swedish in the chapel, during which the Wennerberg male chorus sang "Dåne liksom åskan bröder," and the bishop awarded C.E. Lindberg with the Swedish Order of the North Star. In his remarks the bishop commented that he was very pleased with the "cultural work" and "expressions of Swedishness" he had encountered at Augustana, and promised to convey to the students in Swedish universities that the Augustana students were "worthy descendants of the North."[195]

Another Swedish visitor arrived in Rock Island in April 1902. This was Carl Sundbeck who visited the campus as a part of a study trip to America paid for by the Swedish government.[196] A conservative interested in Swedes and Swedish culture outside of Sweden, he embraced the cultural activities he found among Swedish Americans. The speeches he made during his Swedish-American journey as well as his published account of the trip were all highly complimentary to Swedish America in general, and to the Augustana Synod in particular.

Upon arriving in Rock Island, Sundbeck recorded his pleasure with having arrived in "the Uppsala of Swedish America."[197] He then held a speech in the college chapel in which he praised the educational and cultural work at Augustana College, calling the school "the link between the thousands of young people here in America and the country of their ancestors, which they have never visited, but in their hearts still call their own land, their fathers' land."[198] Sundbeck's visit coincided with the first "Founders' Day" celebrated on campus. (See chapter 5 for more on Founders' Day.)

A visit in November 1904 by Aksel Anderson, a librarian from Uppsala University provided further opportunities for the Augustana community to express its Swedishness in a welcoming ceremony. Both students and faculty greeted Anderson with speeches and singing—the Wennerberg chorus performed "Hör oss Svea,"—and there were cheers for "Sweden in America,"

---

[195] ACL, BdDir, Minutes, 2 April 1902; *Augustana*, 21 November 1901.
[196] Barton 1994, 140–46, Beijbom 1990a, 221–30.
[197] Sundbeck 1904a, 145.
[198] Sundbeck 1904b, 16.

"Sweden in the high North," as well as for Uppsala and Lund Universities.[199]

Another expression of Swedishness at Augustana is the Swedish elocution contests between Augustana and other Swedish-American colleges. In May 1902 the competition was held in Rock Island, and the judges were all notable Swedish-American authors, such as Jakob Bonggren, Ludvig Holmes, and E.W. Olsson,[200] the inclusion of which shows the significance attached to the competition. In the following year the contest was held in Minneapolis and included teams from Gustavus Adolphus College and Bethany College as well, during which the winning team got a prize and a Swedish flag with the American seal superimposed.[201] In 1904 *Augustana* reported about another elocution competition at Augustana, which now was said to be held in Swedish one year and in English the next. The winner in 1904 was C.P. Peterson whose topic was "The role of the Swedish American in the nation's drama," in which he characterized the creation of an American people as a "quiet, but bitter struggle" between all the different immigrant groups in America and asserted that the Swedish Americans had to play their role in this process as well.[202] *Augustana* commented that the competition was "from beginning to end a show of force of the healthy life of Swedish at the college" and ended with "Long live the wonderful language of our fathers!"[203]

The promotion of Swedishness on the Augustana campus after 1890 was also expressed by public lectures by several prominent Swedish Americans on both Swedish and Swedish-American topics. Examples of lectures by Johan Enander include his talks on the Swedish poet and historian Erik Gustaf Geijer in May 1891, an address commemorating the life of Runeberg in February 1904, and a talk on the history and tradition of singing among Swedish university students in February 1905.[204] In March 1900, the author and Augustana pastor Ludvig Holmes gave a talk on "The Swedish-Americans in the towns and in the countryside," and in 1911 the author and book collector G.N. Swan of Sioux City, Iowa was invited to give a talk on Holmes and his "significance for Swedish-American literature." In 1914 Swan also presented an address on the topic "Tegnér and his Fritiofs Saga."[205]

The Phrenokosmian Society

The first of the student organizations to be examined is the Phrenokosmian Society at Augustana College, a literary and debating society of a kind often

[199] *Augustana*, 10 November 1904.
[200] *Augustana*, 8 May 1902.
[201] *Augustana*, 21 May 1903.
[202] C.P. Peterson, "Svensk-amerikanens roll i nationens drama," *Ungdomsvännen* 1904, 168.
[203] *Augustana*, 12 May 1904.
[204] *Augustana*, 14 May 1891, 11 February 1904, 16 February 1905.
[205] *Augustana*, 29 March 1900; SSIRC, GNS. Letters from Jules Mauritzson to G.N. Swan, 2 February 1911, 27 October 1914.

found at American colleges in the nineteenth century.[206] It started in the same year as the college was founded, and its purpose was to "contribute to the cultivation" of the student body by discussions, recitations, and elocutions.[207] The membership was open to the entire student body, and the society's constitution called for a meeting every week, and the proceedings were held alternately in Swedish and English. Judging from the minutes, the frequency of the meetings varied somewhat, whereas the language requirement seems to have been adhered to.

What can be said about the way in which the Swedish and Swedish-American traditions were articulated in this group up until 1900? The reason for ending the examination in that year has partly to do with the availability of source material. In addition, beginning around 1900 several societies specifically devoted to the study of Swedish came into existence at the college.

The discussions during the society's first fifteen years only infrequently addressed issues related to the college's ethnic background, or to the development of the immigrants' heritage in the new homeland.[208] When such topics were discussed, the focus seems to have been on the Swedish language, as on October 24, 1860 when the question posed for discussion was "Are the Scandinavian languages more beneficial than the English for students at Augustana?", or on April 11, 1861 "Are the Scandinavian languages more developed than the English?" Instead, during these early years members of the society seem to have been mostly concerned with religious and moral issues, such as "Has the written word of God had more influence on the salvation of man than the spoken?" on November 7, 1860 or "Which is more beneficial to man: Poverty or Riches?" on May 1, 1861. A few of the discussions seem inspired by contemporary events: on November 23, 1861, for example, the question discussed was "Who has suffered most at the hands of the whites: Indians or Negroes?"

When the school moved to Rock Island and graduated its first college class in the mid-1870s, the topics of discussion in the Phrenokosmian Society had changed considerably. Religious and moral discussions were still frequent, but subjects dealing with Swedish topics were also included, dealing primarily with Swedish literature and history, and we can thus observe a growing sense of a Swedish national feeling in the society. In the literary discussions, the topics reflected the authors who were studied in the Swedish classes in the college. Thus, during the 1870s and 1880s Tegnér and Runeberg were frequently discussed in the society. "Det eviga," "Svea," and "Kungarne på

---

[206] For college literary societies in general, see Lyle 1934.

[207] Catalog 1887/88, 45.

[208] All the subsequent information about topics of discussion in the society comes from the minutes of the Phrenokosmian Society in ACL, PS. Information for the period 1860–1877 is also based on the Record Book of Program Topics in ACL, PS.

Salamis," as well as *Fritiofs saga* are examples of works Tegnér that were read in the society. Frequent selections by Runeberg came from *Fänrik Ståls sägner*,[209] and in 1882, one of the topics for discussion was which of the two authors was the greatest poet.[210] Swedish history was also discussed in the society in the 1880s, although not as frequently as Swedish literature. In 1879 an oration consisted of king Gustav Vasa's farewell address to the Swedish Parliament from the sixteenth century, and one year later another oration dealt with king Gustavus Adolphus' departure for Germany and his participation in the Thirty Years War.[211]

During the 1890s, literary and cultural topics were the most common subjects of discussion, and several Swedish authors were featured at the society's meetings. Some examples include the 1896 meeting devoted to the nineteenth century historian and poet Erik Gustaf Geijer, and the 1897 discussion of the psalm-writer and bishop Johan Olof Wallin, also from the nineteenth century. The Gustavian era in the late eighteenth century, with talks both about King Gustav III and the authors Kellgren, Leopold, and Lenngren was also dealt with several times, and in 1898 the Romantic poet Erik Johan Stagnelius was the featured topic.[212] In 1891 the society devoted at least one meeting to Old Norse mythology and literature.[213] A few topics came from the field of Swedish history, such as a discussion of King Gustavus Adolphus, as well as Swedish history during the middle ages, and the role of Engelbrekt Engelbrektsson, the leader of an uprising in the fifteenth century. The minutes also note that a "patriotic song" preceded the speech on Gustavus Adolphus, which, typically, was held on the anniversary of the king's death in the battle of Lützen on November 6, 1632.[214] The various provinces of Sweden were also discussed a few times, as well as different provincial dialects.[215]

The members of the Phrenokosmian Society also discussed certain aspects of the heritage of their new homeland, although to a lesser degree than they did their Swedish background. As noted before, the early leadership of the

[209] ACL, PS, Minutes: Tegnér: 26 January 1877 (Svea), 28 February 1879 (Svea), 2 May 1879 (Kungarne på Salamis), 24 September 1880 (Det eviga), 27 January 1882 (Kungarne på Salamis), 17 February 1882 (Det eviga), 6 September 1884 (Fritiofs saga), 13 March 1885 (Det eviga), 28 January 1887 (Fritiofs saga). Fänrik Ståls sägner by Runberg was discussed on 14 January 1879, 24 September 1880, 26 November 1886, 25 February 1887.

[210] ACL, PS, Minutes, 24 March 1882.

[211] ACL, PS, Minutes: 3 October 1879 (Gustav Vasa), 3 December 1880 (Gustavus Adolphus).

[212] ACL, PS, Minutes: 13 March 1896 (Geijer), 8 October 1897 (Wallin), 27 November 1891, 28 October 1892 (Kellgren), 6 October 1891 (Lenngren), 19 March 1897 (Gustavian era), 28 October 1898 (Stagnelius).

[213] ACL, PS, Minutes, 10 April 1891.

[214] ACL, PS, Minutes: 1 November 1889 (Engelbrekt Engelbrektsson), 16 October 1896 (the Middle Ages), 6 November 1896 (Gustavus Adolphus).

[215] ACL, PS, Minutes: 19 February 1892 (Nature in Swedish provinces) and 15 November 1895 (Meeting of Swedish provinces), 28 November 1890 (Swedish provincial dialects).

college had encouraged "Americanization" and both American history, geography, politics, and literature were studied in the Augustana curriculum.[216] Although Augustana's Swedish ethnic background received increased attention after 1890, it is clear that Augustana Swedes and Swedish Americans also emphasized their "Americanness" and loyalty to their adopted homeland. Thus, a combination of both Swedish and American elements existed in the Augustana Synod, and the argument was made that no contradiction existed between being a loyal American and at the same time maintaining Swedish cultural traditions.

Some examples will illustrate this point. In 1892, Olof Olsson, the president of Augustana College, emphasized the school's patriotic nature, by saying that as citizens of the United States, "we must be faithful and enthusiastic patriots for the land of the free and the brave." This did not, however, preclude the maintenance of the Swedish language at Augustana College, Olsson continued, and concluded by asserting that if President Harrison were to come to the campus, he would find "no false Americans" but would instead be "moved" by the "true American civic spirit" at the college.[217] Twenty-two years later, in 1914, an article in *Augustana* argued that the purpose of the "preservation of Swedishness" was to contribute an important cultural element to the United States, and in 1916 the paper claimed that "America is not only English," but was, in accordance with the country's motto *E Pluribus Unum* made up many national groups, of which the Swedish Americans were one.

This American emphasis was also reflected in the Phrenokosmian Society, where notable American historical figures were dealt with. One discussion focused on the question "Who was most praiseworthy: Washington, La Fayette, Lincoln, or Grant?" in 1880, the question "Who deserves more praise: Christopher Columbus for discovering America or George Washington for defending it?" from 1896, or the life and achievements of President Lincoln, which were discussed at least once in 1897.[218] Significant events in American history also received attention in the Phrenokosmian Society, such as a program on "The Revolutionary War" consisting of "patriotic songs," a declamation of "The Declaration of Independence" and speeches about the Battles of Saratoga and Yorktown from 1897 and an 1896 lecture on the Civil War.[219]

[216] Although the information in the catalogs is uneven, American history is mentioned already in 1876/77 [Catalog 1876/77, 15.] In 1884/85 both American history and geography were studied [Catalog 1884/85, 23] and in addition to textbooks in American history, the 1892/93 catalog also includes a textbook on the U.S. Constitution. [Catalog 1892/93, 31.] By 1909/10, there were several courses on both U.S. history, politics, and literature. [Catalog 1909/10, 24–43.]

[217] *Augustana*, 27 October 1892, 9 July 1914, and 14 December 1916.

[218] ACL, PS, Minutes: 13 February 1880 (Washington, La Fayette), 23 October 1896 (Columbus or Washington), 12 February 1897 (Lincoln).

[219] ACL, PS, Minutes: 6 March 1896 (Civil War), 29 January 1897 (Revolutionary War).

American and English literature was also discussed, such as a meeting devoted to Longfellow in 1896 or one to American humor and humorists in 1898, and at least one meeting in the early 1890s dealing with the works of William Shakespeare.[220] Contemporary American affairs were also noted a few times, such as a meeting on different American political parties in 1895, or a discussion of the issue of free silver in 1896.[221]

The Swedish and American elements were sometimes directly combined at Augustana. One example is the celebration of Washington's birthday, which the society arranged in 1878. According to the minutes, the celebration took place in the college chapel where "above the speakers, the Banners of the American and Swedish Nations were displayed intertwined. A picture of Washington symbolized the Union." The program contained both Swedish and American elements: it opened with "The Star Spangled Banner" and after a short prayer continued with the Finno-Swedish patriotic song "Vårt Land," which was also popular in Sweden. An oration about George Washington by one of the native-born "American" professors followed, and then the program closed with "My Country 'Tis of Thee."[222] Another such juxtaposition was the 1897 meeting devoted to "famous battles," and two of the *melées* included were the Battle at Hampton Roads from the American Civil War, considered by the participants to have saved the Union fleet and the Battle of Breitenfeld from the Thirty Years War in which the Swedish troops were victorious.[223]

An interest in Swedish-American cultural patterns emerges in the society's activities towards the end of the eighties and in the early nineties. The term "Swedish-American" as a self-description seems to have began to be used towards the end of the 1880s in the Phrenokosmian Society. In 1888, for example, the society discussed "Swedish-American character traits and their influence on the American nationality," and in 1890, when the minutes state that the society moved that "Our Forefathers' Day ought to be celebrated by the Swedish-Americans." Moreover, the nineties saw the first discussions that dealt with the history of the Swedes in America. In 1893 the reasons for Swedish emigration to and Swedish settlements in America in general were dealt with, and in 1897 the Swedish seventeenth-century colony on the Delaware River was the focus of attention for one meeting. In that same year, one whole evening was also devoted to "the Emigrants," during which different speeches dealt with the preparations and farewells in Sweden, the voyage across the Atlantic, and the first years in America. In 1892, finally, an oration was given to the memory of John Ericsson, the Swedish engineer and con-

---

[220] ACL, PS, Minutes: 9 October 1896 (Longfellow), 4 November 1898 (American humor), 3 March 1891, 20 October 1893 (Shakespeare).
[221] ACL, PS, Minutes: 25 October 1895 (political parties), 25 September 1896 (free silver).
[222] ACL, PS, Minutes, 1 March 1878.
[223] ACL, PS, Minutes, 15 March 1897.

structor of the *Monitor* which took part in the Battle of Hampton Roads during the Civil War.[224]

The sense of a Swedish-American distinctiveness in the Phrenokosmian Society can also be seen from an 1896 discussion of the nature of "Swedish-American youth," and a meeting two years later when the topic was "A Swedish-American and His Duties." In 1898, finally, one evening was devoted to "Swedish-American literature", which featured three authors, A.A. Swärd, Ludvig Holmes, and Johan Enander, all of whom were closely associated with the Augustana Synod.[225]

It can be concluded, then, that the discussions in the Phrenokosmian Society dealing with Swedish literature, not surprisingly, mirrors much of the instruction in the college's subject of Swedish, with Runeberg and Tegnér taking center stage early on, but with a gradual expansion into other authors as well. The evidence from the Phrenokosmian Society also suggests that topics dealing with Swedish literature were frequently discussed at Augustana College as early as in the 1870s, which is a further indication of the sustained interest in Swedish at the school, even though the English language was making rapid inroads. In addition, members of the society also discussed topics relating to the history and literature of their new homeland. Prominent American leaders, such as Presidents Washington and Lincoln, together with decisive historical events, such as the War of Independence and the Civil War, found their way into the society's discussions.

It is also possible to see the beginnings of a specific Swedish-American awareness in the society, as, beginning in the 1890s, topics of discussion in the society dealt with both the history and cultural expressions of the Swedish-American group. It can be said that the members had begun to see themselves as "Swedish Americans" rather than "Swedes in America." In addition, selected aspects of the Swedish and American pasts were presented at meetings of the society, often dealing with and juxtaposing patriotic or nationalistic symbols from the respective countries, such as famous Swedish kings or leading American presidents.

Svenska Vitterhetssällskapet
Further evidence of the growth of a Swedish-American identity at Augustana College comes from the four student organizations devoted to the study of Swedish and Swedish-American culture that had been started at the school by

---

[224] ACL, PS, Minutes: 10 March 1893 (Swedes in Minnesota), 13 October 1893 (Reasons for Swedish emigration), 22 January 1897 (Delaware), 7 April 1897 (Emigrants), 13 May 1892 (John Ericsson).

[225] ACL, PS, Minutes: 8 May 1896 (Swedish-American youth), 28 January 1898 (Swedish-American literature), 1 April 1898 (Swedish-American duties).

the turn of the century.[226] The oldest of these groups was the eighteen-member Svenska Vitterhetssällskapet (The Swedish Society for Belles Lettres) formed in 1896 and dedicated to "the study of Swedish literature and culture," and which met on a regular basis for discussions of literary topics, as well as readings of original productions. The society also sponsored public lectures on Swedish and Swedish-American topics.[227] A second literary society was Tegnér-förbundet (The Tegnér Society), organized in 1901, to promote the study of Swedish literature. Both groups were primarily intended for students in the college, whereas the third society, Iduna, organized in 1902 was intended for younger students, primarily in the academy. The fourth group was a Swedish debating club, Torgny, organized in 1904.

Little material is preserved from these groups, except for Svenska Vitterhetssällskapet, for which there is a book of minutes as well as a publication called *Runan* (The Rune). The latter was a handwritten publication that was read aloud at meetings. On three occasions, the group also published a special Christmas issue, called *Julrunan* (The Christmas Rune). A brief overview of the activities of this group will give an additional view of Swedish-related activities at Augustana College during the years following the turn of the century.

With its eighteen members, the group's name obviously alluded to the Swedish Academy (which also was a topic of discussion in 1905[228]), and the first pages of the society's minute book contain a listing with the signatures of the occupants of each of the eighteen "chairs" in chronological order.[229] The 1911 issue of *Julrunan* also proclaimed that the goal of the society was to work for the preservation of "Swedishness and the Swedish language and literature among the Swedish Americans," and added that "Svenska Vitterhetssällskapet seeks to be to America's Swedes what the [Swedish] Academy is to the people of Sweden."[230]

The society seems to have been particularly active during the decade or so after 1900. In 1900, *Augustana* pointed out that during its early years, the group had been "mis-understood," something which was no longer the case.[231] A retrospective article on the society's history, argued that when the group was founded the study of Swedish was on the retreat at Augustana and that many people feared that the Swedish language would die out. Once the society had been founded it was also met with "resistance" and "ridicule," something which, however, changed within a few years, as the group developed an ener-

---

[226] The following listing is based on the information from Catalog, 1909/10, 106–07.
[227] Catalog, 1902/03, 105.
[228] ACL, SV, Minutes, 8 April 1905.
[229] ACL, SV, Minutes, 4–12.
[230] Oscar Montan, "Svenska Vitterhetssällskapets historik," *Julrunan* 1911, 24.
[231] *Augustana*, 7 June 1900.

getic program.[232]

During the first years of the century, Svenska Vitterhetssällskapet met regularly, including a business meeting, which often, but not always, was followed by a program. In almost all the cases the program was either a presentation of one or several authors, or a discussion of a literary work. An examination of the topics discussed at the meetings and of *Runan* shows that topics dealing with Swedish literature were very common, and that the focus was on authors studied in the Swedish curriculum in the college. Runeberg and Tegnér, so popular in the college's Swedish curriculum and in the Phrenokosmian Society, were also discussed in Svenska Vitterhetssällskapet,[233] as well as in its publication *Runan*.[234] Other names mentioned in the society's minutes include Oscar Levertin, Anna Wahlenberg, Viktor Rydberg, Per Hallström, Karl Erik Forsslund, J.O. Wallin, and B. E. Malmström,[235] and in *Runan* Georg Stiernhielm, Zacharias Topelius, king Oscar II, and Sigurd (Alfred Hedenstierna).[236] As shown above, some of these authors, such as Levertin, Heidenstam, and Malmström, were also studied in the college's Swedish curriculum. Others, such as Forsslund and Sigurd, were also popular authors among those imported by the Augustana Book Concern.

Beginning around 1911, fewer authors were dealt with but in seemingly greater detail. In that year at least four presentations focused on works by Verner von Heidenstam, and in December the society started reading and discussing works by August Strindberg, something which continued for more than one year.[237] The minutes from February 1911 stated that special attention would be given to the "national and patriotic" in Heidenstam's writings. In 1914, two meetings each were devoted to Selma Lagerlöf's *Jerusalem* and *Fritiofs saga* by Tegnér.[238] By this time too, Jules Mauritzson, the college's professor of Swedish was taking a more active part in the society, and meetings were apparently becoming more of a direct supplement to the Swedish instruction at the college.

---

[232] F.E. Sard, "När Svenska Vitterhetssällskapet bildades," *Julrunan*, 1905, 23–24; Oscar Montan, "Svenska Vitterhetssällskapets historik," *Julrunan* 1911, 23–24.

[233] ACL, SV, Minutes: Runeberg: 29 January 1902 and 10 March 1909; Tegnér: 6 May 1908 and 22 October 1914.

[234] ACL, SV, *Runan*: 28 March 1903, 28 January 1905, 3 February 1909.

[235] ACL, SV, Minutes: 28 March 1903 (Levertin), 12 October 1902 (Wahlenberg), 10 February 1906 (Rydberg), 15 November 1902 (Hallström), 28 March 1903 (Forsslund), 12 November 1904 (Wallin), 2 March 1910 (Malmström).

[236] ACL, SV, *Runan*: 13 December 1902 (Stiernhielm), no date (Topelius), 10 February 1906 (Oscar II), 28 April 1905 and 3 November 1906 (Sigurd).

[237] ACL, SV, Minutes: Heidenstam: 15 February, 1 March, 26 October, 8 November, 4 December 1911; Strindberg: 2 November, 2 December 1912, 27 January, 10 March, 13 April, 6 October, 3 November, 11 December 1913; 22 January 1914.

[238] ACL, SV, Minutes: Jerusalem: 12 February and 11 March 1914; Fritiofs saga: 22 October and 12 November 1914.

It is apparent that members of the society sought to promote a certain type of Swedish literature, at least during the first years of the twentieth century. In 1902 and 1903 *Runan* claimed that there were only a few good contemporary authors in Sweden. Good literature, the paper argued, was "idealistic" in nature, a quality lacking in much of what was published in Sweden, and the members of the society were encouraged to instead preserve the memory of the earlier idealistic writings.[239]

Several times, *Runan* spoke of the importance of preserving the Swedish language, literature, and history for the Swedish immigrants and their children in America, and of the role that Augustana College and the society played in this process. In November 1902, for example, an article underscored the necessity of maintaining a Swedish cultural heritage, stating that it was indeed possible to be "a good American citizen" while at the same time preserving "one's Swedish language and memories,"[240] and a few months later the society's task of studying Sweden's literary history, especially its "glorious" dimensions such as Tegnér, Runeberg, Franzén, and Geijer, was emphasized, together with the especially great need to convey tradition to those born in America by Swedish parents.[241] In 1906, the paper noted that Augustana College was the "heart of Swedishness in America" where "the pillars of Swedishness in America were reared and educated," a process in which Svenska Vitterhetssällskapet played an important role.[242]

Similar comments were made in conjunction with the establishment of Tegnér-förbundet in 1901, when *Augustana* commented that it was often claimed that the Swedish Americans were becoming Americanized, something which was certainly not true at Augustana. If those who say so, the paper continued, would spend a day among the students here, they would realize that "Augustana College is still the hearth of Swedishness in America, and that it will be difficult to change this."[243]

The society also sponsored literary competitions in the Swedish language. The first suggestion for such a competition was made in 1903, and rules for a competition were drawn up, including poetry, short stories, and pieces on literary and cultural history, with a jury appointed and monetary prizes adopted. No mention is made of winners in 1903, but it seems as if the competitions continued on a regular basis for a few more years.[244] In 1906, the competition was given a high recognition as the jury included the Swedish professors at the

[239] ACL, SV, *Runan*, 11 October 1902, 14 February 1903.
[240] ACL, SV, *Runan*, 15 November 1902.
[241] ACL, SV, *Runan*, 28 March 1903.
[242] ACL, SV, *Runan*, 10 February 1906.
[243] *Augustana*, 9 May 1901.
[244] ACL, SV, Minutes: 11 March 1903, 6 May 1903. Cf. ACL, SV, Minutes: 8 April, 12 November, 10 December 1904; 8 April, 28 June 1905; 10 February 1906.

three leading Augustana Synod colleges, namely Mauritzson, Kilander, and Florén from Augustana, Gustavus Adolphus, and Bethany respectively. First and second prizes were awarded in poetry, whereas only a second prize was given for fiction.[245] Two of the winners, C.A. Lönnqvist and J.F. Englund, expressed their thanks in the November 1906 issue of *Runan*.[246] The literary competitions seem to have ended in 1906, as there are no further mention of them in the society's minutes.

The task of preserving a sense of Swedishness at Augustana did not only mean the promotion of national Swedish literature or the Swedish language. As was the case in the Phrenokosmian Society, Svenska Vitterhetssällskapet also showed great interest in specifically Swedish-American cultural concerns. In December 1904, for example, the topic for deliberations was "Our Swedish-American Christmas literature," in January and February of the following year the focus was on the Swedish-American poet and Augustana pastor A.A. Swärd, and in November 1908 one meeting was devoted to Swedish-American "elocution" and "culture."[247] In 1903 and 1905 *Runan* also included poems by Swedish-American authors, the well-known Augustana pastors Ludvig (pseudonym for Ludvig Holmes) and Teofilus (pseudonym for C.A. Lönnqvist).[248]

The three issues of Svenska Vitterhetssällskapet's special Christmas publication, *Julrunan*, which appeared in 1905, 1911, and 1912 show how Swedish-American cultural concerns were important to the society.[249] An advertisement in *Augustana* for the 1905 issue also noted that it included contributions from "the leading authors in Swedish America."[250] All three issues included many literary contributions—poems and short stories—the majority authored by Swedish-American authors connected with the Augustana Synod. Contributors included such well-known Augustana names as C.W. Andeer, K.G. William Dahl, Ludvig Holmes, Carl Kraft, C.A. Lönnqvist, Anna Olsson, and E.W. Olson.

Several of the stories take place in Swedish America. For example, Anna Olsson's 1905 contribution "Babetistera" deals with contacts between Swedish American Lutherans and Baptists in Chicago, and is written in Olsson's typical linguistic style, mixing Swedish dialects and English, and in 1911 K.G. William Dahl contributed a story about the children Nelly and Peter, also set in Swedish America.[251] A few contributions also deal with the history of the

---

[245] ACL, SV, Minutes: 10 March, 3 October 1906.

[246] ACL, SV, *Runan*, 3 November 1906.

[247] ACL, SV, Minutes: 10 December 1904, 28 January and 18 February 1905, 12 November 1908.

[248] ACL, SV, *Runan*: 28 March 1903, 9 December 1905.

[249] For the following, see *Julrunan* 1905, 1911, and 1912.

[250] *Augustana*, 21 December 1905.

[251] Anna Olsson, "Babetistera," *Julrunan*, 1905; K.G. William Dahl, "Nelly och Pete", *Julrunan*, 1911.

Swedes in America, such as an account of the 1905 Augustana Synod meeting in Stanton, Iowa, or of pioneer life among Swedish immigrants.[252]

Other pieces specifically dealt with the nature of cultural developments among the Swedish-Americans, and are further examples of how a Swedish-American identity was growing stronger at Augustana after the turn of the century. In 1905 Samuel Magnus Hill wondered if a separate "Swedish-American literature" existed, arguing that it was possible to begin to discern such a phenomenon, which reflected the development of life in Swedish America and which was clearly separate from literary developments in Sweden.[253] S.G. Youngert, pastor and editor at the Augustana Book Concern, made a similar point in a reflection on what it meant to be a Swedish American. "It is something more than to be Swedish and also something more than to be American," he stated, incorporating traits that characterize both these peoples, such as the Swedish virtues of honesty, steadfastness, and piety, but also the Americans traits of industriousness, resourcefulness, and courage.[254] A poem by E.W. Olson from 1912, finally, conjured up an image of a Swedish cultural heritage preserved in the New World, in harmony with the traditions of the new land: "In the forests of the North, on the prairies of the West/still Sweden's children recognize their mother/and the flag with the dear Swedish colors/we still hoist next to the Star Spangled Banner."[255]

The Swedish-American tradition which emerged at Augustana College during the final years of the nineteenth century consisted of several parts. It included elements from a national Swedish culture, stressing the established authors of the Romantic era of the nineteenth century and with a focus on idealism and patriotism. The American context in which the immigrants and their children existed was underscored as well, and American cultural icons of a patriotic nature, were also incorporated in the Swedish-American tradition. Finally, the tradition highlighted a Swedish-American culture, focusing on cultural traits and achievements that were seen as specific to the experience of the Swedish Americans, primarily in the Augustana Synod.

The role of ethnicity was thus strengthened at Augustana College around the turn of the century. The previous relative lack of interest in the institution's ethnic background was replaced with an interest not only in certain dimensions of Swedish, and to some extent American, culture, but also with a clear

[252] Christopher Carlson, "Minnen och bilder från Augustana-synodens möte i Stanton," *Julrunan*, 1905; Edor [pseud], "När kyrkan 'restes' i Saron. Bilder från nybyggarlifvet," *Julrunan*, 1912.

[253] S.M. Hill, " 'Vår' litteratur," *Julrunan*, 1905, 11–12.

[254] S.G. Youngert, "Amerika och Svensk-Amerikanerna," *Julrunan* 1905, 21.

[255] E.W. Olson, "Nya banor," *Julrunan*, 1912, 12. It is interesting to note that at this time the Swedish flag had not yet become widely used as a cultural symbol in Sweden. [Jansson 1994, 33.] It seems likely that the prevalent use of the American flag in the U.S. can explain Olson's use of the Swedish flag as a symbol in Swedish America.

emphasis on precise Swedish-American cultural patterns. Given the centrality of Augustana College within the Augustana Synod, the Swedish-American tradition which developed at the college became an important part in the Synod's Swedish-American identity.

The Augustana Student Body

The preceding discussion has illustrated the position and the nature of what I have called a Swedish-American tradition at Augustana College. In this section the question of the nature of the student body at Augustana College that was exposed to this tradition will be addressed. In chapter two, the dominance of the Augustana Synod in Swedish America was discussed and some tentative answers given to the question of who the Augustana Swedish Americans were, through observations about the geographical, generational, and social characteristic of the Augustana Synod; Synod statistics, census data, and contemporary observations by Synod members. Still, the source material available for the Synod as a whole makes it difficult to more precisely establish dimensions such as generational composition and social and geographic background.

Sources are, however, more abundant for Augustana College, and an intensive analysis of the student body at Augustana College will further illuminate the question of Augustana's specific character in Swedish America. Questions to be addressed include the ethnic and generational dimension of the student body, the social background of the Augustana students, and the geographical recruitment patterns of the college. An attempt will also be made to trace the careers of graduates of the college, in order to both discuss the college's role for social mobility among the Augustana Swedish Americans, and to see what role the Augustana graduates played in the larger Swedish-American community.

A Note on the Sources

For this study a number of different sources has been collected in a database and used in the analysis. The most important sources are the printed catalogs for Augustana College from 1871 to 1914, in which all students are listed by name and class in the college, and the forms which each student completed upon registering at Augustana. The registration forms usually include information about birth year, birth place, place of residence, father's occupation, church affiliation, and previous education.[256] Additional information about the students has been gathered through a number of sources: the official annual of

---

[256] Catalogs 1871/72–1914/15; ACL, RF.

the Augustana Synod *Korsbaneret, The Augustana Ministerium,* and the booklet *Who is Who Among the Alumni?,* tracing the further careers of the Augustana graduates, published in 1923.[257]

A total of 1,433 students who matriculated at Augustana College between 1871–1914 have been recorded, and form the basis for the following discussion. The completeness of the sources is, however, uneven and the information is much more complete during the first decades of the period than the latter. Some variables are also more complete than others, such as birth year and place of residence. The latter is noted in 96 percent of the cases. Father's occupation is available in roughly two thirds of the cases throughout the period. During the two first decades, more than 70 percent of the students have noted their father's avocation, whereas this is true of only 56 percent of the students between 1900–1914. The figures are similar for the students' further career and for the generational classification. In no case, however, can one discern a systematic tendency in the way in which the information is missing. Instead, as time progressed, the data collected by Augustana College when its students registered each year became less precise, something which was also true for the church records maintained by the Synod.

Most of the data about birth years, birthplaces, and fathers' occupation has been gathered from the registration forms. It is important to note that all the students in the database did not graduate from the college. Only a little fewer than half of the students attended their senior year at Augustana, leaving a very large group of persons who for some reason left the school after less than the full four years. A small *caveat* concerning the occupational category "farmer" is also necessary. This term, or the American Swedish version of it (*farmare*), is by far the most common word used to indicate that the student's father was working the land—both in Sweden and in the United States. It is used in almost 90 percent of the cases among the occupations which indicate that the fathers tilled the soil. Other categories are used much less frequently: "lantbrukare", "bonde," or "jordbrukare" in seven percent of the cases, and "hemmansägare" in less than five percent of the instances. The word "farmer" in the U.S. context suggests landownership, but, given both the commonality of the word "farmer" in American English and an desire to raise one's social status, it is almost certain that some Augustana students had fathers in Sweden who were not landowners, although they were noted as such.

---

[257] Korsbaneret, 1881–1915; Bergendoff 1980; Who is Who Among the Alumni, 1923.

Generational and Ethnic Composition

Generational composition, has, as noted in chapter two, been an important factor in the discussion of the nature of ethnicity and ethnic identity. An assessment of the generational and ethnic make-up of the Augustana students, and its changing nature over time, is thus of great importance for our further discussion.

The students of Swedish background have been divided into two general categories: first and second generation Swedish Americans. First-generation students are Swedish-born, while the second generation of Swedish-American students includes those American-born students where it can be established that at least one parent (usually the father) was born in Sweden. In addition, those students who were born in the U.S., had typically Swedish-sounding names, lived in typical Swedish-American cities and areas, and had some kind of affiliation with the Augustana Synod (such as being a member of an Augustana congregation, or previously having attended another Augustana Synod academy or college) have also been included in this group. The use of these criteria makes it possible that some third-generation Swedish Americans (i.e., U.S.-born of at least one Swedish-born grandparent) might have been included, as the available sources do not make their identification possible.

In addition, those students who were clearly not of Swedish background have been grouped separately as "non-Swedish." Here, names, religious affiliation, and places of residence have been important in the classification.

During the entire period 1871–1914, Augustana College was clearly dominated by matriculating students with a Swedish background. Only 13 percent of the student body was non-Swedish, mainly consisting of students from the urban area known as the Tri-Cities in Illinois and Iowa where Augustana College was located. Among the students of Swedish background, the number of students born in Sweden and those born in the United States of Swedish-born parents were of roughly the same size, with 45 percent Swedish-born and 42 percent born in the U.S.[258]

The generational constitution of the student body did, however, vary significantly over time, as can be seen in table 2. Since the normal course of study lasted four years, it was possible to be enrolled in the college during two decades, and some students have been thus counted twice. This does not, however, affect our reading of changes in the generational make-up at the college.

During the 1870s and 1880s, the Swedish-born students constituted about three fourths of the student body. During the following decades a decline of the number Swedish-born students started. During the first decade of this century about a third of the students had been born in Sweden, and between

[258] Augustana Student Database.

110

1910–1914, the figure stood at 14 percent. The American-born students of Swedish background increased as the Swedish-born declined. Before 1890, about 20 percent were born in the U.S., but by 1900, the American-born students constituted a majority of all students at Augustana College. The non-Swedish part of the student body, finally, also grew, in particular after the turn of the century. At the end of the period, the non-Swedish students at Augustana constituted about a fifth of the student body.

Table 2. *Generations of Matriculating Students at Augustana College, 1871–1914. In Per Cent.*

	1870s	1880s	1890s	1900s	1910s
Swedish-born	75	73	51	30	14
American-born	22	20	40	57	64
Non-Swedes	3	7	9	13	22
Total	100	100	100	100	100
N	146	303	325	310	266

Source: Augustana Student Data Base

In terms of generational shifts, it is obvious that the decades around the turn of the century were of crucial importance at Augustana College, and they stand out as the period when the American-born generation established a dominance at Augustana. This generational shift can also be seen elsewhere in the college, and it is telling that the first American-born president of the institution, Gustav Andreen, assumed office in 1901.

The shift of generations at Augustana College does not coincide with the course of Swedish immigration to the U.S. Roughly a third of all Swedish immigrants landed on American shores after 1900, when the number of Swedish-born students at Augustana College rapidly grew smaller. It is thus apparent that Augustana College was much less attractive to the immigrants of this later phase, something which we have also observed for the Synod.

Geographical Recruitment Patterns

The geographical recruitment patterns of the Augustana students can also be analysed in order to characterize the student body. An analysis of the data for the first and second generation Swedish-American students at the college shows that five states in the Midwest accounted for more than three fourths of the students. The state with the largest percentage was Illinois, from which a third of the students came. Illinois was followed by Iowa (15 percent), Minnesota (14 percent), Nebraska (seven percent), and Michigan (six percent).

A comparison with the general settlement patterns for the first and second generation Swedish Americans in 1910 shows that the Augustana students had a distinct geographical background. Three fourths of the Augustana students came from the five most popular states, while these states only accounted for half of the total Swedish-American population. Moreover, in 1910 the states of New York and Massachusetts ranked as number three and four among the Swedish Americans, with 11 percent of the population. Only three percent of the Augustana students came from these two eastern states.[259]

The recruitment patterns thus show that Augustana students primarily came from the Midwestern states. Moreover, the patterns also show a considerable stability throughout the period under investigation, as the five leading Midwestern states were as dominant during the 1910s as they were during the 1880s. Augustana's location in the heart of the Midwest on the border between Illinois and Iowa is, of course, one factor that can help explain the geographical origins of the students.

However, it also seems possible to speak of a recruitment tradition at Augustana College, where students kept coming from primarily those Midwestern states that formed the nucleus of the Swedish settlements when Augustana College was founded during the early phase of the Swedish mass-immigration. Moreover, the recruitment patterns are not affected by the generational shift at the college. As we have seen, the student body was largely dominated by the second generation after 1900, and in 1910 the Midwestern Swedish Americans, from whom Augustana recruited heavily, were to a large degree American-born. In Iowa and Nebraska, for example, which were in second and fourth place among the home states of Augustana students, more than 60 percent of the Swedish Americans were American-born.[260] Thus, in the old Swedish-American heartlands, the propensity to go to Augustana was passed down from one generation of Swedish Americans to the next.

Social Background of the Augustana Students

A lively scholarly discussion in social history concerning the social stratification of individuals exists, and a number of classification schemes has been advanced, depending on such factors as theoretical starting points, the nature of the source material, and the need for comparisons.[261] In the present analysis of the social background of the Augustana students, a slightly modified version of a classification scheme that was developed at Uppsala University in the 1970s is used. The scheme aims to place the individuals on a socio-economic

---

[259] Census 1910, vol. I, 927–34.
[260] Census 1910, vol. I, 929–30.
[261] See Andræ 1978 for a discussion of social stratification in Swedish historiography.

scale, where unskilled laborers are found at the bottom, and wealthy property owners at the top. This scheme also corresponds with the classificatory system which developed in the United Sates in the 1960s and 1970s with the advent of the "new social history."[262]

The social background of those Augustana students who enrolled in the college between 1871 and 1914 can be seen in table 3.

Table 3. *Social Background of the Matriculating Augustana Students, 1871–1914 in Per Cent.*

Group	Swedish-born	American-born	Non-Swedes	Total
I	5	30	40	22
II	7	16	31	15
III	57	31	16	39
IV	18	17	13	16
V	13	6	0	8
Total	100	100	100	100
N	345	413	114	872

Source: Augustana Student Data Base

The dominant occupational group among the fathers of the Augustana students was clearly the farmers, to which almost 40 percent of the students belonged. The second largest category was group I, high white collar, which was followed by group IV, skilled and semiskilled workers, and group II, low white collar. The smallest group represented among the Augustana students was the unskilled laborers, to which only eight percent belonged.

There were, however, some major differences among the students of Swedish and non-Swedish background. Although the numbers are considerably smaller for the non-Swedish students, it is clear that they came from a much

[262] The main sources for the classification scheme have been Norman 1974, exkurs 2, and Thernstrom 1973, appendix B. The occupations have been grouped in the following manner:
I: Major proprietors, landowners, higher officials, managers, professionals
II: Petty proprietors, master artisans, clerks, lower officials, semiprofessionals
III: Farmers
IV: Craftsmen, artisans, skilled and semiskilled labor
V: Unskilled labor, domestic service, agricultural labor
For comparative purposes, group I corresponds to the American "high white collar," group II to "low white collar," group IV to "skilled workers" and group V to "unskilled workers." The farmers constitute a problem in this classification, as the occupational notations suggest that almost all are free-holding farmers both in Sweden and the U.S. It has been argued that in the rural Swedish context, such a category of farmers should be classified in a fairly "high" group [Jansson 1982, 55–59.] This may well be the case, and it could be argued that groups II and III should change places in this scheme. Still, to conform with existing Swedish and American practices, I will leave the scheme as it is.

more urban and white collar background than did the Swedes or Swedish Americans. Over 70 percent of the non-Swedes belonged to groups I and II, and 85 percent of them lived in Illinois, almost exclusively in the urban area in which Augustana College was located. Over ten percent of the non-Swedish students had fathers who were ministers in a local American congregation, and other common parental occupations included merchants, physicians, and attorneys. Thus, the non-Swedish students tended to come from fairly well-to-do, often professional, American families in the area, to whom Augustana College was the closest institution of higher education. It is also significant that a fairly small degree of the non-Swedish students actually graduated from the college. Only 25 percent of those students who have been classified as non-Swedish graduated attended their senior year at Augustana. It was very common for these non-Swedish students to enroll at Augustana for one or two years only.

There were also noticeable differences among the students of Swedish background. Although farmers was the largest parental group for both the Swedish-born and the American-born students, it was much more dominant for the Swedish-born students, where more than half of the students were found in this category. Only a third of the American-born students came from farming homes. Moreover, almost a third of the fathers of the Swedish-born students were skilled or unskilled laborers, whereas the corresponding figure for the American-born was about a fifth, suggesting that the college provided an opportunity for inter-generational social mobility among Swedish Americans.

Thus, the American-born students of Swedish background at Augustana were also much more frequently represented in the higher categories than their Swedish-born peers. Almost half of them have been classified as high or low white collar, whereas the corresponding figure for the Swedish-born is 12 percent. It should, however, be noticed that a large group of Augustana pastors is included in the figures for high white collar fathers for the American-born group, and constitute as much as three fourths of all the fathers of American-born students in group I.

The classification of an Augustana pastor as high white collar raises a potential problem. As the Augustana Synod was struggling to get organized, the training of the Augustana pastors was, especially during the first couple of decades, not as rigourous as for the ministers within the Church of Sweden or for other denominations in the U.S., which suggests that they should be included in a lower category. It seems likely that the social prestige of an Augustana minister was less than that of a minister in the Church of Sweden (although Sten Carlsson has shown that an Augustana degree does not seem to have been a major handicap for returning Augustana pastors for a career in the Church of Sweden[263]), but it is also probable that the Augustana pastor did

[263] Carlsson 1984.

enjoy a great deal of respect in the Swedish-American communities, particularly in rural areas. Other common parental white collar occupations among the American born-students include merchants, teachers at Augustana College, and clerks.

There is also a clear shift in occupational background, over time, among both the Swedish-born and the American-born students of Swedish background, as can be seen when the figures for the period 1871–1899 and 1900–1914 are compared in table 4. The analysis is based on a decennial break-down of the student body, and some students attending Augustana during two decades have been counted twice.

Table 4. *Social Background of the Matriculating Augustana Students of Swedish Backgrund, 1871–1899 and 1900–1914 in Per Cent.*

Group	Swedish-born		American-born		Total	
	1871–99	1900–14	1871–99	1900–14	1871–99	1900–14
I	3	17	27	32	11	30
II	6	8	10	20	8	18
III	58	47	40	26	52	29
IV	20	14	19	14	19	14
V	13	14	4	8	10	9
Total	100	100	100	100	100	100
N	356	51	187	286	543	337

Source: Augustana Student Data Base

As can be seen, there was a significant difference in the social background of Swedish-American Augustana students before and after 1900. Before the turn of the century, over half of the students at Augustana came from farming homes, while after 1900 less than a third belonged to that category. Similarly, the share of students from white collar backgrounds (groups I and II) increased from 19 percent during the period before 1900 to almost half after the turn of the century. As was shown in table 3, the social composition of the students is linked to the generational classification, and the quickly growing number of American-born students of Swedish background explains the growing number of students of white-collar background at the school. Augustana College thus developed from an institution which before 1900 primarily attracted students born in Sweden of an agricultural background, to a school which after the turn of the century was dominated by American-born students, the great majority of whom were of Swedish background, and who, to a large degree, came from white collar homes.

Further Careers of the Augustana Students

The final issue which will be addressed concerns the future careers of the Augustana students. What occupations did graduates of Augustana College take up and to what extent did these occupational choices remain within the sphere of the Augustana ethnic institution? These questions will illustrate the social mobility within the group of Augustana students and the significance of Augustana College for maintaining the cohesiveness of the ethnic group.

To establish the further careers of the Augustana students, lists of graduates and their occupations have been used which were published in the college catalogs at some intervals and in a booklet from 1923 published by the Augustana Alumni Association. In addition, the *Augustana Ministerium* (a directory of all ordained pastors in the Augustana Synod) has been utilised. The listings in the catalogs and the Alumni Association publication only include those persons who graduated from the college, which, as noted above, was a little less than half of the enrolled students. Especially during the early years, many of the non-graduating students continued in the Seminary, and can thus be traced in the *Augustana Ministerium*. Except for the Augustana ministers, those students who left the college prior to their senior year are not included in the following discussion. It should finally be noted that among those students who did attend their senior year at Augustana, 17 percent have not been identified.

These *caveats* noted, the evidence suggests that the Augustana students found their future jobs in the white collar categories. Almost all the students who have been identified—95 percent—were employed in the high white collar category (group I), while the remaining persons had low white collar jobs (group II). It is, however, again important to notice that the great number of ministers in the Augustana Synod among the college graduates is included in the high white collar figure, as almost 70 percent of the identified students became ministers in the Synod.

Some differences between the Swedish-born, American-born of Swedish background, and non-Swedish student categories exist. The dominance for the white collar occupations was equally strong among all three categories, but among the Swedish-born students, minister in the Augustana Synod was by far the most popular occupation, including 85 percent of the identified Swedish-born students. Other common occupations among the Swedish-born students included college professor, public school teacher, and physician.

The occupational panorama among the American-born students of Swedish background was more varied. Almost half of them were ordained in the Augustana Synod, while the remaining students found jobs in other professional white-collar employments such as physician, university professor, public school teacher, lawyer, and private businessman. The non-Swedish students, finally, only constituted five percent of all the identified students. The most popular occupation for them was public school teacher, followed by private businessman, physician, and lawyer.

Another way of looking at the subsequent careers of the Augustana students is to try to ascertain what influence they may have exercised both throughout Swedish America at large and within the Augustana sphere of Swedish America. As Augustana College was the leading institution of higher learning within the Augustana Synod, and in many ways functioned as a cultural "motor" for the Synod as a whole, it is of great interest to see how actively associated with Augustana the graduates of the school became. For the present analysis, I have defined a category of "Augustana occupations," which includes the Augustana pastors, teachers at colleges or academies operated by or associated with the Synod, as well as few well-known journalists at newspapers with Augustana sympathies.

This analysis shows that both students born in Sweden and in America of Swedish background demonstrated a strong propensity to remain within the Augustana sphere of Swedish America, as about three fourths of the students did so following their graduation from the college. There are some differences between the Swedish-born students and those born in America of Swedish background. Almost 90 percent of the Swedish-born students remained associated with Augustana in their later lives, whereas the figure for the American-born was 58 percent.

The very large number of Augustana graduates who became ministers in the Synod accounts for many of the "Augustana occupations" among the college graduates. Among the Swedish-born with Augustana occupations, the pastors constituted almost all the cases. The American-born students with Augustana occupations also include more than three fourths of Augustana ministers among its alumni. It should, however, be noted that there was also an increasingly large number of teachers at Augustana-affiliated institutions among this group, approximately 20 percent. In a comment from 1918 on the further careers of the graduates of Synod colleges, *Augustana* also noted that of the 740 ministers in the Synod in that year, only 11 were not educated at a Synod school. These graduates of one of the denomination's colleges were, in *Augustana*'s words, spiritual leaders of more than 300,000 congregation members, but also together with the college professors spearheading "the cultural work which is the unifying force for our people."[264]

It is thus clear that a very large number of Augustana graduates went on to an active professional life within the Augustana sphere of Swedish America.

---

[264] *Augustana*, 18 July 1918.

Most of them became ministers within the Synod, at a time when an ethnic church like the Augustana Synod was important in more than spiritual matters. Local Augustana congregations scattered all over the American continent became linguistic and cultural safe-havens as well, supporting a number of social and cultural activities such as Sunday schools, youth groups, and other undertakings. In most of these settings, the Augustana pastor held a key position. In addition, it was often the local Augustana pastor who encouraged the young and promising members of his congregation to apply for admission to Augustana College, thus further strengthening the ties between the Swedish-American youth and the institution of higher learning in Rock Island.

It is very difficult to determine to what extent the Augustana graduates played a role in the Swedish-American community outside of Augustana. It is, however, not unlikely that the fairly large numbers of professionals, such as physicians, lawyers, businessmen, etc. who resided in places with large Swedish-American populations achieved positions of relative prominence and influence within their respective local Swedish-American communities. An Augustana graduate lawyer or physician in Lindstrom, Minnesota, in Rockford, Illinois, or on the Near North Side in Chicago were almost bound to play an important role in his or her local Swedish-American context. This was also noted by the Synod's official paper in 1918, pointing to the fact that in "dozens of our communities" there were prominent doctors and lawyers who had been "reared in our congregations and [who] studied in our colleges."[265]

Summary

The case study of the student body at Augustana College shows that the 1890s was a particularly important decade. During that decade the institution underwent a generational transformation, so that by the turn of the century the school was dominated by American-born students of Swedish background. The generational shift also coincided with a change in the students' social background, as students from agricultural backgrounds before the turn of the century were replaced by students of parents from white-collar professions after 1900.

During the first phase of Augustana's history, the Swedish immigrants who were attracted to the college, as well as to the Synod in general, came from rural and agricultural backgrounds in Sweden. Given the roots of the Augustana Synod in the Swedish low-church revival of the nineteenth century, it also evident that many of the students came out of that tradition as well. A number of students also came to the college and seminary from Swedish

[265] *Augustana*, 18 July 1918.

118

schools associated with the revival, such as Fjellstedtska skolan in Uppsala.[266] During the college's second phase, American-born students were in the majority, most coming from a non-agricultural background, and belonging to what could be called a Swedish-American middle class. Augustana pastors was the most common parental occupation for the American-born students in this category, but there were also fair numbers of professionals, such as physicians, lawyers, and academics.

We have also observed a considerable geographic stability among the Augustana students, as the majority came from the traditional Swedish settlement areas in the Midwest, both before and after 1900, which also suggests that the college, like the Synod, had difficulties in attracting students from the more urbanized and secularized post-1900 waves of Swedish immigrants.

The analysis of the later careers of the students shows that the Augustana graduates remained largely within the Augustana sphere of Swedish America. To a considerable degree they actively contributed to the various activities of the Augustana Synod, by working in the congregations, in the colleges and academies, in the benevolent institutions, and within the publication endeavors. In this way, the ethnic institution recruited new members from within its own ranks, thus ensuring a significant social and ideological continuity.

Conclusion

Several conclusions can be drawn in assessing the role of Swedish-American education, and in particular that which we have observed at Augustana College, in the construction of a Swedish-American identity. First, it is clear that the role of Swedish ethnicity at Augustana College changed considerably over time, and two phases can be distinguished: one before and one after *circa* 1890. The school developed from a small institution with primarily Swedish-born and Swedish-speaking students from an agricultural background in the 1870s and 1880s, to a larger college with a majority of American-born students of Swedish background, with limited Swedish-speaking ability and from white collar family backgrounds after 1890.

During the first phase the maintenance of a Swedish ethnicity does not seem to have be an issue of major concern. The sense of Swedish identity was weak both in Sweden and at Augustana at this time, and the focus was on teaching the students English and on becoming "Americanized" in President Hasselquist's words. Still, Swedish was taught at the school and the content of the

---

[266] 30 students in the Augustana Student Database noted that they had previously attended one of the school's associated with the Swedish revival. Almost half (14) had come to Augustana from Fjellstedtska. The majority of these students attended Augustana during the 1870s and 1880s. Cf. also Erling 1996, 53.

curriculum largely mirrored that of the Swedish secondary schools. The sense of Swedishness as it existed at Augustana during this early phase, however, seems to have been defined in terms of the use of the Swedish language, as the discussions about the possibility of graduating from the school without having studied Swedish show.

After 1890, when the college was dominated by American-born Swedish Americans, Swedish ethnicity became much more pronounced. A separate department of Swedish was created in 1890, several student organizations devoted to the study of Swedish culture were founded, Swedish visitors were greeted at the campus, and lectures on Swedish topics were presented. The maintenance of this tradition now also became one of the central parts of the school's mission.

During the second phase, a Swedish-American tradition thus developed at the school, in which the Swedish ethnicity was culturally defined, and which, for American-born students without any own direct experiences of Sweden or Swedish culture became something that had to be studied and learned. In this way we can say that Augustana College went from being a Swedish to a Swedish-American institution.

Secondly, it is also obvious that the concern for Swedishness was linked with the concern for religion. Between 1882 and 1890 the subjects of Christianity and Swedish were taught by the same professor, and Christianity was the only subject that still required a reading knowledge of Swedish because of the use of Swedish-language textbooks, at a time when the use of Swedish as a medium of instruction had declined in other subjects. Also, evidence from various official levels in the Synod from the years points to how the maintenance of the Augustana Synod's religious heritage was seen as particularly dependent on the maintenance of a Swedish ethnicity. The visits of Bishop von Schéele, for example, combined the schools commitment to the Lutheran faith and its Swedish identity.

Thirdly, the development of the Swedish-American tradition at Augustana played an important role in defining a specific Swedish-American identity. Even though the curriculum in Swedish literature at Augustana College to a large degree seems to have echoed curricular developments in Sweden, both in terms of books used and authors studied, the Swedish-American context in which it functioned gave it a different meaning than it had in Sweden. At Augustana, the Swedish-American tradition as it was presented through the college's Swedish curriculum, was embedded in Swedish-American circumstances, removed from the Swedish cultural milieu. In that sense, authors like Esaias Tegnér and Johan Ludvig Runeberg and their works, the study of the Icelandic sagas, visits by prominent Swedes, or choir concerts, took on a meaning specific to Augustana's Swedish-American cultural context. The idealized view of Sweden, with an emphasis on romanticism, patriotism, and idealism, which was presented at Augustana could also be said to be representative of the Augustana Swedish Americans, thus providing them with characteristics from their ethnic background that added significant parts to their identity in America.

Finally, we have also seen that the Swedish-American tradition at Augustana included not only aspects of a national Swedish cultural tradition, but also specifically Swedish-American elements. The topics of discussion in the Phrenokosmian Society or in Svenska Vitterhetssällskapet show how a Swedish-American identity was emerging, consisting not only of both selected aspects from the members' two cultural backgrounds, but also as of a focus on the new specific cultural patterns that were developing in Swedish America. In February 1906 C.M. Olander contributed an article to the student newspaper on "Patriotism at Augustana," arguing that even more emphasis ought to be placed on this specific Swedish-American identity and reminding his readers that we must "neither be Swedes, nor Americans but *Swedish-Americans* [emphasis in original]."[267] These elements also became important ingredients in the Swedish-American identity that was emerging within the Augustana Synod at the turn of the century.

In 1903, Gustav Andreen, who assumed the presidency of Augustana College and Theological Seminary in 1901 and then remained in office until 1935, provided a good illustration of how, by this time, Augustana College was seen as central in creating and propagating a specifically Swedish-American identity. Significantly enough, Andreen was American-born, and in a speech about growing up in a Swedish-American community on the prairies of Illinois, he described how he had learned about Sweden, its glorious history, its nature and folk legends through accounts from his parents and other Swedish immigrants, so that a "shimmer from sagas was imbued in the image of the old father country." Andreen also told how his understanding of what it meant to be Swedish and Swedish-American had been furthered by his enrolling as a student at Augustana, echoing the experiences of Charley Washington in the play quoted in the beginning of this chapter. Swedish-American schools like Augustana College, Andreen stated, provided the vehicle through which the Swedish-American youth could be taught to "keep the valuable things we own … the best which we have inherited from a rich history and a historic church." [268]

In a letter to C.A. Swensson at Bethany College in Kansas from 1897, Andreen further elaborated this point by arguing that the Augustana Synod schools must be centers from which this educational program is spread,

---

[267] Augustana *Observer*, February 1906

[268] See the accounts of this speech in "Den svensk-amerikanska kulturen", *Vårt Land*, (Stockholm) 23 March, 1903 and "Svensk-Amerika och dess kulturella arbete", *Aftonbladet*, (Stockholm) 23 March, 1903.

"filling our people with love for our language, our history, our church, our activities—in one word *our* heritage." This particular heritage cannot be taught or conveyed through the regular American colleges and universities, Andreen continues. Thus, it becomes a central purpose for the Augustana Synod schools to ensure that the specific Swedish-American heritage is maintained and passed on to the students at these institutions. At our colleges, Andreen concluded, "one becomes ... such a thoroughly dedicated (*inbiten*) Swedish-American that it never goes away."[269]

---

[269] ACL, GAP, Letter from Gustav Andreen to C.A. Swensson, 30 December 1897.

The Lutheran Augustana Book Concern in Rock Island, Illinois, circa *1900. (Courtesy of Swenson Swedish Immigration Research Center, Rock Island, Illinois.)*

The graduating college class at Augustana College in 1910. (Courtesy of Special Collections, Augustana College Library, Rock Island, Illinois.)

Gustav Andreen (1864–1940), fourth president of Augustana College and Theological Seminary, circa 1910. Note the combination of the Swedish, American, and religious symbols—the Swedish Vasa Order, the American academic cap and gown, and the clerical collar. (Courtesy of Special Collections, Augustana College Library, Rock Island, Illinois.)

Participants in the 1910 fiftieth anniversary celebrations in Rock Island, including Bishop von Schéele from Sweden (#1), Govenor Eberhart from Minnesota (#2), and the President of the Augustana Synod, Erik Norelius (#3). (Courtesy of Special Collections, Augustana College Library, Rock Island, Illinois.)

A view of the 1910 fiftieth anniversary celebrations in Rock Island, with specially constructed Jubilee Hall in the center. (Courtesy of Special Collections, Augustana College Library, Rock Island, Illinois.)

Chapter Four

Introduction

In 1916 Vilhelm Berger, a journalist, author, and astute observer of Swedish-American conditions, published an article on the significance of the Augustana Synod among the Swedish Americans in which he maintained that the Synod had become the "strongest bulwark of Swedishness in the New World." Apart from the work carried out in the individual congregations, Berger specifically mentions several two factors as especially important in the Synod's work for Swedishness: its educational efforts and its publishing endeavors.[1]

Berger's observation about the significance of the publishing (and reading) of Swedish-language materials for the maintenance of a sense of Swedishness in America points to an important link between the spread of printed materials and the rise of an ethnic or national feeling. This chapter will focus on the role Swedish-language publications in the United States played in the forming of a Swedish-American ethnic identity. The major questions to be answered include: What did the Swedish immigrants and their children in America read? What kinds of Swedish-language publications were brought out in the United States and by whom? What kinds of publications did the Augustana Synod promote? And, finally, how did this body of Swedish-language reading matter help shape a Swedish-American ethnic identity in the Augustana Synod?

The question may of course be raised to what extent the act of reading a book, poem, or journal in the Swedish language in America influences the individual reader, beyond the obvious effect of strengthening language retention. But it could be argued, as Brent Peterson has done in his analysis of the nineteenth-century German-American family magazine *Die Abendschule* (The Evening School) published by the German-American Lutheran Missouri Synod, that the readers of such a publication in some ways were influenced by what they read, and Peterson concludes that "[r]eading affected the lives of the readers whose inherited culture was no longer adequate for the situation in which they found themselves" and that the narratives published in *Die Abend-schule* and read by German Americans "contributed to the formation of an

---

[1] Berger 1916, 46–55. Quotation from p. 46.

acquired consciousness—and specifically one variety of German-American consciousness."[2]

For the field of Swedish-American literature, Anna Williams advances a similar argument in her study of the Swedish-American journalist and poet Jakob Bonggren. She shows that he managed to establish himself in Swedish-American cultural circles and uses his writing to illustrate how it contributed to establishing a sense of Swedish distinctiveness in America. Bonggren as a "literary leader" contributed to the construction of a Swedish-American identity or "ideology," as Williams calls it.[3]

From a more general point of view, the connection between printed matter and national feelings has also been emphasized by Benedict Anderson in his now-classic study *Imagined Communities*. According to Anderson, one of the two characteristics of nineteenth-century European nationalism was the "ideological" importance of "national print-languages," and he points to how a gradual codification and establishment of national languages and the spread of printed matter in this language were crucial in forging national sentiments for several European nations.[4]

The first part of this chapter will discuss Swedish-language publishing in general, providing both an overview of the Swedish-American literary institution as well as addressing the question of what was read in Swedish America.[5] In the second part of the chapter, the literary and publishing activities in the Augustana Synod will be discussed in greater detail.

Swedish-Language Reading Materials in the United States: A General Overview

Previous scholarship in Swedish-American history has only cursorily dealt with publishing and printing in Swedish America. The subject has usually been treated in connection with discussions of Swedish-American literature.[6] Göran Stockenström has discussed the Swedish-American publishing houses briefly in an article,[7] the Augustana Book Concern and the Chicago-based Engberg-Holmberg have been analysed by Nils Hasselmo and Raymond Jarvi,[8] and Lars Wendelius has analysed the publishing ventures in Rockford,

---

[2] Peterson 1991, 58. Cf. also 3–5 for similar arguments.

[3] Williams 1991, 209–14. Cf. also Keillor 1992 and Westerberg 1995 for discussions of reading practices among Norwegian and Swedish Americans.

[4] Anderson 1991, chapters 3 and 5.

[5] Parts of the text are based on Blanck 1992.

[6] Cf. Linder 1925a, an overview of Swedish-American literature from the 1920s, which devotes only two paragraphs to the publishers in Swedish America.

[7] Stockenström 1978, 263–65.

[8] Hasselmo 1974, 63–71, Jarvi 1991.

Illinois.[9] The most comprehensive treatment so far is Anna Williams' discussion of what she calls "the Swedish-American literary institution." Her study provides a comprehensive picture of the ways in which the Swedish-language literature was produced, distributed, and read in Swedish America.[10]

Source materials for the publishing enterprises are not abundant, and little archival material has survived from any of the publication ventures. Most companies published catalogs of their books and other imprints with some regularity, but only some of these have survived. The book catalogs give an in-depth review of the different Swedish-language items that were available in the U.S. The majority of the books listed in the catalogs and sold through the Swedish-American publishing houses were not printed in the U.S. but imported from Sweden. At times, the imported books are listed together with those items actually published in the U.S., sometimes making it difficult to distinguish between imported literature and original Swedish-American materials. In addition, a few historical overviews and retrospective accounts of the activities of the various publishers provide supplementary information.[11]

Audience

The Swedish population in the nineteenth century exhibited a high degree of literacy. The Reformation in the sixteenth century had emphasized the need for the individuals to be able to read and understand the word of God. The Church Law of 1686 prescribed that all persons should learn to read and write, and in 1842 a compulsory basic school was introduced, which, especially after some decades, began to be important for the further development of Swedish literacy. There has been some discussion about how well the Swedes could read: did their reading involve a genuine process of understanding unknown writings or was it more of a recognition of already well-known texts? Recent scholarship suggests that the overwhelming majority of the Swedish people had been able to read fairly well for a long period of time when the Swedish mass-emigration to America began, and that Carlo Cipolla's figures of more than 90 percent basic literacy in Sweden in 1850 are not unrealistic.[12]

Moreover, one dimension of Sweden's economic and social transformations in the nineteenth century meant that the growing *bourgeoisie* in the country also changed Swedish literary production and consumption. A literary market

---

[9] Wendelius 1990, 24–31.

[10] Williams 1991, chapter 2.

[11] Examples of such works include for the Augustana Book Concern, Augustana Book Concern 1914 and for the Engberg-Holmberg Company, Olson 1910.

[12] Cipolla 1969, 72–74, 115, Johansson 1973, Johansson 1987, Svensson 1983, 19–21. See also Burke 1978, 250–59 for a discussion of literacy and reading in Western Europe up to circa 1800.

was created, and in the middle of the nineteenth century the number of books and periodical publications published in Sweden increased drastically.[13] Even though the emigrants came from social groups in Swedish society that would not have been great consumers of literature, it has nevertheless been shown that a number of books were printed in large editions and read by substantial numbers of Swedes. Religious literature, such as the hymnal and catechism, were important, but gradually also stories, many of a moralizing nature, became more widespread.[14] The basic reader for the compulsory school, *Läsebok för folkskolan*, which was first published in 1868 and reprinted in ten editions until 1910, was crucial in stimulating reading habits among its audience of those attending the primary schools.[15] The Swedish immigrants who arrived in the U.S. beginning in the latter part of the nineteenth century were thus both fairly literate and had some experience with reading on a regular basis. They constituted a large potential Swedish-language literary market in the U.S. As immigration came to a halt in the late 1920s and as the retention of the Swedish language dropped considerably in the second and drastically in the third generations,[16] one can assume that this market started dwindling by the 1930s. The different bibliographies and book catalogs also indicate that the heyday of Swedish-language publishing in the United States occurred between 1885 and 1925.

Newspapers and Periodicals

The most significant Swedish-language publications that appeared in the United States were periodical publications, and newspapers, journals, annuals, were particularly important in this context. As early as 1922 Robert Park underscored the significance of the foreign-language press for the adjustment of the ethnic group into American society,[17] but the foreign language press' emphasis on materials specific to the needs and interest of the ethnic group helped promote group loyalty and cohesiveness, something which has also been noted by students of the Swedish-American press.[18]

Almost all Swedish-American newspapers were weeklies.[19] The first Swedish-American newspaper was *Skandinaven* (The Scandinavian), published in New York between 1851 and 1852. In 1855 the far more successful

---

[13] Svedjedal 1990, 30–31.
[14] Bennich-Björkman & Furuland 1988, 269–76.
[15] Furuland 1991b. Cf. also Tarschys 1955, 156.
[16] Fishman 1966, 42–43.
[17] Park 1922, 358f.
[18] Björk 1987, chapter I, Lindmark 1971, 219–21.
[19] The following three paragraphs are based on three overviews of the Swedish-American press: Beijbom 1986, 164–88, Linder 1925b, 180–92, and Williams 1991, 29–34.

Hemlandet. Det Gamla och Det Nya (The Old and New Homeland) was started in Galesburg, Illinois, by the prominent Augustana pastor T.N. Hasselquist. The paper moved to Chicago after a few years and was one of the leading Swedish-American newspapers until 1914 when it merged with *Svenska Amerikanaren* (The Swedish American). Throughout its history *Hemlandet* was closely associated with the Augustana Synod, and one of its most influential editors was Johan Enander.

By the beginning of the twentieth century, hundreds of newspapers, magazines, and journals had been established all over Swedish America. The newspapers and magazines followed the settlement patterns of the Swedish ethnic group, and the center for the Swedish-American press became Chicago, where according to one estimate, 187 Swedish-language periodicals were published.[20] Numerous publications appeared in Minnesota, on the East Coast (New York City, Jamestown, N.Y., and Worcester, Mass.), on the West Coast (San Fransisco, Los Angeles and the Seattle area). The only major newspaper in the South was *Texas Posten* (The Texas Post) which was started in Austin in 1896, and continued to be published until 1982.[21]

A number of periodicals were also published in Swedish America, although much fewer in number than the newspapers. A few titles were specifically geared towards literary and cultural subjects, such as *Ungdomsvännen* (The Friend of Youth) and *Prärieblomman* (The Prairie Flower) published by the Augustana Synod. The official organ of the Augustana Synod, *Augustana*, was also a major Swedish-American periodical.[22]

The same social, cultural, and religious divisions that prevailed in Swedish America in general and that have been discussed in chapter two also shaped the attitudes of the newspapers and periodicals. There were newspapers and periodicals associated with the various segments of Swedish-American opinion, as well as more independent ones.[23] The differences in attitude between the Augustana-oriented *Hemlandet* and the secular *Svenska Amerikanaren* with regard to both cultural and ethnic issues are an often cited example of the variety of opinion within the Swedish-American press in particular, and in the Swedish-American community in general.[24]

It is hard to estimate precisely how many Swedish-language newspapers and periodicals were published in North America. Many appeared only for a short while, and mergers with other papers make it difficult to trace individual papers. In 1910 the Swedish-American journalist Axel Söderström recorded

---

[20] Beijbom 1986, 174.
[21] For Texas Posten, see Scott 1991, 195–206.
[22] Cf. Beijbom 1986, 175–76, Williams 1991, 32–33.
[23] Williams 1991, 31–32, 96.
[24] Beijbom 1971, 288–332.

1,158 periodicals,[25] a figure which Ulf Beijbom has lowered to about 650 newspapers and magazines. Thirty-five percent of these were weekly newspapers, 54 percent weekly or monthly magazines, and 11 percent annuals, calendars, or Christmas publications of different kinds.[26]

Most of the newspapers were local, with fairly small circulation figures of a few thousand copies.[27] A small group of newspapers had a much larger and wider circulation, with a readership extending beyond the immediate boundaries of the city of publication. Included here are, for example, the Chicago papers *Svenska Amerikanaren* and *Svenska Tribunen-Nyheter* (The Swedish Tribune News) and the Minneapolis paper *Svenska Amerikanska Posten* (The Swedish-American Post), with publication figures of well over 50,000 copies each week in the 1910s.[28] In 1915 *Svenska Amerikanaren* had the highest circulation among the Swedish-American newspapers with more than 75,000 copies. The largest periodical, *Augustana*, the official organ of the Augustana Synod, had a circulation of some 21,000 copies each week in 1915.[29]

The total circulation for the Swedish-American press in 1910 was just over 660,000 copies. This made it the second-largest of the foreign-language presses in the U.S. at that time, well behind the German-language press with over 3,000,000 copies recorded, but ahead of the Norwegian and Yiddish-language presses with 423,000 and 321,000 copies respectively.[30]

Books in Swedish America

The main source for Swedish-language books in the United States was the many bookstores that carried Swedish books and catered to a Swedish reading audience. Swedish bookdealers and booksellers existed throughout the U.S., mainly in the urban areas where they were a part of the Swedish ethnic communities. The number of bookstores is not known, but Lars Wendelius has recorded several Swedish bookstores in Rockford, Illinois around the turn of the century and for 1880 Ulf Beijbom has noted eight "paper, book and music dealers" in Chicago.[31] The Augustana Book Concern (henceforth A.B.C.) maintained bookstores in Rock Island, Minneapolis, New York, and Chicago,

---

[25] Söderström 1910.

[26] Beijbom 1986, 174.

[27] In 1915 *Vestkusten* in San Francisco and *Texas Posten* in Austin both claimed around 4,000 copies, and newspapers in cities like Moline, Illinois and Ispheming, Michigan had even lower circulation figures. [Björk 1987, 37, 62.]

[28] For circulation figures, see Björk 1987, 61–63 and Lindmark 1971, 330–33.

[29] This figure reflects the situation after the merger between *Svenska Amerikanaren* and *Hemlandet* which took place in 1914. Prior to the merger, *Svenska Amerikanaren* had a circulation of 47,000. [Beijbom 1986, 176.]

[30] Circulation statistics are based on N.W. Ayer 1910, Beijbom 1986, 174, Fishman 1966, 52–60.

[31] Beijbom 1971, 187, Wendelius 1990, 28–30.

and over the years Engberg-Holmberg acquired outlets in Moline, St. Paul, and Boston. Other well-known establishments included Dahlén's in New York, Andrew Lundborg's large bookstore in Worcester, Massachusetts, and Svenska Bokhandeln in San Francisco.[32] Mail order also seems to have been quite common.[33]

The bookstores were not the only channel of distribution for Swedish-language books in the U.S. It was also common to buy books through many of the Swedish-American newspapers and religious publishing houses or in businesses where not only books and paper products were available, but also tobacco, steamship tickets, jewelry, and household appliances.[34] In fact, there was a considerable overlap between authors, publishing houses, newspapers, and booksellers. Frequently, a Swedish-language publishing house also maintained a bookstore for its own and imported titles. Sometimes the publisher even assumed the role of author and marketed his or her own products in the bookstore.[35] A well-known example of the latter combination was the bookstore, publishing house, and general business Dalkullan operated in Chicago by Anders Löfström. Löfström imported and sold books, and published the popular calender and almanac *Dalkullan*, which appeared until at least 1942.[36]

The fact that a Swedish bookmarket existed in the United States was not lost on commercial interests in Sweden, and as Johan Svedjedal has shown, several attempts were made by national Swedish booksellers and publishers to find outlets for their products in America.[37] Two of the major Swedish publishing houses even established their own branches in the U.S., Bonniers in 1910 in New York and Åhlén & Åkerlund in 1912 in Chicago. In 1911, 10,000 copies of Åhlén & Åkerlund's popular Christmas magazine *Julstämning* were sold in Swedish America, and in September the following year the company shipped more than 60,000 copies of both "dime-novels" and more expensive books to its outlet in Chicago.[38] Eventually, however, the interest for Swedish books in the U.S. tapered off, and, in Svedjedal's words, the "rush" for an "un-mined gold field" in Swedish America that the commercial booksellers and publishers in Sweden had hoped for never materialized.[39]

[32] Landelius 1951, 224. This article is one of the few overviews of the Swedish-language bookstores in the U.S.

[33] Wendelius 1990, 29.

[34] Landelius 1951, 216–17.

[35] Williams 1991, 34.

[36] Furuland 1996, Larsson & Tedenmyr 1988, 18.

[37] The following section is based on Svedjedal 1993, 208–13.

[38] "Stort slag för Sverige i Amerika," *Veckojournalen*, 8 September 1912.

[39] Svedjedal 1993, 205 and 213.

Swedish-American Publishers

Readers in Swedish America did not have to rely only on imported publications. A great number of Swedish-language items were also printed and published in the United States. It is impossible to assess exactly both how many Swedish-language titles were published and in how many copies, as no comprehensive bibliography of Swedish-American imprints exists. However, some estimates exist for specific publishers. Nils Hasselmo has calculated that the largest publisher of Swedish-language materials in North America, the Augustana Book Concern, published 746 Swedish-language titles in about 3.3 million copies between 1891 and 1920.[40] The fiftieth anniversary publication for the major publishing house in Chicago, Engberg-Holmberg, lists 185 published titles between 1877 and 1909.[41]

The bibliography of the Tell G. Dahllöf collection of Swedish-language imprints in North America provides the best overview of what has been published in Swedish in the United States. Although the collection is far from complete, it is both geographically and ideologically comprehensive in that it includes publications from all over the U.S. as well as from a large variety of organizations, denominations, and publishing houses. Arnold Barton has called the bibliography the "most comprehensive and useful catalogue of Swedish imprints in America ever published."[42]

The Dahllöf bibliography records 343 different Swedish-language publishing houses and printing outlets in the United States from the mid-nineteenth century on. Several types can be discerned. First, we have a few of what can be called established Swedish-American publishing houses, with a fairly broad publication policy, including religious materials, fiction, schoolbooks, etc. Included here are the Augustana Book Concern, Engberg-Holmberg Publishing Company, Anders Löfström's Förlag of Chicago, Rasmussen's of Minneapolis, and the two Swedish publishers, Bonniers in New York and Åhlén & Åkerlund in Chicago. Although the A.B.C., and to a lesser extent Engberg-Holmberg, had a denominational affiliation and a large part of their publications was religious, they also published non-religious books. Of all these, the A.B.C. was the largest.[43]

A second group of publishers was made up of the different Swedish-Ameri-

---

[40] Hasselmo 1974, 64. It should be noted that a title may have been reprinted several times during the time period, and that the number of original titles is thus smaller.

[41] Olson 1910, 59–64, 156–64.

[42] Barton 1988, 6.

[43] It can be noted that during a discussion in the Swedish-American press about what kind of literature that should be imported to Swedish America from Sweden, the radical paper *Svenska Socialisten* identifies the A.B.C., Engberg-Holmberg, and Rasmussen as those publishers and bookdealers that had dominated the market prior to the advent of Åhlén & Åkerlund and Bonniers around 1910. [*Svenska Socialisten*, 27 February 1913.]

can denominations themselves. Denominational publications comprised one of the major categories among Swedish-American imprints, making up forty percent of the entries in the Dahllöf bibliography.[44] In Chicago, the Mission Covenant Church and the Swedish Methodists maintained Missionsförbundets Bokhandel (later the Covenant Book Concern) and the Swedish M.E. Book Concern. The Swedish Baptists used publishing outlets in Chicago and Minneapolis.[45] In addition to these more or less official denominational publishing houses, many other printing offices also published and printed religious literature.

Third were the Swedish-American newspapers, which published among other things so-called premium books (*premieböcker*). These were handsomely printed and bound volumes of a fairly popular character that were given away as incentives to potential subscribers to the newspaper. *Svenska Folkets Tidning* in Minneapolis, for example, published many premium books, including Strindberg's *Giftas*, Topelius' *Fältskärns berättelser*, and several of Per Thomasson's and Herman Bjursten's works.[46] Many authors also used the printing offices of the newspapers to publish privately printed books. Several of Vilhelm Berger's publications appeared in this way at Nordstjernan's printing offices in New York. [47]

Finally, many smaller print shops and publishers published Swedish-language imprints in the U.S. of a highly varied kind. In Chicago alone, the Dahllöf bibliography lists some forty print shops or publishers with two or fewer titles, many of which seem to have been supported by individuals or organizations.[48]

The practice of issuing lengthy series of fiction which became prevalent in Sweden from the mid-nineteenth century[49] also seems to have caught on in Swedish America. In Minneapolis, Rasmussen's and J. Leachman & Son brought out long series of popular Swedish fiction. Rasmussen's series was called *Svenska Folkböcker* (Swedish Popular Books), appearing as a subgroup of *Skandinavisk National Bibliotek* (Scandinavian National Library), while Leachman's run was known as *Svensk-Amerikanska Biblioteket* (The Swedish-American Library).[50] The Minneapolis-based newspaper *Svenska*

---

[44] 28 % of the publications in Larsson & Tedenmyr 1988 are theological texts—Bibles, catechisms, devotional literature—and 12 % were related to the life of the denomination—minutes, anniversary publications, etc.

[45] Larsson & Tedenmyr 1988, 236–37, 248–49 for the Covenant church, 255–56 for the Methodists, and 95–98 for the Baptists. See also Stephenson 1932, 246–92 for a discussion of publishing activities among the non-Augustana denominations.

[46] Larsson & Tedenmyr 1988, 269.

[47] Larsson & Tedenmyr 1988, 275.

[48] Larsson & Tedenmyr 1988, 234–58.

[49] Lönnroth & Delblanc 1988b, 20–24, 279. Cf. also Furuland 1972.

[50] Little bibliographical information is available for these series, but the titles in the series were often included on the back or inside back covers of individual books.

folkets tidning (The Swedish People's Paper) had its *Svenska nationalbiblioteket* (Swedish National Library) which by June 1898 had issued 119 installments.[51] During the first years of this century, Engberg-Holmberg in Chicago published several historical works, and even seems to have had a series called "romanticized Swedish historical stories",[52] and around the same time Captain Löfström at Dalkullan in Chicago catered to those especially interested in detective stories.[53]

What Was Available in the Swedish-American Bookstores?

An analysis of the books sold in Swedish America has to rely on the catalogs of the Swedish-American bookstores. As noted above, no systematic collection of such catalogs exists and the following discussion is based on an examination of surviving catalogs in different libraries in the United States and Sweden.[54] As can be expected, imported books from Sweden, or pirated editions of Swedish originals, strongly dominate. Most Swedish booksellers in America did carry some Swedish-American imprints, but they make up a small minority of the titles available. It is not always possible to distinguish which books were imports, American reprints, or original Swedish-American imprints, although evidence suggests that the imports dominated heavily. A catalog from the Chicago-based publishing house Engberg-Holmberg from the 1870s lists over 2,700 different titles, of which only 23 were the publishers' own items.[55] The rest were imported from Sweden. Although the publication of Engberg-Holmberg titles increased towards the turn of the century, the company's own books always remained a small share of the books distributed through the firm. No complete listing of the number of titles published at Engberg-Holmberg exists, but no more than 200 books seem to have been brought out prior to 1910.[56] This figure strongly points to the great significance of the imported books from Sweden.[57]

The same tendency can be observed in other Swedish-American bookstores, such as Nya Svenska Bokhandeln in St. Paul, Minnesota, I.T. Relling & Co. in Chicago, A. Österholm & Co. in New York City,[58] and the Swedish book-

---

[51] Bjursten 1898, was issued as number 119.

[52] Larsson & Tedenmyr 1988, 128. It is unclear if more than these three titles were published in this series.

[53] Dalkullan's series was called Populära detektivromaner (Popular Detective Stories). [Larsson & Tedenmyr 1988, 155.]

[54] Catalogs from Swedish-American bookdealers have been located in the Royal Library, Stockholm, the Uppsala University Library, the Tell Dahllöf Collection of Sueco-Americana in the University of Minnesota Library, and in the library of the Minnesota Historical Society.

[55] Engberg, Holmberg and Lindell, 1876.

[56] The compilation is based on the information provided in Olson, 1910.

[57] Jarvi 1991, 260.

[58] Nya Svenska Bokhandeln, Relling katalog, 1878, Österholm Catalog.

stores in Rockford, Illinois.[59] The great majority of the Swedish fiction in these bookstores was not published in the U.S., but imported directly from Sweden. Similarly, in the 1912 catalog from the Augustana Book Concern, about 60 percent of the listings were Swedish imports.[60]

What kind of literature, then, was read in Swedish America? Judging from catalogs of various bookdealers, a great variety of books in Swedish were available in the U.S., including such subjects as religion, education, history, geography, music, theater, schoolbooks, dictionaries, cook-books, how-to books, almanacs, etc. Göran Stockenström has observed that history and education were particularly frequent categories and that while fiction was available, it made up no more than 15 percent of the total number of books sold.[61]

An examination of the fiction and poetry sections of Swedish-American book catalogs reveals a notable difference between the religiously oriented and the secular bookdealers. Fiction, and especially the mass-market-oriented popular fiction that emerged in Sweden (and the U.S. as well) in the second half of the nineteenth century, was a problem for religious groups in Sweden. The Swedish religious revival movement actively promoted the reading of "good literature" of a Christian nature.[62] One representative sent out by the National Evangelical Foundation (E.F.S.) in 1857 reported that he had to struggle against the tendency among Swedes to read what he called "books and newspapers of a harmful nature," among which he included "fairy tales and stories of different kinds."[63] As the Swedish-American denominations had strong roots in the revival movement, similar attitudes toward literature and reading were found in the Swedish-American churches, and are reflected in the literature available at the religiously oriented Swedish-American bookdealers. The A.B.C. literary profile in this respect will be discussed in greater detail below.

The selection of Swedish-language fiction in the non-denominational bookstores was, as Göran Stockenström has pointed out, dominated by popular literature, including novels, romances, detective stories, etc.[64] Historical romances with themes from Swedish history and stories, anchored in a particular province in Sweden, were especially common. An examination of the most popular Swedish authors of fiction in catalogs from Rasmussen's in Minneapolis, Dalkullan and Engberg-Holmberg in Chicago, and Österholm's in New York from around the turn of the century, yields a group of particularly well-

[59] Wendelius 1990, 28–29.
[60] ABC Catalog 1912.
[61] Stockenström 1978, 256.
[62] See Kussak 1982, 21–25 for a discussion of how literature and fiction was viewed among the revival groups.
[63] Pleijel 1967, 40.
[64] Stockenström 1978, 264.

selling authors.[65] By far the two most popular writers were J.O. Åberg and Pehr Thomasson whose romanticized historical romances and accounts of life in rural Sweden[66] were available in great numbers in the Swedish-American bookstores. They were followed by several authors of popular Swedish fiction, including Emilie Flygare-Carlén, Marie Sophie Schwarz, Sara Pfeiffer [pseudonym Sylvia], and Alfred Hedenstierna [pseudodym Sigurd].[67] Authors like Flygare-Carlén, Hedenstierna, and Schwarz wrote in a romantic vein, often focusing on a particular province or area in Sweden.[68] As little information is available on the sales of books, it is difficult to determine the degree to which these books were read. Still, Kermit Westerberg's study of a Swedish-language lending library in St. Paul, Minnesota, confirms the popularity of these authors among Swedish-American library patrons in St. Paul.[69]

The popularity of these authors in Swedish America is hardly surprising, as they were read extensively in Sweden as well, and over 250 titles by Åberg and over 160 by Thomasson were published between 1860–1900.[70] Lars Furuland has noted that Pehr Thomasson was probably the most widely read author of Swedish fiction before August Strindberg (his *Kung Oskar och skogvaktaren* was printed in 43,000 copies in numerous editions), and in 1866 a Swedish magazine commented that emigrating peasants in Gothenburg would buy a Bible, a hymnal, and works by Pehr Thomasson before boarding the ship.[71] In his study of Swedish family magazines in mid-nineteenth century Sweden, Eric Johannesson also shows how some of the authors found in the Swedish-American bookstores were among the most frequent contributors to the Swedish family magazine *Svenska Familjejournalen* (The Swedish Family Journal), including Emilie Flygare-Carlén, Marie Sophie Schwarz, and Sara Pfeiffer.[72]

---

[65] The analysis is based on Rasmussen Catalog 1907, Dalkullan 1910, Engberg-Holmberg Catalog [no date is given for the Engberg-Holmberg catalog, but no Swedish fiction published after 1901 is included, suggesting this year as the latest year of publication], and Österholm Catalog [no date is given for the Österholm catalog, but the years 1890/91 have been added in pencil on the copy in the Royal Library in Stockholm].

[66] For Åberg see Svenskt litteraturlexikon 1970, 636, for Thomasson see Furuland 1962, 147–57.

[67] The total number of titles listed for each author in the catalogs were Åberg 276, Thomasson 138, Flygare-Carlén 71, Schwarz 66, Pfeiffer 45, and Hedenstierna 37.

[68] Svenskt litteraturlexikon 1970, 167 (Flygare-Carlén), 229 (Hedenstierna), and 496 (Schwarz).

[69] Westerberg 1977, 87–90. The Swedish authors with the highest circulation figures were Herman Bjursten, Emilie Flygare-Carlén, Marie Sophie Schwarz, Pehr Thomasson, and J.O. Åberg.

[70] Linnström 1961, Bok-Katalog 1866–75, Bok-Katalog 1876–85, Bok-Katalog 1886–95, and Bok-Katalog 1896–1900. Furuland 1962, 148–49.

[71] Furuland 1962, 149.

[72] Johannesson 1980, 122. Cf. also Svedjedal 1994 for a discussion of the popularity of several of the noted female authors.

Similar conclusions have been reached in analyses of books in various lending libraries in Sweden. An examination of the most frequently borrowed books in a local library in central Sweden in the 1880s shows that Pehr Thomasson and Alfred Hedenstierna were particularly popular, and that the kind of historical and biographical works, by, for example, J.O. Åberg that were so common in Swedish-American bookstores, were also frequently read in Sweden.[73]

It should also be noted that a number of popular authors of non-Swedish background had their works translated, at times imported from Sweden, and read in Swedish America, such as the French authors Eugène Sue, Alexandre Dumas, and Paul de Kock, who were well represented in the Swedish-American bookstores. These authors were also widely read in Sweden at the time, although not always viewed with approval. The middle-class oriented *Svenska Familjejournalen* criticized works by Sue, Dumas, and de Kock as "dangerous" and "inflammatory."[74] The same also seems to have been true elsewhere in Europe. In France *Les Mystères de Paris* (Mysteries of Paris) and *Le Juif Errant* (The Wandering Jew) by Sue were "explosive successes" and printed in totals of 60,000 and 50,000 copies respectively before 1850.[75] In Ulster, novels by Paul de Kock were controversial and, according to J.R.R. Adams, viewed "with horror by the right-thinking people of Britain."[76] It seems fair to assume that these sentiments would have been shared by many leading representatives in Swedish America as well. In Swedish America the above-mentioned titles by Sue were available in Swedish translations as *Paris mysterier* and *Den vandrande juden* through Dalkullan in Chicago in 1910.[77]

The most important source of Swedish-language fiction and poetry was, however, the Swedish-American press,[78] where the serialized stories, which could run for several months, were particularly important. In 1930 readers of two Swedish-American newspapers in Moline and Rock Island, Illinois, indicated that the serials were the second-most popular feature in the newspapers, rivalled only by news from Sweden and Swedish America.[79] Unfortunately, no systematic study of the kind of literature that was made available to Swedish-American newspaper readers exists. It seems likely, however, that the same patterns that have been noted in the Swedish-American bookstores and in the publishing houses also characterized the literary selection in the Swedish-

---

[73] Berg 1969, 124–25. See also Lundevall 1953, 176–77.
[74] Johannesson 1980, 159.
[75] Lyons 1987, 90–92.
[76] Adams 1987, 163.
[77] Dalkullan 1910, n.p.
[78] Furuland 1990, 107.
[79] 60 % of the readers listed news from Sweden and Swedish America, while 20 % mentioned the serials. The two newspapers studied were *Svenska Amerikanaren* and *Svenska Tribunen-Ny-heter*. [Schersten 1933, 55.]

American press. In her study of *Svenska Amerikanaren*, Anna Williams also notes that the most frequently serialized Swedish authors in that newspaper were Emilie Flygare-Carlén, Georg Starbäck, Marie-Sophie Schwarz, and Sigge Stark (pseud. Signe Björnberg), a selection which seems to confirm this assumption.[80]

Summary

One of the consequences of Swedish mass immigration to the United States was the establishment of a Swedish-American literary institution. Swedish immigrants were, by and large, literate and brought with them reading habits to the new land. The most important part of the Swedish-American literary institution consisted of newspapers and periodicals, which apart from regular news items also included a great deal of fiction. Books in Swedish were also readily available in Swedish America. The majority were imported from Sweden, but a fair number of books were also printed in the U.S. at one of the many Swedish-language printing outlets.

If the fiction and poetry available in selected commercial Swedish-American bookstores are taken as an indication of what was read in Swedish America, popular fiction, often with a historic and local attachment, was particularly popular. This selection also mirrors general reading habits of popular literature in Sweden at the time. Many of these bookstores and publishing outlets were thus responding to literary demands from the Swedish-American community, and their sales policies can thus be assumed to be largely commercially motivated.

It is also clear, however, that bookstores and publishing outlets associated with one of the Swedish-American denominations show much more deliberate publishing and import policies. Here it is possible to find publishing profiles, that show fairly precise notions of what kind of reading matter was desirable or undesirable. Obviously some of the boundaries were determined by the religious dimensions of the bookstore or publishing house. As the significance of ethnicity increased towards the turn of the century, it is also possible that ethnic cultural considerations came to be important as well. This question will be discussed below with regard to the A.B.C.

Given this general background, we will now examine the Augustana Book Concern in greater detail and the role it played in both in the larger framework of Swedish-American publishing and in the creation of an ethnic identity in the Augustana Synod.

---

[80] Williams 1991, 119–20. Cf. also Wendelius 1990, 97 for similar results from *Rockford-Posten*.

Publishing in the Augustana Synod

The Augustana Book Concern—A Brief History

The annual meeting of the Augustana Synod in 1889 was held in Rock Island and Moline, Illinois. At this synodical meeting, several years of work towards creating a publishing house owned and operated by the Augustana Synod came to fruition, as it was decided on June 18 to establish a Board of Publication, the purpose of which was to "achieve better uniformity in the use of textbooks in the parochial schools and our colleges and to publish and supply such books and newspapers that the Synod may deem suitable."[81] In September 1889, the Lutheran Augustana Book Concern (from 1904 the Augustana Book Concern) was formally incorporated in the State of Illinois, remaining the official publishing house of the Augustana Synod until the merger of the Synod into the Lutheran Church in America in 1962.

The Augustana Book Concern was not the first publication endeavor associated with the Augustana Synod. Discussion about publishing activities had begun as early as 1854, six years prior to the establishment of the Augustana Synod when the early Augustana leaders L.P. Esbjörn, T.N. Hasselquist, and Erland Carlsson discussed the need for a Swedish-language newspaper promoting the religious interests and needs of the Swedish immigrants.[82] As noted above, in 1855 T.N. Hasselquist started the newspaper *Hemlandet. Det Gamla och Nya*, and four years later *Svenska Lutherska Tryckföreningen* (The Swedish Lutheran Publication Society in the United States) was organized in Chicago for the purpose of publishing *Hemlandet*, as well as "books of general usefulness, especially Christian books and above all those of the Lutheran confession."[83] This organization never turned a profit, and in 1872, the ownership was transfered from the Augustana Synod to the board of Augustana College and Theological Seminary for the financial benefit of this institution.[84]

In 1872, the Augustana Synod found itself in a serious economic situation.[85] Faced with the choice of continuing to operate the educational institutions or the publication activities, the Synod leaders opted for the former. They sold off *Hemlandet* to Johan Enander and G.A. Bohman in Chicago and the Swedish Lutheran Publication Society, which had been the Augustana Synod publication outlet since 1859, was sold to the firm Engberg- Holmberg, also in Chicago. The Synod guaranteed not to publish any further newspapers that

---

[81] Referat 1889, 25–26.
[82] Olson 1910, 5–6.
[83] Nystrom 1962, 10.
[84] Nystrom 1962, 14.
[85] For the following, see Nystrom 1962, 14–28, Augustana Book Concern 1914, 35–41.

could be seen as competitors to *Hemlandet*, and representatives of Engberg-Holmberg claimed that the Synod would not be able to start another publishing house again. Still, following the move of Augustana College and Seminary to Rock Island in 1875, several private publishing enterprises were started, such as "Ungdomens Vänner" (The Friends of Youth) in 1877. In 1889, the Synod as a whole decided to reestablish a formal publication enterprise.[86]

The A.B.C. quickly established itself as a major force in Swedish-American publishing. Due to the lack of a comprehensive Swedish-American bibliography, it is difficult to determine the exact size of the A.B.C. in relationship to other publishers, but Anna Williams identifies the A.B.C. and Engberg-Holmberg as the two leading publishing houses.[87] These two are also the leading publishers in the Dahllöf bibliography, with 354 titles recorded for the A.B.C. and 154 for Engberg-Holmberg,[88] thus pointing to the dominant position of the A.B.C. on the Swedish-American book market.

By 1910 the A.B.C. also operated bookstores in Rock Island, St. Paul, New York City, and Chicago, as well as a mail order service, through which the publisher's own books were available, as well as significant numbers of imported books from Sweden.[89] Its strong position is also shown by the fact that it was the only Swedish-American publisher that had contacts with Svenska Bokförläggareföreningen (The Swedish Publishers Association).[90]

What Did the A.B.C. Sell and Publish?

By the turn of the century, the A.B.C. had become the dominant Swedish-American publisher, as well as a major importer of Swedish-language books. How did the A.B.C. fit into the larger picture of the Swedish-American literary institution sketched above? What kinds of books were sold and published by the A.B.C., and what does this tell us about the view of Swedish literature and culture presented by the A.B.C.?

An examination the Swedish-language books available for sale through the A.B.C. shows that it had its own literary perspective. An analysis of the 1912 A.B.C. catalog reveals that, as noted above, 60 percent of the titles were im-

---

[86] The organization of the A.B.C. resulted in a prolonged conflict with Engberg-Holmberg who claimed that the Synod had forfeited its publishing rights through the sale of the Swedish Lutheran Publication Society, and that Engberg-Holmberg should be considered the Synod's official publishing house. This conflict would characterize much of the relationship between the A.B.C. and Engberg-Holmberg for almost the next three decades. [For the Engberg-Holmberg position, see Olson 1910, 75–116.] Following several years of negotiations, the much larger A.B.C. bought Engberg-Holmberg in 1917. [AFP, ABCMin: 10 May, 27 June, and 11 October 1911, 30 January 1912, 1 July 1913, 7 July and 6 October 1914, 26 June and 21 August 1917.]

[87] Williams 1991, 34–36.

[88] Larsson & Tedenmyr 1988, 230–94.

[89] Nystrom 1962, 96–100.

[90] Svedjedal 1993, 210.

ported from Sweden. In the category of Swedish fiction and poetry, the A.B.C. placed almost all its emphasis on the established authors from the latter part of the nineteenth century. Authors frequently represented in the commercial Swedish-American bookstores, such as Pehr Thomasson and J.O. Åberg, were conspicuously absent at the A.B.C.[91] The most popular authors in the 1912 catalog included Zacharias Topelius (30 titles), followed by Oscar Levertin (27), Mathilda Roos (21), Viktor Rydberg (18), Verner von Heidenstam (14), Selma Lagerlöf (10), Johan Ludvig Runeberg (7), Carl Snoilsky (7), and Esaias Tegnér (6).

The Swedish literature available through the 1912 A.B.C. catalog was thus much more of an "elite" nature than in many other bookstores. It was the more established and critically acclaimed authors who were presented to prospective Swedish-American readers. This focus on authors established in the Swedish literary canon is also evident from an announcement that the A.B.C. had become the sole American sellers of the edition of the collected stories by Selma Lagerlöf published by Bonniers in Stockholm, as well as by an advertisement for the 25-volume *Sveriges Nationallitteratur* (Sweden's National Literature), a multi-volume series of Swedish literary history that was underway in Sweden.[92]

The A.B.C.'s focus on established nineteenth-century Swedish authors is also reflected in several anthologies of Swedish literature published at the A.B.C. around 1900. Johan Enander brought out two books of poetry, *Eterneller och vårblommor* (Evergreens and Spring Flowers) (1892) and *Ur svenska sången* (From the Swedish Song) (1901), which according to the prefaces and advertisements in the A.B.C catalogs were geared towards youth clubs and literary societies among the Swedish Americans.[93] The circulation was small, with the total number of copies for each title coming to 2,000 copies.[94] Both anthologies include principally national Swedish poetry from the nineteenth century with an emphasis on romantic, historical, and patriotic pieces. The selection in *Eterneller och vårblommor*, for example, includes among others Johan Olov Wallin, K.M. Malmström, Carl David af Wirsén, and C.W. Böttiger, and a number of "historical" selections present contribu-

[91] The following is based on an examination of the titles under the section "Vitterhet" in ABC Catalog, 1912.

[92] ABC Catalog 1912, 180, 188.

[93] Enander 1892b and 1901. Cf. also ABC Catalog 1912, 29 and 89.

[94] A.B.C. database. [See note 100 for an explanation of the database.] It should, however, also be noted that *Eterneller och vårblommor* first appeared at Hemlandet Publishing Company in Chicago, (judging from the preface, probably in 1888,) at which time Enander was editor of *Hemlandet*. In 1891, Engberg-Holmberg bought "half the share" of *Eterneller*, and some time "later" it was sold to the A.B.C. where it first appeared in 1892. [Olson 1910, 157.] Still, a copy of the book with the Engberg-Holmberg imprint from 1894 exists in the Uppsala University Library, a fact which illustrates the difficulties in establishing the exact bibliographic provenance for Swedish-American imprints.

142

tions by Erik Gustaf Geijer and Esaias Tegnér; ["Manhem," "Odalbonden," and "Vikingen" by Geijer, and selections from "Svea" and *Fritiofs Saga* by Tegnér.][95] In the commentaries that accompany the poems, Enander also asserts that the different poems embody various Swedish national character traits, such as the unbroken freedom of the Swedish peasant embodied in "Odalbonden" or the fact that the Viking journeys described in "Vikingen" were "the school of our fathers, the emigration of our old fatherland during ancient times."[96] The selection in *Ur svenska sången* was similar, but, as will be shown below, its selection of poems was not uncontroversial, and it resulted in a discussion in the Swedish-American press about the A.B.C.'s literary perspective.

Given this literary focus, it should come as no surprise that the A.B.C.'s selection of established Swedish literature excluded some examples of modern writers, in particular representatives of the more realistic and radical literature of the so-called modern breakthrough. One of its most notable representatives, August Strindberg, was only represented by one title in the 1912 catalog—*Sagor*, a collection of literary fairy tales—while his more controversial works were missing. Few of the female authors of the Swedish 1880s were also represented in the A.B.C. catalog.[97] Strindberg's work was available elsewhere in Swedish America. A. Österholm in New York and Nya Svenska Bokhandeln in St. Paul, for example, each listed eight Strindberg titles around the turn of the century, and *Svenska Folkets Tidning* in Minneapolis published the controversial *Giftas* in 1888, which went through three editions in two years.[98]

Let us finally examine the publication profile of the A.B.C. What kinds of reading matter did the A.B.C. publish under its own imprint? The examination covers the years 1890–1919, during which period a total of some 3.9 million copies were printed. The Swedish-language imprints dominated greatly, accounting for 81 percent of the total copies printed. As Nils Hasselmo has shown, the number of English-language publications began to grow in earnest only after 1915. Prior to that year, only nine percent of the copies printed at the A.B.C. were in English, and it was not until after 1920 that the number of English-language titles and number of copies printed at the A.B.C. exceeded those in Swedish.[99]

Given the A.B.C.'s role as a denominational publishing house, it is only natural that religious publications serving the needs of the growing church

---

[95] Enander 1892b.
[96] "Historiska anmärkningar," following the selection of poems in Enander 1892b.
[97] A.B.C. Catalog 1912. Strindberg is noted on p. 189.
[98] Larsson & Tedenmyr 1988, 128.
[99] Hasselmo 1974, 63–65.

body were significant.[100] Just over 50 percent of all copies printed at the A.B.C. between 1890–1919 belonged to what can be called denominational publications. Religious music was the most important group, accounting for 17 percent of the copies published at the A.B.C. between 1890–1919. Included here were various hymnals and song books, with the very popular *Hemlands-sånger* (Homeland songs) accounting for well over a third of the books printed. Its popularity was particularly pronounced before 1900 when it was used as a hymnal in the Augustana congregations and represented over two thirds of the copies printed in the category of religious music. Sunday school materials accounted for about ten percent of the total copies published and were followed by a group including Bibles, New Testaments, and catechisms making up some five percent of the total.

Not quite half of the A.B.C. publications were of a non-denominational nature. This is a high figure in comparison with other Swedish-American denominational publishing houses. Both the Mission Covenant Book Concern and the Baptist Publication Society published very few non-religious publications,[101] whereas by 1910 the A.B.C. had clearly developed a publishing profile that went beyond the more direct denominational needs of the church body. The non-denominational publications can be divided into several categories. The largest was almanacs which accounted for 16 percent of the total A.B.C. copies printed between 1890–1919, followed by stories, primarily intended for children and youth (14 percent), schoolbooks (ten percent), and various literary periodicals (six percent). Some national Swedish literature was also reprinted at the A.B.C. (one percent), as well as a small group of original Swedish-American fiction and poetry (half a percent), and books about Swedish America (one percent). Those publication categories that were particularly important for the A.B.C.'s role in shaping Augustana's Swedish-American identity will be discussed below.

[100] All information concerning the publications of the A.B.C. has been gathered into a database from the annual reports of the A.B.C. between 1890 and 1919, which are printed in the Synod's minutes each year. The 948 titles have been grouped in 23 categories according to contents, which form the basis for the following analysis. As many titles were reprinted, the total number of copies has been chosen to indicate the relative sizes of the groups. The identification of each publication is not always easy as no systematic bibliographic references are given in the reports. In most cases the circulation figures are included, but for a total of 31 titles they are missing. The information from the annual reports has been supplemented with data from the printed A.B.C. catalogs and with individual books with A.B.C. imprints located in various libraries, missing in the annual reports. It is thus likely that some A.B.C. imprints are missing from the A.B.C. database. Still, it provides the best approximation that we have of the A.B.C. imprints. Printed A.B.C. catalogs exist in the E.L.C.A. Archives in Chicago, in the Royal Library in Stockholm, and in the Uppsala University Library.

[101] The publication profiles of the Mission Covenant Book Concern and the Baptist Publication Society are based on Larsson & Tedenmyr 1988. Cf. note 45.

Suitable Reading Material at the A.B.C.

In 1908, *Augustana* carried an article stating that Swedish-Americans ought to read "good, elevated [*uppbygglig*] literature."[102] In the same year, the position of a literary secretary was established at the A.B.C., whose duties it was "to encourage the authorship of such works as it may be in the best interest of the Book Concern to publish."[103]

As has already been suggested, a vision of suitable reading matter existed in the Synod, and it thus becomes important to identify what the Augustana Synod meant by "good" literature that would be in the "best interest" of the denomination. The Synod's view of literature must be seen against the background of the general attitude toward culture and education within the Augustana Synod, in which, as has been underscored earlier, the religious dimension, and more precisely the Lutheranism associated with the Synod, was fundamental. The question of upholding and promoting what were perceived as basic Christian values was, as we have seen, a very important concern for the Synod leadership.

The A.B.C. made its specific position with regard to suitable reading material clear several times. In his annual report to the Synod in 1884, President Erland Carlsson pointed to complaints from Minnesota and Kansas where the "bad newspapers and magazines" had gained influence among Swedish Americans. He voiced concern not only over the non-Christian tendencies in these publications, but also pointed to the danger associated with reading the serialized novels in these publications, which "inevitably destroy a person's sense of right and wrong" and stated that it was the duty of parents, pastors, and the churches to ensure that "good and Christian" books and magazines were read.[104] He noted with pleasure, however, that youth organizations "guided by a true Christian spirit" had been formed in the Synod, which provided its members with lending libraries that contained "good books."[105]

This attitude remained one of the basic elements in the Augustana Synod's view of literature. In 1893, *Augustana* warned against the kind of literature that appealed to the "lack of morality and materialism" among Swedish Americans, instead advocating reading materials that were founded on Christian religion and that had played a very important role in "the moral and intellectual growth of the Swedish people."[106] As noted above, fifteen years later, *Augustana* cautioned against reading "cheap and sensational" books, and maintained that Swedish Americans ought to read "good, elevated litera-

---

[102] *Augustana*, 4 June 1908.

[103] AFP, ABCMin, 14 July 1908; ELCA, CJB, Letter to C.J. Bengtson from the Augustana Book Concern, 14 July 1908.

[104] Referat 1884, 20.

[105] Referat 1884, 18.

[106] *Augustana*, 12 January 1893.

ture."[107] In 1910, when the A.B.C. published *Ett klöfverblad* (A Clover Leaf) by Maragrete Lenk, a story for children, *Augustana* recommended it strongly as a "healthy and simple story" in a time when so much material "of a doubtful nature, especially for the youth" was being published[108] and again in 1912 "bad literature" was called a threat against the church, as was the reading of novels dangerous, as it diverted attention from "serious subjects."[109]

A further example of the process of how the A.B.C. sought to promote "good literature" appropriate for Swedish-American readers comes from the discussion about "trash literature" (*smutslitteratur*) in 1913,[110] sparked by attempts by the two Swedish publishing houses Bonniers and Åhlén & Åkerlund to gain a foothold in the Swedish-American market. Protests were heard in many quarters in Swedish America, including the Augustana Synod, against the kind of "trash literature"—sensational and popular fiction—that these publishers imported, and an appeal was published in *Svenska Journalen* (The Swedish Journal) in Rockford in early 1913 calling for writers of higher quality, such as Fröding, Heidenstam, Lagerlöf, and Strindberg.[111]

Karl-Otto Bonnier of Bonnier's publishing house responded to the Swedish-American accusations, saying that Bonniers simply marketed what Swedish Americans wanted, an "older literature," including August Blanche, Emilie Flygare-Carlén, and Marie Sophie Schwarz. Erik Åkerlund added that this was not the first time his publishing house had been attacked by Swedish Americans, suggesting that part of the reason was fear of competition on the part of the A.B.C. He also noted that the A.B.C. had refused to publish advertisements for Åhlén & Åkerlund's Christmas magazine *Julstämning* in 1912, of which a substantial part of the 300,000 copies printed had been set aside for the Swedish-American market.[112]

A quick response appeared in *Augustana*,[113] which pointed out that the Synod agreed that a great deal of undesirable literature promoting free love and drunkenness and attacking religion was imported to Swedish America. But *Augustana* did not abide by all the suggested replacements by *Svenska Journalen*, noting that "many of Strindberg's works cannot be recommended

[107] *Augustana*, 4 June 1908.

[108] *Augustana*, 17 November 1910.

[109] "En beaktansvärd varning," *Augustana*, 25 April 1912.

[110] I would like to thank Eric Johannesson for drawing my attention to this discussion.

[111] "Smutslitteratur," *Svenska Journalen*, 17 January 1913. It is interesting to note the parallel to the discussion in Sweden a few years earlier about the dangers of popular and inexpensive fiction, which came to be symbolized by the stories about the detective Nick Carter. Cf. Boëthius 1989.

[112] For statements of Bonnier and Åkerlund see "Svensk smutslitteratur till Amerika?," *Svenska Dagbladet*, 23 January 1913. For information about Åhlén & Åkerlund and *Julstämning* see "Stort slag för Sverige i Amerika," *Veckojournalen*, 8 September 1912.

[113] For the following, see "Svensk smutslitteratur till Amerika," *Augustana*, 20 February 1913.

to our people." Concerning *Julstämning*, Augustana admitted that advertisements had been refused, but cited aesthetic grounds rather than commercial for their exclusion. Many of the illustrations in the magazine were of such nature that Augustana found it highly surprising that they were considered suitable for distribution in Sweden, concluding that no members of the Augustana Synod could "tolerate *Julstämning* on their parlor tables."[114]

The situation does not seem to have been resolved, and three years later, in 1916, the issue was discussed by the Executive Committee of the Board of Directors of the A.B.C., when it was stated that an A.B.C. Christmas magazine was "urgently needed" in order to "obviate the evil influence of certain Swedish Christmas magazines with very offensive contents" that were imported to Swedish America every year. It was also decided to publish such a Swedish-American Christmas magazine, to be edited by E.W. Olson, on the staff of the A.B.C. The magazine which was to be "adapted to the needs of the Swedish Americans in general without regard to their church affiliation," it would "furnish a literary publication of good moral tendency," and contain articles of interest to Swedish Americans, dealing with "their history, their cultural progress and matters of similar import."[115] Contributors were carefully selected, and the title *God Jul* (Merry Christmas) settled upon.[116]

God Jul became a Swedish-American Christmas magazine.[117] A number of leading Swedish-American authors and artists contributed to the publication, both from within and without the Augustana sphere in Swedish America, suggesting both the degree to which a Swedish-American identity had developed in the Augustana Synod by 1916, and the leading cultural position the Synod had in Swedish America. It included artwork by Olof Grafström, G.N. Malm, Henry Reuterdahl, and Birger Sandzén, and literary contributions came from Jakob Bonggren, David Nyvall, E.W. Olson, Ernst Skarstedt, Mauritz Stople, and Leonard Strömberg. Some contributions specifically dealt with what it meant to be Swedish-American, and will be discussed in the latter part of this chapter.

Selecting Reading Matter at the A.B.C.

Because the Augustana Synod had a vision of the kind of proper or suitable reading material that it wanted its members, and especially youth, to read, the process through which these reading materials was selected is important to analyse. The workings of this process can be observed in the screening of suit-

---

[114] Most likely, Augustana was referring to the colored illustrations by Zorn and others of dancing and bathing women, sometimes not fully clothed.

[115] AFP, ABCMin, 11 April 1916.

[116] AFP, ABCMin, 2 February, and 27 June 1916.

[117] God Jul 1916.

able manuscripts at the A.B.C. as well as in discussions following the publication of certain books. One example is the publication of a book of poetry by the well-known journalist and editor of *Svenska Amerikanaren* in Chicago, Jakob Bonggren, who submitted a manuscript for a book of poetry in 1899. As Anna Williams has shown, Bonggren was one of the leading persons in the Swedish-American cultural circles at this time, and to publish a book of his poetry would clearly have strengthened the Swedish-American profile of the A.B.C.[118] Following the submission, a committee was appointed to "edit the manuscript,"[119] and in July 1900, the A.B.C. encouraged Bonggren to send in the poems he would like to publish to "the official scrutinizer S.G. Youngert" who would then determine which of the poems "from the point of view of the A.B.C. ought not to be published."[120] No versions of the manuscript have survived, but it seems likely Bonggren's text did undergo some kind of a screening process. The A.B.C. decided to publish the book in 1901,[121] and it appeared under the A.B.C. imprint in 1902 as *Sånger och sagor* (Songs and Sagas).[122] Apparently, the publishing house was pleased with the publication, as the book was kept in stock at the A.B.C. at least until 1912.[123]

An example of a publication rejected on the grounds of not being suitable comes from 1901 when the former science professor at Augustana, Joshua Lindahl, at the time living in Cincinnati, offered the A.B.C. a translation into English of *Singoalla* by Viktor Rydberg, an offer which was rejected because works of this nature were not considered to be "within the sphere of activities of the Augustana Book Concern."[124] It was not explicitly stated why this was the case, but one factor may be that *Singoalla* partly deals with forbidden love between a married man and a young, seductive Gypsy girl.[125]

Another illustrative example of the gatekeeping function that A.B.C. exercised comes from 1902 and a discussion about the publication of *Ur svenska sången*. This was an anthology of Swedish songs and poetry from 1800–1850 edited by Johan Enander, offered to the A.B.C. in 1899,[126] and published shortly before Christmas 1901. According to the preface and the advertisements in the Swedish-American press, this "poetic reader" was intended to be read and used in "Swedish-American homes, youth groups, and literary societies."[127]

[118] Williams 1991, 178–82, 185–86.
[119] AFP, ABCMin, 12 April 1899.
[120] AFP, ABCMin, 10 and 11 July 1900.
[121] AFP, ABCMin, 15 May 1901.
[122] Bonggren 1902.
[123] ABC Catalog 1912, 81.
[124] AFP, ABCMin, 14 August 1901.
[125] Lönnroth & Delblanc 1988b, 165.
[126] AFP, ABCMin, 12 April 1899.
[127] Enander 1901, 3–4.

The book was fairly widely reviewed in the Swedish-American press, and a debate ensued about the selection of the poems that had been included. The Chicago-based *Fosterlandet* criticized Enander for having excluded some of "the most beautiful" poems by the poet and bishop Frans Michael Franzén because they dealt with drinking both champagne and beer. In this way, Enander showed a bias, *Fosterlandet* argued, favoring those groups who advocated abstinence of alcohol.[128] On the other hand, two other leading papers in Chicago, *Hemlandet* and *Svenska Amerikanaren*, found no problems with the selection of poems in the book. *Hemlandet* emphasized that the selection of poems was "carefully done" and recommended the book "warmly" to "youth groups, literary societies, homes and schools in Swedish America."[129] A similar opinion was expressed by J.B. (Jakob Bonggren) in *Svenska Amerikanaren*, who stated that the selection of poetry was "good and done with care" and that the book would satisfy a "felt need among us Swedish Americans."[130]

A week after the first reviews had appeared, the discussion continued in *Svenska Kuriren*, another Chicago paper, where *Fosterlandet*'s criticism against the book was noted. *Kuriren* defended Enander's job as editor, claiming that he had only done what the publisher, the A.B.C., had wanted the editor to do. He was given the task of putting the book together "following the same principles that the synod wishes to implement in all the education of the youth that it sees as its mission to educate," *Kuriren* wrote.[131] These principles, *Kuriren* continued sarcastically, obviously included the "exclusion" of all pieces from the first half of the previous century that expressed "joy of life," included even mild swear words, or hinted that all "fermented beverages," except for weak beer (*svagdricka*) would have an exhilarating effect. These biases were to be expected, as Enander followed only "the Augustana perspective" (*Augustanasynpunkten*) in his editing policy. Had he been able to act independently, without having to pay attention to the views of the Augustana Synod, *Kuriren* was convinced that he would not have given "such a terribly mutilated view of Swedish poetry".[132] A week later, *Kuriren* commented further on the issue of including poems in which champagne was drunk, asking if it did not seem strange if Augustana ministers, who at the recent banquet in honor of bishop von Schéele were seen "happily consuming one glass of champagne after the other," were to impose different moral standards for their parishioners.[133]

---

[128] *Fosterlandet*, 4 December 1901. An identical review was published on the same date in *Svenska Tribunen*, another Chicago newspaper.

[129] *Hemlandet*, 4 December 1901.

[130] *Svenska Amerikanaren*, 3 December 1901.

[131] The following is based on "Något om en viss kritik," *Svenska Kuriren*, 10 December 1901.

[132] The original Swedish reads: "en så förfärligt stympad bild av den svenska poesin."

[133] *Svenska Kuriren*, 17 December 1901.

The book was also reviewed in *Augustana*, which presented it in a very positive manner, specifically stating that Enander's selection of poetry was "the best from the time period in question," and that the book would be a suitable anthology for Swedish-American youth, societies, and educational institutions.[134] *Augustana* also responded to the criticism by *Fosterlandet*, defending the exclusion of certain poems. It was notable that a newspaper "for church and home" would lament the fact that poems such as "Gode gosse, töm glaset" and "Champagnevinet" were missing. "We consider it a strength (*en verklig förtjänst*) that the collection is free from drinking songs, and only contains such poems that can be read both at home and in church, or in company where "church and home' are revered."[135]

Fosterlandet responded to both *Augustana* and *Svenska Kuriren*.[136] To *Augustana*'s criticism that *Fosterlandet* condoned drinking songs, the paper said that "fiction and poetry ought to be able to be what they are and not be subjected to arbitrary excising and interpretations in such a biased manner that every single piece could be read in church." *Augustana*'s opinion that "church and home" required the elimination and annotation of poetry by Wallin and Franzén was rejected and the paper repeated its position "let our people get our Swedish literature un-mutilated! Let young and old themselves choose what suits them!"

In response to *Kuriren*, *Fosterlandet* maintained that Enander as editor had not been unduly influenced by the A.B.C., as *Kuriren* had claimed. The paper asserted that it knew for a fact that the Augustana Book Concern published the manuscript just as it had been received from Enander. The selections in the book were thus made by Enander, and should not be seen as an attempt by the Augustana Synod to "strangle or mutilate the Swedish poetry." Moreover, *Fosterlandet* wondered how was it that it anyone who wished could order books by "the other Swedish poets," from Bellman to Fröding, through the Book Concern, if the A.B.C. was engaged in such vicious attacks against Swedish poetry? They also pointed to the recently published volume of the literary annual *Prärieblomman* where "the Augustana Synod poet par excellence" Ludvig Holmes had a poem, which, although devoted to the "glory of coffee," also "praises "Spiritus Stimulus'."

Enander himself, finally, commented on the debate in *Augustana* a few weeks later, saying that, although those poems which had been excluded could well have a literary and artistic value, they were "less suitable" for a book intended to be used in "homes, churches, schools, youth associations, and lit-

[134] *Augustana*, 7 November 1901.

[135] *Augustana*, 12 December 1901.

[136] The following two paragraphs are based on *Fosterlandet*, 25 December 1901. This article was also printed simultaneously in *Svenska Tribunen*.

erary groups."[137] Further, he noted that he knew that the A.B.C. "did not approve" of such songs, nor "would have been willing to publish or distribute" them and that it thus would have been impossible to publish a book along the lines that his critics wanted. And, said Enander, "I am convinced that if *Ur svenska sången* had included such "gems' as Franzén's drinking songs, both I and the publishing house would have been just as much criticized as we have been now." It is also worth noting that in the preface to the book, Enander stated that he had avoided those poems that included words and expressions that may seem "offensive" in certain circles, in order that the book may be useful for *"all countrymen"*(emphasis his).[138]

The debate over *Ur svenska sången* illustrates the fact that a "special perspective" existed within the Augustana Synod regarding the nature of suitable reading matters, especially in a publication that was directed towards the homes and the young. Poems which could be seen as endorsing drinking were not suitable—not even if they were written by a Swedish bishop— and thus not possible to publish, as both Johan Enander and *Augustana* pointed out. The debate also shows that the secularly oriented newspaper *Svenska Kuriren* used this discussion as an opportunity to attack the view on literature and culture in general in the Augustana Synod, claiming that it sought to "mutilate" Swedish poetry.

It is not surprising that *Hemlandet* gave the book a very positive review, as the paper was closely allied with the Augustana Synod. It is perhaps more noticeable that *Svenska Amerikanaren*, *Hemlandet*'s old rival and antagonist, which in the past had been very critical of the cultural narrow-mindedness in the Augustana Synod, also treated the book in positive terms and approved of the selection of poems. This can partly be explained by the fact that, as Anna Williams has pointed out, the "cultural gap" between *Svenska Amerikanaren* and the Augustana Synod by this time was beginning to grow smaller.[139] Moreover, it should be noted that the reviewer in *Svenska Amerikanaren* was the same Jakob Bonggren, who had had his *Sånger och sagor* published by the A.B.C. six months prior to the review.

The significance attached to the process of selecting suitable A.B.C. publications eventually resulted in the establishment of a position as literary secretary at the A.B.C. in 1907. Such a position had been discussed in 1894, when the need to ensure that "only truly good works" were published had been noted.[140] But it was not until the annual meeting of 1907 that the Synod

---

[137] The following is based on Johan Enander, "En liten vidräkning," in *Augustana*, 9 January 1902.
[138] Enander 1901, 5.
[139] Williams 1991, 167.
[140] Referat 1894, 63.

created the position of literary editor at the Book Concern, and Pastor C. J. Bengtson was appointed to the job in 1908.[141]

The literary editor was to review manuscripts submitted to the A.B.C. and recommend to the Board on the suitability of publication. In judging the various manuscripts, the editor considered both literary and financial aspects of the publications. An example of the latter comes from 1909 when the manuscript "Ungdomsbilder i biblisk belysning" (Youth Pictures in a Biblical Light) by E.J. Werner was considered to be "a credit to the author" but hardly economically viable to publish.[142]

Bengtson served as literary editor for two years, when he was replaced by Pastor O.V. Holmgrain, who had served as assistant editor at the A.B.C. Two other applicants had, however, applied for the job, but the Executive Committee of the A.B.C. did not feel that either one was suitable, and therefore picked Holmgrain, who was considered the best candidate because of his "many years of experience of literary questions, sound judgement in literary matters, and general expertise and suitability."[143] Holmgrain remained as literary editor until 1918.

Summary

Publishing activities were an important part of the work of the Augustana Synod. Its publishing house, the Augustana Book Concern, became the dominant Swedish-American publisher, as well as a major bookseller of imported and domestic titles. The preceding discussion has shown that the A.B.C. developed a definite literary profile, in which religious and moral concerns were important, both in terms of the books published, as well as the books sold in the A.B.C. bookstores. In terms of books imported from Sweden, the most frequent authors represented the established elite authors from the latter part of the nineteenth century, while many of the authors of Swedish popular fiction of the time, widely read in both Sweden and Swedish America, were excluded at the A.B.C. Apart from religious publication for denominational use, the publisher's own publication list included almanacs, stories for children and youth, schoolbooks, as well as a small amount of original Swedish-American fiction, poetry, and books about Swedish America.

The analysis of the contemporary discussion about the kind of books sold and published shows the significance that the A.B.C. attached to its publication profile. Suitable reading matter for Swedish Americans was a part of the cultural struggle in Swedish America and the A.B.C. functioned as a gate-

---

[141] Referat 1907, 55; AFP, ABCMin, 14 July 1908.
[142] AFP, ABCMin, 20 April 1909.
[143] AFP, ABCMin, 19 April 1910.

keeper. We have seen how the publishing house carefully selected the books to be sold and published, in this way maintaining an "Augustana perspective" on literature, as critics labeled it in the debate over *Ur svenska sången*. Religious and moral considerations set boundaries for what was considered acceptable, and what was not. In this way, the literary selections at the Book Concern provided a selected number of literary building blocks that became an important ingredient in the Augustana Synod's Swedish-American identity.

The Augustana Book Concern as a Source for Swedish-American Identity

The religious dimension in the publication profile of the A.B.C. was not only important in terms of denominational publications, but, as noted above, the general Christian tenor that informed the Augustana view of culture and education also set an ideological framework for the non-denominational publications. In his 1901 annual report to the Synod, President Norelius also noted that the Augustana Synod was a "civilising" force among Swedish Americans. He characterized the Augustana Synod as the only denomination, which through schools, literary activities, and maintenance of a Swedish Lutheran faith, had done anything significant for the "maintenance of Swedish language, literature and spirit [*anda*]" in the U.S.[144]

This statement is a reflection of the fact that the "ethnic element" in the Augustana Synod in general was beginning to be emphasized around the turn of the century in what I have called the second phase of the Synod's history. In chapter three, we have seen how a Swedish-American tradition was taking form at Augustana College after *circa* 1890 in its curriculum, student societies, etc. We will now examine the specific role of the A.B.C. in the creation of a Swedish-American ethnic identity in the Augustana Synod, or what can be called the "ethnic element" in the A.B.C. publishing profile. This will be done through an analysis of several types of A.B.C. publications that were especially important for shaping the Swedish-American ethnic identity.

An analysis of the "ethnic element" at the A.B.C. will rely on three types of publications: stories for children and youth, schoolbooks, and publications specifically dealing with Swedish-American topics. One of the main concerns of the Augustana Synod was keeping the children who were growing up in America as members of the denomination. Given the secular and mainstream American cultural environment, keeping youth within the religious and cultural confines of the Synod became a serious matter. As we have seen, the Synod supported a great number of activities directed towards the youth, in

---

[144] Referat 1901, 8, 11.

which various forms of instruction, such as Sunday schools, confirmation schools, parochial schools,[145] as well as the academies and colleges, were important elements. In addition, special youth organizations were started, promoting both religious and ethnic loyalties.[146]

The publications at the A.B.C that were directed towards children and youth included a wide array of magazines, books, and pamphlets. The youth publications are a good source for examining the ideas that the Synod considered to be important for the socialization of the young.

The A.B.C. publication list shows that publications for youth were one of the main concerns of the publishing house.[147] Stories in book form made up 14 percent of all the copies published between 1890 and 1919 (538,000 copies).[148] Eight-one percent of the copies printed were in Swedish, and it was not until after 1910 that any significant number of stories in English for children and youth were published.

In addition, at least six literary serials or annuals especially directed towards juvenile readers existed, which appeared either once—usually before Christmas—or several times per year containing literary selections of varied nature. These made up almost five percent of the total copies published.[149] Finally, the A.B.C. published a number of monthly or semi-monthly magazines directed at children and youth, which went out in quite large editions, averaging between 20,000–30,000 copies per issue.[150]

A second category of publications that can be assumed to have had a more direct role in the promulgation of a Swedish-American identity consists of schoolbooks, including readers of both elementary and more advanced nature, as well as anthologies of selected Swedish fiction and poetry. Schoolbooks constitute an obvious example of how values are transmitted from generation to generation, and it can be argued that they are important elements in the construction and maintenance of national identities.[151] The creation of an ethnic identity is in some ways parallel to the socialization process in schools,

---

[145] See Minneskrift 1910, 361–90 for an overview of these educational activities up until 1909.

[146] Minnesskrift 1910, 391–410.

[147] All the following statistics come from the A.B.C. database.

[148] The classification of the various titles as reading matter for children or youth is not always obvious, but the main rule has been to follow the A.B.C.'s own guidelines. When the book contains a subtitle such as "readings for the young" etc., the book is automatically grouped as reading for children or youth.

[149] They accounted for 177,500 copies. This figure excludes *Prärieblomman*. [A.B.C. Database]

[150] A.B.C. Database.

[151] Andersson 1986, 15–22 and Brink 1992, chapter 7 include useful discussions of the role of canons and schoolbooks in Sweden. Cf. also Elson 1964 and Tingsten 1969, part II for further discussions of both American and Swedish conditions.

154

and one can thus assume that similar processes are at work here. Schoolbooks were also the fourth largest category of publications at the A.B.C., behind stories for children and youth, accounting for some 10 percent of the total copies printed. All of the schoolbooks that will be examined were published in Swedish.

A final group of publications related directly to Swedish-American culture. Included here is original Swedish-American literature, titles dealing with different aspects of Swedish-American history, and books reflecting on the nature and character of Swedish America. Contributors and authors in this group include established Swedish-American writers and opinion makers, such as C.W. Andeer, Jakob Bonggren, Johan Enander, Oliver Linder, Johan Person, and Anna Olson. In addition, *Prärieblomman* and *Ungdomsvännen* also included material which merits their inclusion in this category of the A.B.C. publications.

It is this group of publications at the A.B.C. which most explicitly deals with Swedish-American culture and the issue of what it meant to be Swedish in America. Still, it must be underscored that it made up only a fraction of the A.B.C. imprints—just 1.5 percent. *Sånger och sagor*, the 1902 collection of poetry by Jakob Bonggren, was printed in a run of 2,500 copies,[152] and remained in stock for at least a decade, and *Prärieblomman*, which was considered a show window for Swedish-American culture, never exceeded 3,000 copies.[153] Though quantitatively a small group of publications, from the point of view of how a Swedish-American identity was formed in the Augustana Synod, they are of great qualitative interest. In the remaining parts of this chapter, these three categories of publications will be examined in greater detail.

Stories for Children and Youth

Books
Virtually none of the books published at the A.B.C. for children were written by Swedish-American authors. They were instead either reprints (or towards the end of the period translations into English) of national Swedish children's literature or translations into Swedish (or sometimes English) of non-Swedish materials.

Since the A.B.C. was the largest Swedish-language publishing house in the United States, one could assume that large quantities of national Swedish children's literature would have been published. However, the position of such Swedish literature was surprisingly weak, as only about 15 percent of the copies printed where the national origin of the author can be established was

---

[152] A.B.C. database.
[153] Svensson 1994, 32.

Swedish.[154] The most popular authors from Sweden were Mathilda Roos, whose books appeared in 12,000 copies (of which 10,000 were in English translation), Elisabeth Beskow (better known under her pseudonym Runa) with 14,000 copies (of which 6,000 were in English translation), and Emily Nonnen with 15,000 copies.

It was rather translations of German authors into Swedish (and to a lesser extent English) that dominated among the books for the young at the A.B.C. More than two thirds of all the children's books printed for which the background of the author is known were of German origin.[155] The top three German authors, who accounted for a fourth of the copies printed, were Maragrete Lenk, who was printed in 33,000 copies (of which 5,000 were in English translation), Nikolaus Fries with 21,000 copies, and Minna Rüdiger with a total run of 12,000.

As Margareta Hamrin has pointed out, the children's literature published in Swedish America did not reflect the intensive debate about children's reading going on around the turn of the century in Sweden, and stories containing elements of fantasy were very rare in Swedish America.[156] Most of the authors mentioned above tended to write books conveying a basic message of Christian morality to their readers, in which traditional moral values such as being content, obeying one's elders, doing good deeds, etc., prevail, and in which in many cases end with the protagonists finding salvation in God. The stories exhibit the same characteristics that Åke Kussak has found in his analysis of the short stories published by Svenska Missionsförbundet in its various publications after 1910, with an emphasis on the Christian faith and "how to become a Christian and how to act as a Christian."[157] Of the German authors at the A.B.C. who can be found in the standard encyclopedia of German children's literature, all are described as having written stories with religious tendencies, and several of them were published at German religious publishing houses.[158]

How closely did the A.B.C. follow the publication profiles of similar

---

[154] The identification of the national origin of the author is not always easy. In many cases when the author's name is not given, I have still been able to classify the books since it is often noted in the book that it is a translation from a particular language. In some cases, the A.B.C. catalogs also supply that information. In this way, I have been able to classify the national origin of 54 % of the total number of copies of children's literature published at the A.B.C.

[155] Total copies printed for those authors where national origin was established: 257,785. Of those identified 42,250 copies were of Swedish origin and 179,835 copies of German. [A.B.C. database.]

[156] Hamrin 1979, 74.

[157] Kussak 1982, 158. See also chapter 4, 94–141. A similar situation has been noted regarding the reading habits in a youth temperance lodge in Sweden 1909–1920, which of course emphasized abstinence of alcohol but also good morals, honesty, and industriousness. [Rydbeck 1995, 220–23.]

[158] See Doderer 1973–1982, 4 vols. The authors are: Frida von Kronoff, vol 2, 270, Maragrete Lenk, vol 4, 369–70, Sophie von Niebelschütz, vol. 4, 427–28, Karl Gustav Nierirtz, vol 2, 555–57, Christoph von Schmid, vol 3, 290–92 and Ottile Wildermuth, vol 3, 804–07.

religious publishing houses in Sweden? Did it merely mirror what was being done on the other side of the Atlantic, or did it choose to pursue a more independent policy? We have seen that the share of national Swedish children's literature was relatively small at the A.B.C. Translated children's literature dominated in Sweden from 1870 until 1920 as well, even though the German share of translations in Sweden was gradually replaced by English-language originals at the turn of the century.[159] Many of the authors, and to some degree titles, that came out at the A.B.C. were also published in Sweden, primarily by Evangeliska Fosterlandsstiftelsen (EFS) but also by other religiously oriented publishing houses.

At EFS the literature for children and the young was dominated by translated works,[160] and the three top German writers at the A.B.C.,—Lenk, Fries, and Rüdiger—were also frequently published at EFS. During the decades around the turn of the century, 21 titles by Lenk, 16 by Fries, and nine by Rüdiger appeared in Sweden, with the great majority at EFS.[161] Of these titles, two by Lenk and Fries and one by Rüdiger also appeared at the A.B.C.[162]

Still, the majority of the titles by Margarete Lenk and Nikolaus Fries as well as a number of other authors at the A.B.C. do not seem to have been published in Sweden.[163] Moreover, a physical examination of those titles published in both countries shows that the American editions are not just American republications of the Swedish editions.[164] The translations were done in the United States, and judging by the names or initials of the translators given, usually by someone associated with the A.B.C. or Augustana College. In at least one case the A.B.C. preceded EFS in bringing out a Swedish translation of one of the German titles, later published in both countries.[165]

This suggests that the A.B.C. maintained an independent publication profile in the selection of individual titles, although it quite naturally operated within a similar cultural sphere as did, for example, EFS in Sweden. It also seems

---

[159] Mählqvist 1977, 59–61. See also Klingberg 1973, 81–82.

[160] EFS 1906, 55.

[161] Bok-Katalog 1866–75, Bok-Katalog 1876–85, Bok-Katalog 1886–95, Bok-Katalog 1896–1900, Bok-Katalog 1901–05, Bok-Katalog 1906–10, Bok-Katalog 1911–15, Bok-Katalog 1916–20. The time periods in question are for Lenk 1901–1920, Fries 1866–1919, and Rüdiger 1906–1915.

[162] The figure might be higher, as some of the books might have been published under different titles in Sweden and at the A.B.C. Moreover, several of the A.B.C. titles are collections, which may have been put together by the A.B.C. under its own title.

[163] The A.B.C. titles have been checked against the same sources as noted in note 161. Six titles by Lenk not published in Sweden appear at the A.B.C., and four by Fries. It must, again, be kept in mind, however, that the titles under which books appeared in Sweden and Swedish America might have been different, which could account for some of the discrepancies.

[164] Pirated editions of Swedish books were not uncommon in Swedish America, and it was not until 1911 that a copyright treaty was signed between Sweden and the U.S. [Williams 1991, 36].

[165] Fries 1904 (A.B.C.), Fries 1908 (EFS). Cf. also Stein 1893 (A.B.C.) and Stein 1911 (EFS).

likely that the A.B.C. was influenced by the publication profiles of other Lutheran publishing houses in the U.S. The large number of translations from German were probably inspired by German-American Lutheran publishing houses in the United States. One such example is Nikolaus Fries' *Irrlichte. Eine Erzählung*, which was published in Pelcher, Pennsylvania, in 1880 and was brought out at the A.B.C. in 1904 as *Vid Fyrelden*.

Literary Serials and Annuals for Children

Six different serials or annuals in Swedish aimed at the younger readers have been identified in the A.B.C. publication list.[166] Four of them, *Julklockorna* (The Christmas Bells), *Juvelskrinet* (The Jewel Box), *Blommor vid vägen* (Roadside Flowers), and *Lekkamraten* (The Playmate) were published mainly before the turn of the century and appeared in total editions of between 9,000 and 14,000,[167] totals considerably smaller than for those titles published after 1900. *Julklockorna* was a Christmas annual,[168] whereas *Juvelskrinet* and *Blommor vid vägen* contained "stories for children," and *Lekkamraten* included "illustrations for the young with text."[169] The content in these publications was heavily religious and in rather simple language, obviously directed at fairly young children.

Around the turn of the century two new serials were started that reached much larger editions, *Nytt bibliotek för barn och ungdom* (New Library for Children and Youth) and *Vid Juletid. Vinterblommor samlade för de små* (At Christmastime. Winter blossoms for the Young). In both serials, the language was considerably more advanced than in those published before the turn of the century, the intended audience being young persons with a good basic knowledge of Swedish. Their content was also of a different nature. *Nytt bibliotek*, published at least between 1906–1915, appeared in a minimum of 47,000 copies and contained a number of short stories and a few poems. It included stories of an edifying and religious nature. Although all authors have not been identified, those that have, including such as Josef Grytzell, Anna Lybecker, Karl Karlsson, Lina Sandell-Berg, and Sigrid Wiedemann, were active in the sphere of religious publishing for children and youth in Sweden associated with denominations such as EFS or Svenska Missionsförbundet.[170]

---

[166] No complete runs of these literary serials have been located, and the analysis is therefore based on incomplete material. The A.B.C. annual reports do not always include the literary serials, which makes it hard to compute the size of the editions and establish exact years of publication. The best holdings of the literary serials exist at the Swenson Swedish Immigration Research Center at Augustana College in Rock Island and in the Royal Library in Stockholm.

[167] Figures from A.B.C. annual reports in Referat.

[168] ABC Catalog 1912, 40.

[169] ABC Catalog 1912, 40, 44.

[170] See Åhlén 1942, vol 1, 260 (Grytzell), 393–94 (Karlsson), 517–18 (Lybecker), vol 2, 886 (Widermann). Cf. also Kussak 1982, 206–07.

Vid Juletid, published between 1896–1910 in a total edition of at least 72,000 copies, was an even more ambitious publication. It was edited by professors of Swedish at Augustana College, first Ernst A. Zetterstrand, and from 1904 Jules Mauritzson. It was a Christmas magazine similar to those published in Sweden at the turn of the century. In fact, *Vid Juletid* drew heavily on texts from these Swedish magazines, and many of its contributions were *Kunstmärchen* by such well-known contemporary literary fairy tale authors in Sweden as Elisabeth Beskow, Hugo Gyllander, Hedvig Indebetou, Amanda Kerfstedt, and Harald Östenson. Most of these fairy tales had already been published in Sweden and, although there was a basic tone of Christian morality to many of the stories, they are much less explicitly religious than the contributions in the other magazines discussed.[171] *Vid Juletid* thus shows a high cultural profile in comparison with the other periodicals and was the Christmas magazine that was most like its Swedish counterparts.

It should be noted that other American denominations also published periodicals for children, with a didactic, moral, and religious content similar to that found among the Augustana publications. According to Barbara Snedeker Bates, over 200 denominational periodicals for children were published between *circa* 1840 and 1960, reaching millions of children. This is, however, an area of research within which relatively little work has been done.[172]

Summary

How did these publications for children and youth relate to the creation of a sense of Swedishness at the A.B.C.? First, the language aspect must be stressed. By reading these books and magazines, young Swedes and Swedish Americans were given an opportunity to learn or to maintain the use of the Swedish language. Some publications, such as books by Mathilda Roos or Margarete Lenk and *Vid Juletid*, required a good command of the Swedish language, thus also contributing to the use and knowledge of a more advanced level of Swedish in America.

Secondly, some are set in a Swedish milieu. This is of course particularly true of the contributions by Swedish authors but also visible in some of the collections of stories.[173] A few collections of stories also include Swedish-American settings, such as *Vid Jesu krubba* from 1908, where a Christmas story contrasts a wealthy, but non-Christian Swedish-American family in Chi-

---

[171] See Nordlinder 1991, 43–94, for an analysis of the *Kunstmärchen* in Swedish Christmas magazines. Eva Nordlinder has also helped in the identification of unsigned contributions to *Vid Juletid*.

[172] Bates 1980, 13–18.

[173] Cf. e.g., Hanna Frosterus Segerstråle, "Den lille studentens 'julgåfva'," and "Var barmhärtig" in Vid Jesu krubba 1907, and "Frihet" in Guds vägar 1908.

cago with a much poorer, but pious one in the same city.[174] Although the moral and religious elements in the stories undoubtedly were most significant, the Swedish or Swedish-American geographical settings also singled out and placed Swedish and Swedish-American milieus in special circumstances for the readers, helping create a frame of reference in which Sweden and Swedish America were natural elements.

Finally, it is important to note that certain fairly well-known Swedish authors for children were also introduced into the Swedish-American cultural milieu, especially through *Vid Juletid*. Among all the periodical publications for youth, *Vid Juletid* was clearly the most ambitious and included contributions that went beyond the basic Christian morality in many other works. Several contemporary national Swedish authors were represented in the journal, who thus also became a part of the Swedish-American cultural tradition.

Schoolbooks

As noted above, schoolbooks were the fourth largest category of publications at the A.B.C., following behind stories for children and youth among the non-denominational publications. The category includes elementary Swedish language books, primers for various grades, anthologies of Swedish literature, and a few titles to be used in the instruction of Swedish at the college and university level. The great majority of the publications were in Swedish, and those few titles which appeared in English were the Swedish college and university text books.[175]

The publication of these schoolbooks was of great significance for the Augustana Synod: indeed it was one of the motives behind the establishment of the publishing company in the first place. When a Board of Publications was appointed at the Synod meeting in 1889 and empowered to buy the then privately owned Augustana Book Concern on behalf of the Synod, one of the main reasons given was, as noted above, to "achieve better uniformity" in the use of schoolbooks in the schools associated with the Augustana Synod.[176] Moreover, during the A.B.C.'s first decade school-books comprised the leading category on the A.B.C. publication list, both in terms of number of titles and number of copies. These books were thus significant both as they assisted in the maintenance of the Swedish language and in helping the more advanced

---

[174] "Tvenne olika julaftnar," in Vid Jesu krubba 1908.

[175] One example is a Swedish grammar, printed in just over 5,000 copies between 1912–1917 (Vickner 1917); others are editions with commentary and vocabularies for different Swedish texts, such as Tegnér's *Fritiofs saga* (Tegnér 1914) and Runeberg's *Fänrik Ståls sägner* (Runeberg 1915).

[176] Referat 1889, 25.

readers shape a view of Sweden and Swedish America. In the following sections, we will pay particular attention to the role these schoolbooks played in the forging of a Swedish-American ethnic identity in the Augustana Synod. The main focus of the analysis will be on the primers, as these were printed in the largest number of copies. Although the elementary language books were printed in many large runs as well, their contents focused exclusively on linguistic exercises, a material which is not of particular use for a content analysis. The two anthologies of Swedish literature that were at least partly intended to be used in schools—Johan Enander's *Eterneller och vårblommor* and *Ur svenska sången*—have already been discussed above.

The first primer at the A.B.C. was *Församlingsskolans läsebok* (A Primer for the Congregational Schools), edited by Anders Bersell, professor of Greek at the college, and meant to be used in the Augustana congregational schools. The matter of suitable textbooks was brought up at the Synod meeting in 1890 when it was decided that the Synod publish its own primer.[177]

Församlingssskolans läsebok became one of the most venerable titles at the A.B.C.; from its first publication in 1890 it was reprinted 16 times—last in 1915[178]—and appeared in more than 38,000 copies.[179] In 1897 Bersell brought out another primer called *Barnens andra bok* (The Children's Second Book), which according to the preface was intended to complement *Församlingsskolans läsebok*, since the latter was sometimes considered to be too advanced, especially for younger children. With the publication of *Barnens andra bok*, however, the editors proudly noted that there now existed a "relatively complete series of Swedish school-books" to be used by the Swedish-American children as they were learning to use and love "their fathers' resounding language."[180] *Barnens andra bok* was also printed in a large edition: it appeared in 15 printings between 1897 and 1914 in a total of 57,800 copies.

After the turn of the century, a series of three primers appeared: *Första läseboken för skolan och hemmet* (The First Primer for Schools and Homes), *Andra läseboken för skolan och hemmet* (The Second Primer for Schools and Homes), and *Tredje läseboken för skolan och hemmet* (The Third Primer for Schools and Homes). The first two were edited by Hulda Magnusson and first appeared in 1908 and 1910; Augustana Swedish professor Jules Mauritzson brought out the third in 1917. Both the Magnusson books were aimed at chil-

---

[177] Referat 1890, 25.

[178] As far as can be determined, the book remained virtually unchanged through all the printings. In 1898, the title page notes a second edition and the book is one page longer than the previous printings. No texts have, however, been changed, and the preface notes that the only alterations include the usage of the new spelling rules in Sweden according to Sundén's principles. [FL 1898, 4.]

[179] A.B.C. database.

[180] Bersell 1897, 4.

dren learning Swedish, and contain simple reading exercises. *Tredje läseboken*, which appeared in one printing of 2,000 copies, however, assumes a good reading knowledge of Swedish, as it includes a number of selections from poetry, fiction, and historical writings, and although it was aimed at the congregational schools, the publishers felt that "the Swedish youth in America" and "Swedish-Americans of all ages" could read and enjoy this book.[181]

The two schoolbooks published by the Augustana Book Concern that best lend themselves to a content analysis from an ethnic point of view are thus *Församlingsskolans läsebok* and *Tredje läseboken*. In the following sections they will be analyzed and compared. Their dependence on similar Swedish primers will also be discussed.

Församlingsskolans läsebok

An examination of *Församlingsskolans läsebok* shows that it was obviously inspired by similar primers in Sweden, perhaps most prominently *Läsebok för folkskolan* (A Primer for the Elementary Schools), which was used in the nineteenth-century Swedish elementary schools.[182] This primer first appeared in 1868 in 25,000 copies, and within the next two years another 75,000 copies were printed. These very high circulation figures meant that *Läsebok för folkskolan* in its many editions became very influential in shaping reading habits and minds of generations of Swedish school children.[183]

The book was carefully edited by prominent academics and teachers; even the Minister of Education F.F. Carlson took an active part. The object of the book was to cover most of the fundamental subjects in elementary school, and it therefore included sections on Swedish and world geography, nature, and history, as well as pieces on natural phenomena, technical inventions, etc.[184] The book also included fictional reading selections, with stories, fables, and poetry. According to Lars Furuland, the primer sought to instill a sense of national feeling in its readers. A number of selections from Swedish literature and history helped create a "national canon of persons and events" that was rooted in the Romanticism of the nineteenth century, in part emphasizing what were seen as the ancient Swedish virtues of freedom and independence associated with the Swedish peasantry, as well as exalting Swedish nature and the different provinces.[185]

The name of the Augustana primer alludes to its Swedish counterpart, especially as the Swedish book was almost always referred to as *Folkskolans*

---

[181] ABC Catalog 1920, 53.

[182] For further information about the book and it its history see Furuland 1991b.

[183] Lo-Johansson 1988, 265–66 is an account by one of the leading Swedish workingclass authors about the role that *Läsebok* played for him as a child.

[184] Furuland 1991b, 66–73.

[185] Furuland 1991b, 72.

läsebok instead of its actual title. In the preface to *Församlingsskolans läsebok* the editor also notes that "there is no lack of primers for Swedish elementary schools" but that the present volume is still needed since there is no book that is especially suited for "our congregational schools in this country."[186] The purpose of the book is to include selections that are "suitable for our Swedish-American circumstances" and that "have a clean, moral character" and emphasize "positive Christian" aspects.[187] The A.B.C. catalog from 1900 further states that the selections have been made so that a "domestic viewpoint is kept, so that nothing appears strange or alien to the young readers."[188] Similar points were made in various advertisements in the press at the time of publication.[189] To ascertain the nature of a book "suitable" for "Swedish-American circumstances," it will be useful to compare the two primers.

Församlingsskolans läsebok included two parts: spelling exercises followed by shorter or longer texts. There is a gradual progression in difficulty in the reading section, beginning with a simple piece on "The Child," ending with a fairly advanced item on Henry Wadsworth Longfellow. The primer is slightly more than half the size of its Swedish counterpart[190] and includes a similar division into geography, history, natural phenomena, etc., as well as shorter stories, fables, and poems. At least thirteen of the items are direct copies or in a few cases modified versions of pieces from *Läsebok för folkskolan*, sometimes with slightly different titles, mostly shorter poems, often with a religious touch.[191] Other pieces that were borrowed, often in an abbreviated form from the Swedish primer, include short biographies of historical figures or events, such as the emperor Charles the Great, the Crusades, and Esaias Tegnér.[192] Furthermore, a number of the items in *Församlingsskolans läsebok* have the same titles as in *Läsebok för folkskolan*, particularly pieces dealing with different animals, such as elephants, reindeer, and camels. Although the texts are different and mostly shorter in the American primer, there are no substantive

---

[186] "Förord" in FL 1890, 3.

[187] FL 1890, 3. The original Swedish reads: "lämpadt efter våra, svensk-amerikanska förhållanden", "har en ren, sedlig prägel", "positivt kristliga."

[188] ABC Catalog 1900, 49.

[189] E.g. *Augustana*, 6 November 1890 and 5 February 1891.

[190] In my comparisons between the two books, I will use the 8th edition of *Läsebok för folkskolan* [LfF] printed in Stockholm in 1878. As the 9th edition appeared in 1890, it was the 8th edition that was available as the work with *Församlingsskolans läsebok* [FL] was underway in Swedish America. LfF 1878 runs 629 pages, whereas FL 1890 is 384 pages long.

[191] E.g. "Hvem gjorde skyn" FL 1890, 209–10 is identical to "Guds Godhet," LfF 1878, 1–2, and "Under höbergningen," FL 1890, 248–49 is identical to "I Husaby (Under Höbergningen)," LfF 1878, 36.

[192] "Karl den store," FL 1890, 323–24, also published as "Carl den store," LfF 1878, 530–31, "Korstågen," FL 1890, 325–29 is an edited version of "Det första korståget," LfF 1878, 531–32 and "Esaias Tegnér," FL 1890, 372–76 is an edited version of "Esaias Tegnér," LfF 1878, 415–19.

differences in the mode of presentation between the two books, as they both give a straightforward presentation of the subject matter at hand.

There are, however, some major differences between the books. Roughly half of the selections in *Församlingsskolans läsebok* are stories and poems, while they only comprise about a fourth of the items in *Läsebok för folkskolan*. Slightly more than a third of the pieces in *Församlingsskolans läsebok* deal with geography, natural phenomena, or geology, whereas almost half of the items in the Swedish book are found in this category. Historical and biographical pieces, both Swedish and general, finally, make up not quite a third of the selections in the Swedish book, but only about a tenth in the Swedish-American primer. The Swedish-American primer thus places much more emphasis on selections with a general moral and religious content, with inspiring stories of how faith in God or good behavior is rewarded. Very few of the selections from Swedish literature of the kind included in *Läsebok för folkskolan* have been identified in *Församlingsskolans läsebok*.

As noted above, the Swedish primer became important in shaping a Swedish national feeling by emphasizing Swedish nature and certain aspects of Swedish history and literature. A similar national element can also be found in *Församlingsskolans läsebok*, although to a lesser extent. The emerging national element in *Församlingsskolans läsebok* shows a duality, in that the book includes a number of selections that deal with both Sweden and the United States. Evidently, the editors of *Församlingsskolans läsebok* wanted to make sure that the intended readers among the Swedish-American youth were exposed to both the Swedish and American cultural heritages.

This emerging duality is found among the selections dealing with history, famous persons, and general cultural phenomena. The Swedish historical selections include pieces on ancient Swedish history (the Stone, Bronze, and Iron ages), the Viking voyages, the Swedish patron saint, St. Erik, the Christianization of Finland, Ansgar, Engelbrekt Engelbrektsson (a political leader of the 1430s,) the Reformation, and the kings Gustav Vasa and Gustavus Adolphus. Two prominent authors are also given short biographies: Georg Stiernhielm and Esaias Tegnér. Two pieces on the Swedish language are also included, one descriptive and one laudatory poem, as well as the poem "Sverige" by Erik Gustaf Geijer. In addition to the entry on Swedish geography, the reindeer and the Lapps (Sami) are also presented.

The selections dealing with the cultural background of the adopted homeland include biographical sketches of Christopher Columbus, George Washington, Benjamin Franklin, Washington Irving, and Henry Wadsworth Longfellow. There is also a general description of American geography, a piece on the Niagara Falls and Yellowstone Park, and entries on two American animals, the buffalo and the prairie dog. It is also interesting to note that *Församlingsskolans läsebok* devotes very little attention to Swedish-American experiences.

Only one item in the book deals specifically with such a theme, namely an overview of the history of the Swedish Lutheran church in America, that is the Augustana Synod itself.

Many of the themes that deal with the Swedish background in *Församlingsskolans läsebok* can be found in *Läsebok för folkskolan* as well, although the entries in the Swedish-American primer are often modified and shortened. This is the case with the items on ancient Swedish history, Ansgar, St. Erik, Stiernhielm, and Tegnér, where parts of the text have been borrowed verbatim. It should be noted that a mild criticism of Tegnér in the Swedish primer—that there are different opinions of his role as bishop—[193] has been omitted in the American book. The discussions of Engelbrekt, Gustav Vasa, and Gustavus Adolphus share the same basic assumptions in the two books, and all three figures are portrayed in very positive terms, as guarantors of freedom, independence, and religion as well as being noble and intelligent. *Församlingsskolans läsebok* tends to put a somewhat stronger emphasis on the religious dimensions, and Gustav Vasa, who by the grace of God, said to have become as powerful and wise as King David, is praised for having saved the country from slavery and carried out the Reformation,[194] and Gustavus Adolphus is hailed for his bravery, steadfastness, and defense of religious liberty.[195]

None of the pieces dealing with the American cultural background is found in the Swedish primer. The historical biographies of Washington, Franklin, and Lincoln all emphasize their significant contributions to the new homeland of the readers of *Församlingsskolans läsebok*. A keyword for all three figures is "freedom": Washington, with the help of God, led the English colonies to freedom from England;[196] Franklin, as the "noble citizen" worked for freedom of the slaves;[197] and Lincoln, finally, was the "instrument of God" in saving the U.S. in its times of trouble and defending the freedom of both the nation and the slaves.[198] The two American authors who are highlighted for the Swedish-American audience, Washington Irving and Henry Wadsworth Longfellow, are both characterized as the most popular writers of prose and poetry in the U.S., writing in a simple and clear style, yet also with "depth" (Irving) and "compassion" (Longfellow).[199]

The choice of the Swedish cultural symbols in *Församlingsskolans läsebok* is perhaps not surprising. Almost all of the Swedish symbols can also be found

---

[193] LfF 1878, 419.
[194] FL 1890, 360–61.
[195] FL 1890, 362–67.
[196] FL 1890, 336–39.
[197] FL 1890, 340–43. Quotation from p. 340.
[198] FL 1890, 343–46. Quotation from p. 343. It should be noted that the entry on George Washington relates the legend of young George and the cherry tree, although in the Swedish-American version it has become a peartree.
[199] FL 1890, 376–79. Quotations from p. 376 and 378.

in Sweden at the time, and the American primer can thus be said to reflect the situation in Sweden. Still, in our comparison with *Läsebok för folkskolan*, we can note that fewer Swedish cultural symbols are included in the American primer. Also, there is a clear emphasis on religion and freedom, as Swedish-American readers learned about the accomplishments of Ansgar and St. Erik in bringing Christianity to Sweden and Finland respectively, of Engelbrekt and Gustav Vasa in defending the freedom and independence of Sweden, and of Gustav Vasa and Gustavus Adolphus in promoting the Lutheran faith at home and abroad. Two Swedish authors receive special notice, both poets: Stiernhielm from the seventeenth century and Tegnér from the nineteenth. The concern in America for preserving the Swedish language may partly explain the inclusion of Stiernhielm, as one of his main contributions was his importance for the development of the Swedish language.[200] As noted above, the primer also includes two pieces on the Swedish language itself, one of which is a poem by Johan Enander glorifying the Swedish language.[201] Tegnér is praised as Sweden's greatest poet, and was, as we have seen, together with Johan Ludvig Runeberg, among the most popular authors both at Augustana College and in the Swedish secondary schools in the late nineteenth century.

The choice of American historical symbols is not surprising either. Washington, Franklin, and Lincoln were among the most important symbols of American nationhood around the turn of the century. Ruth Elson has shown how important these persons were in mainstream American primers at the time,[202] and Peter Karsten has charted the rise and fall of American "patriot-heroes" in the nineteenth century with similar results.[203] Lincoln receives the greatest attention. This corresponds to a growth in Lincoln's popularity at the expense of Washington and others during the end of the nineteenth century.[204] Regarding the American authors included, it should be noted that Longfellow enjoyed a great deal of prestige in Swedish America, as he both visited Sweden and translated some of the works of Tegnér into English,[205] which the entry in *Församlingsskolans läsebok* also duly notes. Augustana College President Olof Olsson used him in justifying the study of the Swedish language at Augustana College in the 1890s, when he rhetorically wondered if "it reduce[d] the honor of Longfellow that he appreciated Swedish as one of the cultured living languages?"[206]

---

[200] FL 1890, 372.
[201] FL 1890, 367–69.
[202] Elson 1964, 188–206.
[203] Karsten 1978, chapter 5.
[204] Karsten 1978, 98–101.
[205] Hilen 1947, chapter 4.
[206] Olsson 1896, 13–14.

Tredje läseboken

Quite a different picture is presented in *Tredje läseboken för skolan och hemmet*, which was brought out by the A.B.C. in 1917, some 25 years after *Församlingsskolans läsebok* first appeared.[207] As we have seen, this book was the third and most advanced in a set of Swedish primers published by the A.B.C. after 1908 and was targeted not only to schools but also to a larger Swedish-American audience. The two earlier books had been edited by Hulda Magnusson, but when she submitted the manuscript for the third book, the literary editor at the A.B.C. Oscar Holmgrain reported that the manuscript was not suitable.[208] Instead, it was decided that Jules Mauritzson be engaged as editor, and make a selection of materials as he saw fit.[209] The new manuscript was submitted in early 1917, and after some discussions of revisions (necessitating an extra meeting of the Executive Committee of the A.B.C. Board), the manuscript was finally approved.[210]

The content of *Tredje läseboken* is much more oriented towards building a sense of Swedish-American identity than any other of the schoolbooks published by the A.B.C. The 326-page volume consists of three sections. The first, roughly a third of the book, includes a selection of stories and poems. The second section, slightly less than half the book, deals with the "Swedish people in old and recent times," whereas the book's third and shortest section, about a fifth of the contents, includes contributions "from America."

The stories and poems in the first section are mostly Swedish. In Mauritzson's selection of materials, two national Swedish primers by Hammmer and Wallgren, *Första läseboken* and *Andra läseboken*,[211] seem to have been a source of inspiration for *Tredje läseboken*'s first section, and four items are specifically noted as being based on these books. The dependency particularly on *Andra läseboken* is in fact even greater, as three fourths of the selection in the first section of the Swedish-American primer also appear in *Andra läseboken*.[212] Authors represented in this selection include, for example, Zacharias Topelius, Karl-Erik Forsslund, and Anna Maria Roos, which were well-known names in literary selections for children in turn-of-the century Sweden,[213] and

---

[207] TL 1917.

[208] AFP, ABCMin, 17 October 1916.

[209] AFP, ABCMin, 17 October 1916.

[210] AFP, ABCMin, 10 April 1917.

[211] FL 1915, AL 1916.

[212] The following items appear in both TL 1917 and AL 1916: "Skyddängelns röst," "Nu blir det vår," "När bina vaknade," "Vad vinden gjorde," "Sommarens första ros," "En farlig väv," "Gammelgäddan i vassviken," "Sagor om björn och räv," "En tam björn," "Kom hör min vackra visa," "Det är Vilhelm," "Mors varghistoria," "Den underbara gröten," "Vita blomster," and "Haren". The following items appear in both in TL 1917 and in FL 1915: "Snöklockans sång," and "Tores julgran."

[213] Nordlinder 1991, 31, 55.

whom we have met in other A.B.C. publications as well. It is, however, noticeable that a few selections by August Strindberg in Hammer and Wallgren's *Andra läseboken* have not been included in the Swedish-American primer. Strindberg's name was still controversial, and few of his works were available at the A.B.C.

The section dealing with Swedish history and culture included historical and biographical items as well as a few selections of poetry. The historical selections are almost all based on national Swedish textbooks in history for the elementary school, notably by those by Carl Grimberg and Anders Fryxell. A comparison between *Tredje läseboken* and Grimberg's *Sveriges historia för folkskolan* shows that eight selections in the American book are based on Grimberg. The American versions are slight modifications of the Swedish original, most commonly shortened versions. No particular tendency seems evident in the modifications, except perhaps in the part dealing with Swedish life during the ninth century: the American entry omits a section on the pagan religion in Sweden.

The view of Swedish history presented to the prospective Swedish-American readers in *Tredje läseboken* emphasized the Viking Age, Engelbrekt, Gustav Vasa, and Sweden's Age of Greatness during the seventeenth century. Religion is still important, as the first missionary to Sweden (Ansgar), St. Birgitta, (a Swedish saint from the Middle Ages), Martin Luther, and the nineteenth-century bishop and hymn-writer Johan Olov Wallin are featured. Other prominent individuals from Swedish history are Jonas Alströmer, Linnaeus, Per Ling, Peter Wieselgren, and Alfred Nobel. Two authors are also highlighted through biographical sketches and examples from their literary production, Anna Maria Lenngren and Esaias Tegnér.

The third section in *Tredje läseboken* includes contributions which, according to the table of contents, come "from America." In this context, America actually means Swedish America, as all of the selections deal specifically with the history and circumstances of Swedes in the New World. This is a marked difference from *Församlingsskolans läsebok*, which only included one such selection. In addition, the items dealing with Anglo-American mainstream culture found in *Församlingsskolans läsebok* are missing in *Tredje läseboken*.

It is thus largely a view of Swedish-American conditions that is presented in *Tredje läseboken*. However, the longest contribution, taking up more than a fourth of this section, deals not with the Swedish-American community of the nineteenth and twentieth centuries, but with Swedes in America in the seventeenth century in the New Sweden colony.[214] The selections are drawn from a national Swedish primer for elementary school children, written by

---

[214] TL 1917, 275–91.

Märta Edqvist, that dealt with various aspects of the history of the Swedish church.[215]

In *Tredje läseboken* readers are presented with a romanticized version of the history of the colony, set in 1691 when the old colony had passed into the hands of the English. The story is set in the house of Carl Springer, a Swede who had arrived in the area after Sweden's loss of the colony. Springer has invited a group of Swedes, including one of the original colonists, Peter Rambo, to greet the Swedish visitor Anders Printz, the nephew of Johan Printz, the first governor of the colony. Rambo relates stories of the early years of pioneer hardship for the colonists and asserts that the Indians were treated fairly by the Swedes, since, as he puts it, "we were Swedes, and Swedes respect the rights of others."[216]

Springer tells the visitor of the churches built in the colony and of its religious life. Unfortunately, no minister is left any longer to conduct services. Moreover, the Swedes are forgetting their language, and Springer wishes that there were "school teachers and Swedish books available."[217] The remaining Swedes on the Delaware had written to Sweden asking for assistance, but have not received a response. Anders Printz is moved by what he hears, and promises to do what he can upon returning to Sweden.

The story also gives a picture of an "Indian camp" that Printz visits.[218] In very positive terms the Indians tell of their friendship with the New Sweden colonists and speak with particular reverence of Pastor Campanius Holm who translated the catechism into Lenapi. Printz is amazed by the thought that, at one time, both children in Sweden and Indians in their wigwams had been studying the Swedish catechism. Upon returning to Sweden, Printz acts on the behalf of the Delaware Swedes, and the story ends in 1697 with the arrival of three ministers from the Church of Sweden for the old Swedish churches in the area, which the Swedes see as the answer to their prayers.

There is an historical background for this story. Carl Springer and Peter Rambo lived in the New Sweden area at this time and had appealed to Sweden for new ministers to the old Swedish churches. Anders Printz did visit the old colony in 1691, and a group of new ministers from the church of Sweden did land in Delaware in 1697.[219] The significance of this story is that it establishes a continuity and kinship between the prospective readers—turn-of-the-century Swedish Americans—and the Swedish colonists on the Delaware and their descendants. First of all, in the story the New Sweden colony is characterized as a historical link between the two groups, suggesting a much longer Swedish

---

[215] Edqvist 1915, 145–81.
[216] TL 1917, 282–83.
[217] TL 1917, 286.
[218] The following is based on TL 1917, 289–90.
[219] Norman 1995, 195–96.

history in America than that of the recent phase of immigration. Moreover, the similarities between the two groups of Swedish migrants is further underscored through the portrayal of the colonists and their life in old Swedish Delaware as pioneers who had struggled against harsh conditions but succeeded in building a prosperous community. The parallels to the Swedish immigration of the nineteenth and early twentieth centuries are obvious. The positive attitude toward the Indians expressed by the colonists also reflect favorably on the Swedes both of the seventeenth and nineteenth centuries. Finally, it is interesting to note that the immigrants in the story, the descendants of the New Sweden colony in 1691, are concerned about the same issues that were confronting the Swedish-American community in general and the Augustana Synod in particular around the turn of the century, namely how to maintain the language and religion of their Swedish ancestors.

After the section on New Sweden, *Tredje läseboken* moves on to nineteenth-century Swedish America. A chapter is devoted to the inventor John Ericsson, who is portrayed in very positive terms, emphasizing his role as the designer of the *Monitor*, which headed off the attacks by the Confederate *Merrimac* at the Battle of Hampton Roads in 1862 during the American Civil War.[220] According to *Tredje läseboken*, this achievement was greeted with great joy and made Ericsson known as "the liberator of four million slaves."[221] The primer also notes that although Ericsson was a true American patriot, he also remained loyal the country of his birth and requested that he be buried there.

The primer also includes an account of how "our fathers" participated in the Civil War, as well as a description of Swedish pioneer life in rural Minnesota in the 1870s.[222] The latter piece depicts the hard work of the homesteading immigrants, emphasizes the importance of the arrival of a Lutheran pastor, and portrays how the monthly services turn into joyous festivities for the entire community.

Three pieces deal specifically with the history of the Augustana Synod: one an overview of the Synod's history, one an account of life at the Augustana Deaconess Institute in Omaha, Nebraska, and one a humorous account of student life at Augustana College.[223] The two final pieces deal with life among contemporary Swedish Americans. The first is a narration of Christmas celebrations among Swedish Americans in the fictitious rural community of Betlehem, while the last item in *Tredje läseboken* describes a Fourth of July celebration among Swedish Americans somewhere on the prairies.[224]

---

[220] The following is based on TL 1917, 292–303.
[221] TL 1917, 300.
[222] "Våra fäder deltaga i inbördeskriget" and "Nybyggarliv," TL 1917, 303–08.
[223] "Augustana-synodens stiftande," "Ett studentupptåg," and "En morgon vid diakonianstalten," TL 1917, 308–24.
[224] "Julen i 'Bethlehem'" and "Fjärde juli på prärien," TL 1917, 324–36.

Summary

The schoolbooks published by the A.B.C. served several purposes. One important aim of the more elementary A.B.C. books and primers was obviously to teach Swedish-American children to read and write Swedish. A second objective, especially in the more advanced books and in particular *Församlingsskolans läsebok* and *Tredje läseboken*, was to provide children with edifying reading and to teach them about various subjects.

In *Församlingsskolans läsebok* the greater emphasis was on edifying reading of a religious and moral nature, but the book also included a number of selections which dealt with geography, natural phenomena, history, and culture. In the latter pieces, it is possible to discern a duality in emphasis, as both conditions in Sweden and the United States are presented. Prominent leaders of the respective countries are featured, and values such as freedom and religiosity, said to be typical for the two countries, are underscored. *Församlingsskolans läsebok* from 1890 thus provides its Swedish-American readers with cultural elements from both Sweden and the United States which, when they were juxtaposed, formed the foundation for the identity of the Augustana Swedish Americans.

The history and culture of the Swedish Americans themselves play a small role in *Församlingsskolans läsebok*. Only one piece deals explicitly with Swedish-American conditions, namely a section on the history of the Augustana Synod. In this respect, *Tredje läseboken* from 1917 is markedly different. Here, those pieces that deal with the U.S. are all concerned with Swedes in America, beginning with the New Sweden colony and extending to contemporary Fourth of July celebrations among Swedish Americans. *Tredje läseboken* provides its readers with cultural ingredients for an identity that are drawn from a joint Swedish and Swedish-American cultural repertoire. In 1917 Augustana's version of a Swedish-American identity was not only rooted in Sweden and the United States, as it had been 27 years earlier in *Församlingsskolans läsebok*. Now cultural expressions and patterns focusing on Swedish America itself were important elements of the ethnic identity, suggesting an important shift in the way the Augustana Synod had begun to perceive a Swedish-American identity in the intervening years.

A parallel movement was simultaneously underway among the Norwegian Americans. Schoolbooks of a similar nature to those discussed were also published by different Norwegian-American Lutheran synods. Anne Hvenekilde has shown how, as in the Augustana Synod, the different synods' views of culture and religion were reflected in these books. With regard to the role these books played for a Norwegian-American ethnicity, Hvenekilde shows how the ethnic dimension gradually became more important. Before circa 1900, she notes little material about Norway or Norwegian America that could be used as a basis for an ethnic identity in Norwegian-American primers. After that time, however, a shift takes place, and the primers become exponents for Norwegian-American ethnicity, primarily through a literary and historical perspective.[225] Thus, there seems to be a parallel among Lutheran groups in Norwegian America to developments in the Augustana Synod, as the schoolbooks after the turn of the century play a more explicit role in shaping an ethnic identity among the immigrants.

Specifically Swedish-American Oriented Publications

The A.B.C. also published a number of titles that dealt directly with Swedish-American conditions, and that are specifically useful for an analysis of the Swedish-American identity at the A.B.C. Publications in this category can be divided into Swedish-American literature, Swedish-American history, and works that reflected on the nature of the Swedish-American community. In addition, the two cultural and literary periodicals *Prärieblomman* and *Ungdomsvännen* frequently deal with Swedish-American topics and can thus also be included in this category. Quantitatively, this group of publications includes few titles, published in small editions. Qualitatively, however, these books were significant. They provided both the authors and the publishing house with a possibility to articulate their opinions about Swedish America and what it meant to be a Swedish American, and these publications thus became the exponents of the new Swedish-American culture that was being created in the United States. Included here are both original Swedish-American literature and texts dealing with the life and history of Swedish America.

Swedish-American Literature
Although it made up no more than one percent of the total copies published at the A.B.C., Swedish-American literature was one qualitatively important category of Swedish-American publications at the A.B.C. These Swedish-language imprints included works of poetry and fiction, and the authors represented were a fairly small group of persons, most of them associated with the Augustana Synod. We have already met some of these names in the analysis of the discussions of Swedish-American culture in both the Phrenokosmian Society and in Svenska Vitterhetssällskapet at Augustana College. Eric Johannesson and Anna Williams have shown that an awareness of the existence of a distinct Swedish-American literature had developed by the turn of the century,[226] and the A.B.C. was one of the leading publishers of this kind of literature.

---

[225] Hvenekilde 1992, 584–86. I thank Urban Dahllöf, Uppsala for providing me with this reference.
[226] Johannesson 1991b, Williams 1991, 42–48.

The first title was published in 1896 and was a selection of poetry called *Ludvigs dikter* (Ludvig´s Poems) by Ludvig Holmes, an Augustana pastor. The collection appeared in a fairly modest run of 950 copies. Holmes was the leading author of Swedish-American literature at the A.B.C. and brought out two more volumes of poetry.[227] He has been characterized as the national poet of the Augustana Synod, and was the author of a number of commemorative poems written especially for different Augustana jubilees. He was also recognized as a major literary figure in Swedish America by contemporaries who wrote histories of Swedish-American literature.[228]

During the next two decades, a small group of authors was to follow Holmes at the A.B.C., most of them connected with the Augustana Synod in some way, often as ministers or professors at a synod college. The Rev. C.W. Andeer brought out several collections of short stories that dealt with life in Swedish America in general and in the Augustana Synod in particular, such as *I brytningstid. Skisser från det svensk-amerikanska folklifvet* (In Changing Times. Sketches from Swedish-American Life) from 1904 and *Augustanafolk. Bilder och karaktärer ur vårt kyrkliga arbete* (Augustana People. Pictures and Characters from Our Religious Work) from 1911, with a second volume appearing in 1914.[229] As already discussed, in 1902, the collection of poetry *Sånger och sagor* by the editor of *Svenska Amerikanaren* and leading Swedish-American author Jakob Bonggren was published by the A.B.C.[230] Another Augustana pastor, C. A. Lönnqvist, published two volumes of poetry in 1907 and 1916,[231] and Anna Olsson, daughter of Augustana president Olof Olsson, brought out her *Från Solsidan* (From the Sunny Side) in 1905 and in 1917 her well-known account of life on the Kansas prairies *En prärieunges funderingar* (Thoughts of A Prairie Child).[232]

In 1913 the A.B.C. established a publication series of Swedish-American literature, called *Svensk-amerikansk vitterhet* (Swedish-American Belles Lettres) which can be seen a further sign of the significance attached to this genre. The Board of the A.B.C. decided to publish each year "a literary work by some Swedish-American author of good repute." Two manuscripts were discussed as the first volume in this series, one by Johan Person and one by Oliver Linder.[233] Eventually the A.B.C. settled for Linder's *I Västerled* (In Western Lands)[234] which, according to advertisements for the book, was par-

---

[228] Holmes 1896, Holmes 1904, Holmes 1911.
[228] Johannesson 1991b, 96, 109.
[229] Andeer 1904a, Andeer 1911, Andeer 1914.
[230] Bonggren 1902.
[231] Lönnqvist 1907, Lönnqvist 1916.
[232] Olsson 1905, Olsson 1917.
[233] AFP, ABCMin, 28 January, 6 October 1914.
[234] Linder 1914.

ticularly suitable since it dealt with Swedish America and was characterized by "a Swedish-American temperament." Linder was described as a "typically Swedish-American" author and as one of the first who had "naturalized his Swedish pen and consequently is able to give us something genuinely Swedish-American in his writings."[235]

Swedish-American Literary and Cultural Periodicals
As noted above, the A.B.C. published two periodicals between 1900 and 1918 that were of great importance for the maintenance and formulation of a Swedish-American ethnic identity. The first was the annual *Prärieblomman* which appeared shortly before Christmas each year.[236] The first issue of the calendar, which appeared in December 1899, was published by the Chicago-based group "Vitterhetens vänner" (Friends of Culture), in which the journalists and authors Anders Schön and Johan Enander, who were both associated with the Augustana sphere in Swedish America, played an important role.[237] In April 1900 the calendar was offered to the A.B.C., which decided to take on the publication and appointed Schön editor. The second issue of the calendar was published in December 1901.[238] Schön remained editor of *Prärieblomman* until it ceased publication in December 1913.[239] Its circulation was between 2,000 and 3,000 copies per year.[240]

In her study of *Prärieblomman*, Birgitta Svensson argues that the calendar became an exponent for a Swedish-American ideology. Svensson shows that the majority of the writers in the calendar were leading Swedish-American authors, such as Jakob Bonggren, Johan Enander, Ernst W. Olson, and Anders Schön,[241] and that, although some contributions to *Prärieblomman* dealt with national Swedish topics, the main emphasis was on Swedish-American themes, with a noticeable emphasis on Swedish-American history.[242] *Prärieblomman* also became an important vehicle for the Swedish Americans to demonstrate to Sweden how a separate Swedish-American culture had developed in the United States, and Svensson calls it a "cultural manifestation toward Sweden."[243]

Ungdomsvännen was a monthly publication, started by two Augustana pastors in St. Paul, Minnesota in 1898. A year later, it, too, was offered for

---

[235] *Augustana*, 10 December and 26 December 1914.
[236] Svensson 1994 is an in-depth study of *Prärieblomman*.
[237] Svensson 1994, 25.
[238] AFP, ABCMin, 25 April 1900, 15 May 1901.
[239] Svensson 1994, 42–43.
[240] Svensson 1994, 32–33.
[241] Svensson 1994, 36–40.
[242] Svensson 1994, chapter 3.
[243] Svensson 1994, chapter 5.

sale to the A.B.C., which assumed responsibility for the magazine from 1900. The first editor appointed by the A.B.C. was S.G. Youngert, an Augustana pastor who was also active within the A.B.C.[244] Youngert remained editor until 1913 when the responsibility was shared by O.V. Holmgrain and E.W. Olson.[245] From 1915 E.W. Olson assumed the sole editorship, a post he held until April 1918 when he was forced to resign over a controversial article that was claimed to show disloyalty during the ongoing world war.[246] In October the same year, the magazine was officially discontinued.[247] At its peak in 1912 it had a circulation of close to 10,000 copies, but two years later the figure had declined by half.[248]

Ungdomsvännen contained more varied material than *Prärieblomman*, focusing on Swedish and Swedish-American topics, but also on other motifs, such as religion, history, literature, and cultural topics, and there were both Swedish and Swedish-American contributors. [249] The articles were grouped under different headings, which for example, in 1911 included "Edifying articles," "Poems," "Sketches, stories, and articles of general nature," and "Biographies." *Ungdomsvännen* also richly illustrated.[250] It was, as indicated by its name, aimed toward the youth of the Augustana Synod, and in contrast to *Prärieblomman*, seems to have been more inwardly directed toward the Augustana Synod, rather than toward the rest of Swedish America or Sweden.

The magazine maintained a balance between religion and articles of a more general cultural nature which varied over time. The religious element was more dominant during the magazine's first decade of publication, but with the change of editorship in 1913, the new management recommended that *Ungdomsvännen* become "a purely literary magazine," and that a new journal be started for reports from religious youth groups that had previously been included in *Ungdomsvännen*. Following a "lengthy discussion," the A.B.C. Board of Directors agreed that the material dealing with youth religious groups be discontinued, but also stated that *Ungdomsvännen* would remain "a positively Christian literary magazine."[251] The following year, when the magazine's low circulation figures were discussed, the A.B.C. Board of Directors once again emphasized the journal's religious dimension, stating that it should

[244] AFP, ABCMin, 25 October 1899.
[245] AFP, ABCMin, 9 October 1912.
[246] AFP, ABCMin, 23 April 1918.
[247] AFP, ABCMin, 8 October 1918.
[248] "Ett ord till Ungdomsvännens prenumeranter," *Ungdomsvännen* 1918, 268.
[249] No systematic study of *Ungdomsvännen*, such as Svensson's for *Prärieblomman*, exists. It has not been possible to conduct a complete examination of *Ungdomsvännen* within the framework of this study. Evidence from the journal will instead be given to illustrate the general developments.
[250] *Ungdomsvännen*, 1911, Table of Contents.
[251] AFP, ABCMin, 1 July 1913.

include both more articles of a Christian nature and by writers from the Augustana Synod,[252] and in 1917 two new sections of specifically religious materials were also added.[253]

Both *Prärieblomman* and *Ungdomsvännen* were discontinued due to a lack of interest among its readership. Svensson suggests that *Prärieblomman* may have suffered from the competition with *Ungdomsvännen,* but also underscores economic difficulties.[254] *Ungdomsvännen's* circulation figures declined after 1912, making it economically difficult to continue publication. In 1917 the A.B.C. Board of Directors decided to circulate a questionnaire to all pastors and other interested to solicit ideas about the future of the magazine,[255] which showed that a majority of the respondents were dissatisfied with the magazine, as it was perceived as "too advanced" and difficult for its intended readership.[256] This decline in subscriptions, taken together with the accusations of disloyalty to the war effort, sealed the fate of *Ungdomsvännen.*

Swedish-American History

A few titles dealing with Swedish-American history were also published by the A.B.C., most of them authored by the Synod's official historiographer, Erik Norelius. In 1891 he brought out his monumental *De svenska lutherska församlingarna i Amerikas historia* (The History of the Swedish Lutheran Congregations in America) that contains a wealth of information about the early phase of the immigration of Swedish Lutherans and of the Augustana Synod.[257] Norelius was scheduled to bring out a second volume within a few years, but it took until 1916 and many reminders, including a visit by a delegation from the publisher to Norelius' home in Vasa, Minnesota, before it finally appeared.[258] Norelius was also the author of a biography of T.N. Hasselquist, the dominant figure during the early years of the Augustana Synod, published in 1900.[259] In conjunction with the fiftieth anniversary of the Augustana Synod in 1910, the A.B.C. also published two overviews of the Synod's history—one in Swedish and one in English—as well as an account of the celebrations in Rock Island.[260]

---

[252] AFP, ABCMin, 6 October 1914.
[253] The two new sections were called "Our Christian Faith and Doctrine" and "Our field of work." AFP, ABCMin, 27 June 1916.
[254] Svensson 1994, 42–44.
[255] AFP, ABCMin, 31 October 1917.
[256] "Ett ord till Ungdomsvännens prenumeranter," *Ungdomsvännen* 1918, 268.
[257] Norelius 1891.
[258] Norelius 1916. AFP, ABCMin, 19 January 1909, 19 April 1910, 19 July 1910, 24 April 1913, 29 May 1913.
[259] Norelius 1900.
[260] Augustana History 1910, Minnesskrift 1910, Minnen 1911.

Johan Enander's 1893 book *Nordmännen i Amerika* occupies a special place among the historical works published by the A.B.C. This book was published in conjunction with the 1893 World's Fair in Chicago, called the "Columbian Exposition" in commemoration of the 400th anniversary of Columbus' landing in the New World. In face of all the focus on Columbus, the author draws attention to the Viking journeys to North America around the year 1000, making the claim that the "Norsemen" were the first Europeans to reach the American continent.[261] A.B.C. publications dealing with history will be discussed in greater length in chapter five.

Reflections on Swedish America

The A.B.C. also published three books that reflected on the life and times of the Swedish-American community, one by a Swedish visitor and two by Swedish-American journalists. The first book was written by Carl Sundbeck, who, as noted in chapter three, visited Swedish America in 1902, and was received with particular warmth by the Augustana Synod. In 1903 Sundbeck offered a book manuscript of his journey to the A.B.C., and after a very positive evaluation by C.J. Bengston, the book was accepted for publication.[262] It appeared in 1904 under the title *Svensk-amerikanerna. Deras andliga och materiella sträfvanden* (The Swedish Americans. Their Spiritual and Material Developments),[263] and according to Arnold Barton, the book became a "bestseller" on the Swedish-American market,[264] giving a highly positive account of conditions among Swedish Americans. In particular, it was very complimentary to the Augustana Synod, suggesting that the Synod provided the best support for Swedishness in America.[265]

The two Swedish-American books were Johan Person's *Svensk-amerikanska studier* (1912), and Vilhelm Berger's *Svensk-amerikanska meditationer* (1916).[266] Both Person and Berger were well-known journalists in Swedish America[267] and their respective books are collections dealing with Swedish-American topics. The articles explore a variety of subjects, such as the history and social, cultural, and political characteristics of the Swedish immigrant community, as well as its future.[268]

Vilhelm Berger also published his book *Vårt språk* at the A.B.C. in 1912.[269] It is a collection of articles on the Swedish language in America and how it

---

[261] Enander 1893.
[262] AFP, ABCMin, 11 November 1903.
[263] Sundbeck 1904a.
[264] Barton 1994, 142.
[265] Barton 1994, 142–46.
[266] Person 1912, Berger 1916.
[267] On Person see Björk 1993, and on Berger see Beijbom 1981, 64–81.
[268] See Barton 1994, 222–28 for a summary of these books.
[269] Berger 1912.

had been influenced by English. Published previously in the newspaper *Nordstjernan* (The North Star), and it was one of the first studies of the development of the Swedish language in America. Berger was clearly interested in getting the book published at the A.B.C., as he already began correspondence with the A.B.C. Board member G.N. Swan on the topic in 1910.[270]

A Swedish-American Identity at the A.B.C.

What do these relatively few publications dealing with specific Swedish-American topics tell us about the significance of the Augustana Book Concern for the construction of a Swedish-American identity? First, the time dimension should be noted, as these publications appeared during the second, post-1890 phase in the history of the Augustana Synod, corresponding to the renewed emphasis on ethnic identity visible elsewhere in the Synod as well at this time. Ludvig Holmes' first volume of poetry from 1896 was followed by several volumes of Swedish-American poetry and fiction over the next twenty-odd years. In 1900, the A.B.C. also took over the publication of the two leading cultural periodicals *Prärieblomman* and *Ungdomsvännen*, and beginning in 1904 the three books reflecting on the nature of the Swedish-American community by Sundbeck, Person, and Berger were published. The series on Swedish-American literature was established in 1914, and shortly thereafter *Ungdomsvännen* tried to raise its literary and cultural profile more than before.

Secondly, many of these books show an awareness of a distinct Swedish-Americanness, suggesting that a new set of cultural patterns had developed in America, different from those in Sweden. Ludvig Holmes' first volume of poetry from 1896, for example, is dedicated to "the Swedish-American youth," which he identifies as a group of persons with roots in both Sweden and America, and who "love" both countries equally.[271] In his poem "The Swedish-American", included in *I Västerled* from 1914, Oliver Linder speaks of an emigrant from Sweden who has become a Swedish American, "keeping the bonds of memory" with the land of his parents, but at the same time building his home in America, which has become his new homeland.[272] Holmes also pointed to the cultural developments taking place in America in an article from 1903, "Hälsning till det gamla landet" (A Greeting to the Old Country). There he described how a new Swedish culture had developed in America, which, because of its separation from Sweden, had grown particularly strong.[273] In 1913 Augustana pastor Alfred Bergin also concluded that "Swedish America is a reality" and that the Swedish Americans constituted a

---

[270] SSIRC, GNS. Letters from Vilhelm Berger to G.N. Swan, 1 December 1910, 20 April 1911, 12 September 1911.
[271] Holmes 1896, 11–12.
[272] Linder 1914, 288.
[273] Ludvig Holmes, "En hälsning till det gamla landet," *Ungdomsvännen* 1903, 20.

"respectable nation." Swedish America was not a geographic entity, Bergin continued, but was made up by a common language, religion, and press, and existed "wherever the Star Spangled Banner flew."[274]

Examples can also be found of how Swedish America was conceived of as a new nation and Swedish Americans as a new people. As discussed in chapter one, in his *Svensk-amerikanska studier* (1912) Johan Person noted how the eight-day Atlantic crossing laid the foundations for the transformation of the Swedish immigrants into "a Swedish-American people." Although not fully understood by either the Americans or the Swedes, the Swedish-American people had "a common language, common memories, common traditions, and common interests," which, according to Person, were "neither Swedish, nor American ... but a combination of both." As long as these attributes existed in America, Person concluded, a Swedish-American people would exist.[275] Person's ideas were explicitly endorsed in a preface to the book, by E.W. Olson, editor at the A.B.C. He wrote that too many uninformed accounts of Swedish America had been published, but that the A.B.C. could without hesitation recommend Person's book, as it was written by a knowledgeable Swedish American.[276]

In his work on the Swedish Americans from 1904, Carl Sundbeck had also spoken of a "Swedish-American nationality" containing "the best of both the old and the new homelands."[277] To Sundbeck, the future of the Swedish-American nationality depended on the existence of a religious movement, namely the Augustana Synod, and he identified three particularly important dimensions of the cultural work of the Augustana Synod: the Lutheran religion, the Swedish language, and Swedish cultural traditions (*svensk bildning*).[278]

Similar sentiments were expressed in an article in *Ungdomsvännen* in 1905. The author (who uses the pseudonym E-n, probably Johan Enander) argued that since the Swedish Americans had established themselves economically in America, conditions existed for the development of a Swedish-American culture, or, in his words the creation of "a new Swede." We are fortunate, he said, to be the "heirs of freedom and personal independence" as Americans, and the children of the "peculiar creative talents of the North" as Swedes. As Swedish Americans, this makes us one of the "the best equipped" cultures of the world, as we have developed a "harmonious cultural combination" of both American

---

[274] Alfred Bergin, "Hafva vi som svenskar några gemensamma lifsintressen?" *Ungdomsvännen* 1913, 86. Cf. also Vilhelm Berger, "Vår tidningspress," *Ungdomsvännen* 1913, 273–74, for similar sentiments.
[275] Person 1912, 9–10. Cf. also Svensson 1994, 109–10 for a discussion in *Prärieblomman* of how Swedish America's unique characteristics were misunderstood in Sweden.
[276] Person 1914, 5.
[277] Sundbeck 1904a, 62.
[278] Sundbeck 1904b, 17.

and Swedish traits. The American elements in this identity included independence and industriousness, while the Swedish contributions encompassed Nordic honesty, preservation, and faith.[279]

As we have seen, the Christmas magazine *God Jul* was started in 1916 to provide a specifically Swedish-American Christmas publication, and included many leading Swedish-American authors and artists as contributors. The first issue featured an article by David Nyvall, a leading educator in the Mission Covenant Church called "Bort med bindestrecket?" (Shall we do away with the hyphen?), in which Nyvall discussed the advantages of being a hyphenated Swedish-American in ways similar to those of Ludvig Holmes or Johan Person. Those who wish to do away with the hyphen will become orphans and familiar with only one culture, Nyvall argued, ignorant of either their Swedish background or of the conditions in the new country. By retaining the hyphen, however, a balance can be struck, which would allow the Swedish Americans to affirm both their American and Swedish backgrounds, much like the "harmony of a rainbow."[280]

The focus on a specific Swedish-American experience can also be seen in some of the Swedish-American fiction published by the A.B.C. One illustrative example is *I brytningstid*, the collection of short stories by Augustana pastor C.W. Andeer, published in 1904. Most of the stories take place in Swedish America, often in rural settings with the local Augustana Lutheran church playing a significant role, where life is portrayed in very positive terms. A common theme in these stories is the attraction that the good life in Swedish America has, and several stories deal with how unhappy protagonists of the stories, often Swedes or recent Swedish immigrants, find happiness in Swedish America, and become "good Swedish Americans."[281]

The story "The Swedish-American" specifically shows the superiority of Swedish America over Sweden. Arvid Norén, a Swedish-American college professor, returns to the village where his father had been a crofter before emigrating to America. He is received with great disdain by a group of Swedes, who thinks Swedish Americans are nothing but rabble. Still, Norén gets the better of his hosts, as the Swedish-American professor is highly educated, eloquently defends America and Swedish America, and speaks better French, German, Italian, and Latin than the Swedes. Before he returns to America, Norén falls in love with young Miss Anna Stjärnfält, on whose estate Norén's father had worked. Despite the differences in social status, Anna's father, Count Stjärnfält, agrees to their marriage, as he has taken a great liking

---

[279] E-n, "Den svensk-amerikanska litteraturens framtid," *Ungdomsvännen* 1905, 88.

[280] David Nyvall, "Bort med bindestrecket?", *God Jul* 1916 (n.p.). Quotation from the last line.

[281] See, for example, "Olika falla ödets lotter," "Ett löst problem," "Mörker-ljus," "En faktor i samhället," in Andeer 1904a.

to the young upstanding Swedish-American, and the young happy couple leaves for America.[282]

The American side of the Swedish-American identity was less often featured in the A.B.C. publications, but it was dealt with in some articles in *Ungdomsvännen*. In 1903, an address by Olof Olsson, the former president at Augustana, on the nature of "true Swedish-American patriotism" was published, claiming that although the Swedish Americans from a religious, cultural, and linguistic standpoint had ties to Sweden, they were without any doubt loyal to the American republic and its form of government.[283] Examples of the relatively few American topics in *Ungdomsvännen* often focus on the political or civic dimensions of American life such as articles on the Declaration of Independence, George Washington, American presidential elections, and the centennial of the American national anthem.[284]

Conclusion

Reading was important in Swedish America. As most Swedish immigrants were literate, a Swedish-American literary market developed in the United States during the second half of the nineteenth century, replete with newspapers, periodicals, books, bookstores, and publishing houses. Most books available in Swedish America were imported directly from Sweden, but a number of Swedish-American publishing houses also existed. The Swedish-American reading patterns followed the cultural and ideological divisions within the community, and there was a noticeable difference between the secular and religious spheres.

The Augustana Book Concern was one of the most important building blocks in the creation of a Swedish-American identity within the Augustana Synod. As has been noted several times, it was the largest Swedish-American publishing house as well as a major importer of Swedish-language reading materials to the U.S. The literary profile of the A.B.C. must, like the general cultural work in the Synod, be seen as one part of the interaction of religion and nationality. Obviously the immediate concerns of the Synod were religious, and they defined its ideological framework. This emphasis is also evident at the A.B.C. Almost half of its publications were directly geared toward synodical use, and the religious element was also a basic determining factor for the "non-denominational" publications.

---

[282] "Svensk-amerikanen," in Andeer 1904a.

[283] Olof Olsson, "Något om sann svensk-amerikansk patriotism," *Ungdomsvännen* 1903, 201–03.

[284] *Ungdomsvännen*: Declaration of Independence 1900, 208–10, George Washington 1904, 53, American presidential elections 1909, 118–21, American national anthem, 1914, 277.

Still, it is possible to establish a sense of Swedish-American identity at the A.B.C., and much of the reading material provided by the publisher became an important ingredient in the Swedish-American ethnic identity that emerged within the Augustana Synod. We have also seen that this process began during the years around the turn of the century, when a stronger emphasis on the Swedish element also can be found elsewhere in the Augustana Synod.

Three categories of publications have been analysed: publications for children and youth, schoolbooks, and books specifically dealing with Swedish-American conditions. The publications for children and youth cannot be said to have contributed directly towards the growth of a Swedish-American ethnic identity. Their main contribution was rather indirect, through promotion of the language and general references to Sweden and to Swedish milieus. It is instead among the latter two categories that the growth of an explicit Swedish-American identity can be more directly observed. Through the schoolbooks, Swedish, American, and Swedish-American cultural traditions were presented, and in *Församlingsskolans läsebok*, for example, Swedish-American students could read about Swedish historical figures such as Gustav Vasa and Gustavus Adolphus as well as the American presidents Washington and Lincoln. Increasingly, the schoolbooks also included materials dealing with the specific conditions and history of the Swedish immigrants and their children in America.

The concern for specific Swedish-American conditions is also clearly manifest in the third group of publications—those dealing directly with Swedish America. Stories by C.W. Andeer on life in Swedish America, accounts of Swedish-American history, reflections on what it meant to be Swedish American by leading Swedish-American authors, or high profile literary and cultural publications such as *Prärieblomman* or *Ungdomsvännen*, suggest a conscious effort on the part of the Augustana Book Concern to assist in the process of shaping a Swedish-American identity in the Augustana Synod. This meant that the opportunities for Swedish-American cultural work increased within the general cultural and religious boundaries of the Synod. It is possible to speak of a cultural opening-up that took place within the Synod, which provided for a Swedish-American identity to be formulated, an identity in which the religious and ethnic elements complemented each other.

Finally, it can be noted that the nature of the Swedish-American identity and views of Swedish America that were expressed through the publications at the A.B.C. became influential also outside the Augustana sphere of Swedish America, and, as the cultural struggles in Swedish America from the 1870s and 1880s were abating, it was Augustana's definition of what it meant to be Swedish American that was becoming dominant.[285] David Nyvall's views on the dual heritage of the Swedish Americans and the desirability of maintaining

[285] Cf. Williams 1995, 214–17.

this identity as expressed in his article in *God Jul*, as well as elsewhere,[286] is one example of similarities of opinion between the Augustana Synod and the Mission Covenant Church. Another example is the inclusion of Jakob Bonggren's *Sånger och sagor* (1902) on the A.B.C. publication list which might seem surprising, given Bonggren's earlier antagonistic position toward the Augustana Synod.[287] Still, as Anna Williams has shown, Bonggren had by the turn of the century abandoned his more radical and anti-clerical positions and had instead approached the cultural views of the Augustana Synod. The selection of poems in *Sånger och sagor* included poetry of a nature much more acceptable to the Synod.[288] The book was also favorably advertised in *Augustana*, where Bonggren was called one of the "foremost" Swedish-American authors, and his writings "true poetry" both in terms of form and contents.[289]

A final example is the cultural magazine *Valkyrian* (The Valkyrie) published from 1897 to 1909 in New York. According to Gunnar Thander, the Augustana Synod exercised a similar influence on the content of *Valkyrian*, which Thander maintains was started as a secular alternative to publications in the Augustana Synod, especially *Prärieblomman*.[290] Still, several prominent Augustana authors, such as Ludvig Holmes, C. W. Andeer, and A.A. Swärd, also contributed to *Valkyrian*,[291] and Thander concludes that although the journal sought to establish a cultural distance from the Augustana Synod, this proved difficult. The Synod affected *Valkyrian's* attempt at creating its separate Swedish-American culture and, according to Thander, instead became "willing promotor" of Augustana's view of Swedish-American culture.[292] The fact that the A.B.C. purchased *Valkyrian* in 1910 is also suggestive of the proximity between the journal and the A.B.C.[293]

---

[286] Cf. Erickson 1996, 126–28 and Barton 1994, 119–20.

[287] Williams 1991, 97–101, 167.

[288] Williams 1991, 185–87.

[289] *Augustana*, 27 November 1902. Cf. also the positive review in *Augustana*, 25 September, 1902.

[290] Thander 1996, 26–27. Ms. provided on diskette by author.

[291] Thander 1996, 115.

[292] Thander 1996, 156.

[293] AFP, ABCMin, 26 January 1910.

Chapter Five

Introduction

As noted in chapter one, myths of origin and descent and a sense of a shared history are important in the construction of both national and ethnic identities. Kathleen Conzen has argued that a fundamental part of ethnicity is the sense of "commonality that results from being part of the same extended conversation about where we came from and how we got where we are,"[1] and Orm Øverland has called attention to the role of what he calls "home-making myths" used by immigrant or ethnic groups to claim a special status in their new circumstances.[2] This means that a sense of history is an important building block in the creation of ethnic identities. Historical events and persons were appropriated by those who were defining a particular ethnic identity, and, as they were put to use in new circumstances, they were given a new meaning, specific to the context in which they were used.

Raymond Breton has given an even more precise discussion of the role of history for ethnic communities. He notes that ethnic communities need "a location in time" which entails "the reconstruction of the past and/or the creation of a mythical past." Ethnic pasts can thus be literally created or fictitious (that is, with no empirical grounding) or be reconstructions, in which the meanings of past events are redefined. Breton emphasizes the need to examine the degree to which ethnic pasts are created or recreated, as well as the importance of examining the content of the ethnic pasts. Questions of particular importance for the content of the past include whether it pertains to the country of origin or to the receiving country and whether it emphasizes the negative or the positive experiences of the group. Finally, Breton also emphasizes the cultural competition going on between ethnic groups and the dominant host culture or segments of it.[3]

An important part of the construction of an ethnic identity in every ethnic group in the United States was to establish and write the group's own history in the new land. This was not unique to the Swedish Americans, but something which characterized not only ethnic groups in America, but also, as

[1] Conzen 1995, 49.
[2] Øverland 1996, 2.
[3] Breton 1992, 7–8.

184

noted in chapter one, the new American republic as a whole, where the definition of what really constituted American history was an important part of the formation of an American national identity in the nineteenth century.[4]

On one level this process can be observed through the numerous books that have been published by members of the ethnic group about themselves, or by the creation of societies devoted to the history of the ethnic group ("organizations in search of the past" as Harald Runblom has called them[5]). Creating a sense of history in a new environment and land became a way of legitimating the group's status vis-à-vis both the Anglo-American host society and other immigrant and ethnic groups, with whom interaction and often competition took place.

The interest in documenting the immigrant group's history in the new land can be seen in the Augustana Synod as early as in the first decade after the founding of the denomination when a "Committee for Historical Documents" was active in the Synod, collecting "historical information on our diverse parishes and settlements, of value to the history of our Synod." The committee had begun its work as early as 1866,[6] with Pastor Erik Norelius as the driving force. At the synodical meeting in Moline, Illinois, in 1869, Norelius was appointed "historiographer" of the Synod.[7] And, as we have seen in chapter four, Norelius eventually wrote a comprehensive two-volume study of Swedish Lutheran settlements in the U.S. which in great detail discusses religious and general conditions among the Swedish immigrants connected with the Augustana synod, and a biography of T.N. Hasselquist. Norelius also contributed historical articles to *Prärieblomman*.[8]

Jubilees were particularly well suited occasions for historical retrospectives: the publications in connection with the fiftieth anniversary of the Augustana Synod in 1910 serve as a good illustration of this.[9]

In this chapter, the process by which Swedish Americans in the Augustana Synod fashioned a past for themselves and its significance for the construction of their identity will be discussed. As the Augustana Swedish Americans set out to construct a Swedish-American historical tradition, they were able to draw on three main sources for their history, namely those of Sweden, the United States, and of Swedish America. Taken by themselves, these historic traditions could be seen as referring to the separate histories of Sweden, the U.S., and Swedish America. By using a combination and selection of these

[4] Cf. Commager 1967, 3–27, Appelby, Hunt & Jacob, chapter 3.
[5] Norman & Runblom 1988a, 206.
[6] Referat 1867, 9.
[7] Referat 1869, 20.
[8] Norelius 1891, Norelius 1900, Norelius 1916. Erik Norelius, "Den första svenska invandringen till Förenta Staterna," *Prärieblomman*, 1900, 1 (1899), Norelius "Nybyggarelif. Teckningar från Minnesotas tidigare dagar," *Prärieblomman,* 1903, 3 (1902).
[9] Augustana History 1910, Minnesskrift 1910, Minnen 1911.

histories, however, the leaders of the ethnic group created a new historical tradition, which we can call a Swedish-American history. This history was specific to the needs of the Swedish immigrants and their children in the U.S. and must thus be seen from the American and Swedish-American context in which it was created and presented. In that sense, it was a history created by the needs of the present, to use the phrase of Chapman, McDonald, and Tonkin.

The questions that will be addressed include: What did the version of the past as presented by the Augustana Swedish Americans look like? Who were the heroes and heroines? Which historical persons and events were singled out? What aspects of the past were put to use in the Augustana Synod's version of a Swedish-American history?

It is not possible to examine in detail all the expressions of an historical awareness that developed within the Augustana Synod. Instead, certain important dimensions of the historical tradition that emerged within the Synod will be discussed. One important source will be materials from historical celebrations and anniversaries at Augustana College and elsewhere. Another important source will be selected materials dealing with historical topics from the leading Augustana literary and cultural publications *Prärieblomman* and *Ungdomsvännen*. Both these publications included a number of historical and biographical articles which, taken together, will present a good overview of the Synod's Swedish-American history. The historical writings of the leading Swedish-American author and opinion-maker Johan Enander is also considered separately, since Enander was the leading historical ideologue in the Synod and in Swedish America.

The Early Presence in America

One important dimension of the Swedish-American historical tradition was the establishment of an early presence for Swedes in America. Several scholars have emphasized the fact, that since the United States in the nineteenth century was a young nation, American nationalism as it took shape during the country's first century was an "ideological construct" in which a set of national heroes was necessary for the creation and maintenance of American nationalism.[10] In this context, the early pilgrims, the colonists, or the founding fathers of the Republic emerged as vital historical figures, and individuals such as George Washington and Thomas Jefferson became "patriot heroes" in American nationalism of the nineteenth century.[11] Beginning in the final decades of

[10] Zelinsky 1988, 16.
[11] Karsten 1978, chapter 5.

the nineteenth century, a number of organizations which attached significance to connections with early American history, were founded. Such groups included the Colonial Dames of America, the Society of Mayflower Descendants, the Sons of the American Revolution, and the Daughters of the American Revolution.[12] As David Lowenthal has recently argued, this need for "being first" was not unique to the United States, although he, too, underscores its importance for "reborn nations," in which he includes the United States.[13]

Immigrant groups also sensed this need to find early roots in what was to become the United States. This phenomenon has been noted by Joshua Fishman and Vladimir Nahirny who maintain that the ethnic groups in this way sought to establish a "bilateral" line of descent to both the American colonial past as well as to their own "Old Country." As examples of "the colonial connection" they cite various immigrant groups who have discovered their respective ancestors "among the contemporaries of John Smith, George Washington, and Abraham Lincoln."[14] To borrow a contemporary Canadian term, one can say that this represents an attempt by the ethnics to become "charter peoples" of the American republic instead of being perceived as "immigrants," trying to measure themselves against the original British cultural and political tradition of the New England colonists.

New Sweden

To the Swedes, the most important aspect of their colonial history was the New Sweden colony on the Delaware, which Sweden maintained between 1638 and 1655 and which left a rather small imprint on subsequent American history. The opportunity to put the New Sweden colony to use as a means of establishing an early presence in the New World was not lost on the nineteenth-century Swedish immigrants in America. Although links between the Swedes on the Delaware in the mid-seventeenth century and the Swedish Americans some two centuries later were virtually non-existent, nineteenth-century Swedes in America did their best to portray the New Sweden colonists as their forerunners, and all the virtues that could be associated with the colonists could then, by implication, be carried over to the immigrants in the nineteenth century. In this view, Swedish colonists had been on American soil, showing the beginnings of an organized Swedish-American society, a mere eighteen years after the landing of the *Mayflower*.

One of the earliest instances of the colony's use in the construction of a

---

[12] Kammen 1991, 218. Cf. also Davies 1955.
[13] Lowenthal 1996, 173–91.
[14] Fishman & Nahirny, 1966, 350.

Swedish-American history was a major celebration of the 250th anniversary of its founding, held in September 1888 in Minneapolis.[15] It is telling that the celebrations took place in Minneapolis, a rapidly growing center for nineteenth-century Swedish Americans, and not at the original site in Delaware. The celebration included a parade, which attracted some 15,000 persons, as well as a number of prominent speakers from different segments of the Swedish-American community, religious and secular alike, and was characterized as the most grandiose Swedish-American celebration to date.[16]

One of the main thrusts of the celebration was to establish the fact that the Swedes had been a colonial people in America. Hans Mattson, one of the best-known Swedes in Minnesota, who served as a Colonel in the Union army in the Civil War and Secretary for the Minnesota State Board of Immigration, phrased it well in his speech, stating that a few colonial peoples—the English, the Dutch, the Swedes, the Scotch, and the French—had settled the New World and had all contributed to its growth. "History" had, however, been "partial" in favor of the English, leaving the other peoples "forgotten or ignored," making it urgent to remedy this historical error by letting the Swedes assume their rightful place in American history.[17]

The Augustana Synod was also represented at this celebration. In the parade that preceded the speeches, the Synod delegation marched in the second division, and the invocation at the meeting was given by T.N. Hasselquist, the president of the college and seminary in Rock Island. Other speakers included such well-known Augustana Synod representatives as C.A. Swensson, president of Bethany College, and Johan Enander. In his speech, the latter emphasized two legacies of the New Sweden colony—one religious and one political. He maintained that the Swedish colonists led a life "completely governed by Christianity" and that they had also proved instrumental in bringing Christianity to the Indians in the area. From a political point of view, the Swedish immigrants brought a commitment to "freedom" to America. Most notably, Enander maintained, there was personal freedom—and absence from slavery—in the colony, showing that the Swedes "were ahead of their times" on this important issue, which would render them "eternal honor."[18]

Both Enander and C.A. Swensson tried to establish a connection between the New Sweden Colony and the Swedish-American community of the late nineteenth century. Enander maintained that since the establishment of the colony, Swedish immigration to the United States "has never completely stopped,"[19] and Swensson made a connection between the past and the present

[15] For an account of this celebration, see Blanck 1988, 5–20.
[16] Söderström 1899, 319.
[17] Mattson 1888, 4–5.
[18] Mattson 1888, 26–27.
[19] Mattson 1888, 25.

by calling the present celebration a "wedding occasion" in which "the first two hundred and fifty years of Swedish-American history" had "been united with bonds of love and memory to the common history of the American nation."[20] This connection also meant that parallels between the New Sweden colonists and their compatriots of 250 years later could be drawn. Both groups were deeply religious, and both were committed to the ideals of freedom. For example, just as the Swedish colonists abhorred slavery, Enander exclaimed, the nineteenth-century Swedish immigrants answered to the call to defend the cause of freedom in the Civil War in which "thousands" of Swedes "bled and died heroic deaths."[21]

New Sweden's centrality to the Swedish-American history emerging in the Augustana Synod can also be seen in the cultural and literary publications *Ungdomsvännen* and *Prärieblomman*. In *Ungdomsvännen*, the New Sweden colony was the topic for a series of no less than 19 articles published between 1901 and 1903 called "The Swedes on the Delaware." The author of these articles was Anders Schön, whom we have already met as the editor of *Prärieblomman* and a close collaborator of Johan Enander, and clearly anchored within the Augustana sphere in Swedish America.[22] In these articles a very positive account of the colony is given, emphasizing the colony's good contacts with the Indians, the spread of Christianity to the Indian community, and the colony's general peaceful, religious, and politically stable development.[23] *Prärieblomman* also dealt with the topic several times, including biographical articles about Governor Johan Printz and his wife, the latter subtitled "a profile of a woman from seventeenth-century Swedish America."[24]

Enander's role in connection with the New Sweden colony was vital. Spurred by the American centennial in 1876, Enander published a series of articles in his newspaper *Hemlandet* that presented American history to the newspaper's Swedish readership.[25] The articles were also printed in a book called *Förenta Staternas historia utarbetad för den svenska befolkningen i Amerika* (The History of the United States, Written for the Swedish Population in America), brought out by Enander's own publishing house between 1874 and 1877. In the section of the book dealing with the history of the thirteen colonies from 1607, the New Sweden colony is featured prominently. The colony receives almost twice as much attention as Enander gives to the history of Pennsylvania, and, excepting a fairly lengthy treatment of the Virginia and

---

[20] Mattson 1888, 37.

[21] Mattson 1888, 28.

[22] Svensson 1994, 34–36.

[23] "Svenskarna i Delaware," *Ungdomsvännen*, 1901 (8 articles), 1902 (8), and 1903 (3).

[24] Amandus Johnson, "Johan Printz. Nya Sveriges guvernör 1643–1653," *Prärieblomman*, 1912, 12 (1911); Anders Schön, "Fru Anna på Printzhof. En kvinnoprofil från 1600–talets Svensk-Amerika," *Prärieblomman*, 1903, 3 (1902).

[25] Beijbom 1980, 265.

the New England colonies, the New Sweden colony is the first one discussed, before, for example, Pennsylvania, Maryland, and the Carolinas.[26] Enander describes the life of the New Sweden colony in very positive terms, emphasizing the friendly relations with the Indians and the Christian and the politically stable nature of life in New Sweden,[27] themes that would be repeated many times during the years to come.

The person who perhaps did most to establish the colony's position in Swedish-American historiography was Amandus Johnson who cemented the position of the colony's history in Swedish America and the historical literature. There was a direct continuity between Enander and Johnson, as the latter's interest in New Sweden had been awakened by a lecture Enander gave that Johnson had attended in 1903 at Gustavus Adolphus College. This spurred him to on become an historian, publishing widely on the history of the colony—his *The Swedish Settlements on the Delaware* appeared in 1911—as well as making him the prime mover behind the American Swedish Historical Museum in Philadelphia.[28]

One consequence of establishing the colonial status of the Swedes was the opinion that the colony should be viewed as one of the earliest example in the creation of a longer, continuous Swedish-American historical context, extending into the present. For example, Erik Norelius, the official Augustana historiographer, explicitly included the Delaware colony in his conception of Swedish-American history in an article in *Prärieblomman* from 1900, in which he wrote that Swedish immigrants were sometimes called "greenhorns and aliens,"—a characterization that was incorrect since the Swedes could "point back to 1638 and answer that the first New England colonists came to this country only 18 years before the first Swedish colonists."[29] It is also interesting to note that in 1914 and 1915 the Augustana Synod actually discussed purchasing the land at the site of landing in Delaware in order to erect a monument, a project which, however, came to naught as the price asked was considered too high.[30]

Another example of placing the Delaware colony in a longer Swedish-American historical tradition comes from 1906 when the recently founded organization *Svensk-Amerikanska Historiska Sällskapet* (The Swedish-American Historical Society) had its first annual meeting in Chicago. Although not exclusively a group based on the Augustana Synod, a number of leading persons from the Synod were active members in the society. Present at the meet-

---

[26] Enander, 1877, 3–45.
[27] Enander 1877, 27–32.
[28] Beijbom 1980, 276–77.
[29] Erik Norelius, "Den första svenska invandringen till Förenta Staterna," *Prärieblomman*, 1900, 1 (1899), 37.
[30] Referat 1914, 163 & 1915, 171.

ing in 1905 when the organization was founded were, for example, Pastor L. G. Abrahamsson, Gustav Andreen, and Anders Schön. The first president of the group was, significantly enough, Johan Enander.[31] In his address at the meeting in 1906, the Secretary Anders Schön extended Swedish-American history to include not only the era of the nineteenth-century immigrants, but also their compatriots from the seventeenth century. He noted that the Society met on the day marking the 268th anniversary of the Swedish landing in Delaware, and said that one of the main tasks for the Swedish Americans was to learn to know their history and themselves better, a history which had already begun during America's era of colonization.[32] Another important task for this newly founded Society was also, according to Schön, to erect memorials at "important Swedish-American sites," defined not only as such nineteenth-century pioneer settlements as Pine Lake, Wisconsin, and Bishop Hill, Illinois, but which were also extended chronologically and geographically to include Delaware.[33]

The Vikings

Another important dimension in the creation of a Swedish-American history was the Viking journeys to, and supposed settlements in, North America in the eleventh century. Here, the self-styled cultural leadership did its best to promote and prove that the Vikings had indeed been the first Europeans in the New World, thus giving the Swedes (as well as other Scandinavians) a special birthright in America. This was an attempt not only to bring the Swedish immigrants up to the same level as the New England colonists, whom the Swedish immigrant cultural leadership clearly perceived as a core group of the American republic, but to go actually beyond the colonial history and claim the right of discovery for at least the Scandinavians. Although the Viking journeys did indeed become an important ingredient in Swedish-American history, the controversy surrounding the nature of the settlements and the lack of physical evidence meant that it was probably more difficult to advance the case of the Vikings than of the New Sweden colony. This did not, as we shall see, deter Swedish Americans and Scandinavian Americans from putting the Vikings to use.

Enander was one of the main proponents of these ideas. He maintained that the American notion of freedom had come to the New World not only via the New England colonists, but that its origin was instead in Scandinavia. It had migrated from Scandinavia to England through the Vikings in Normandy and

[31] Swan 1915, 45–46.
[32] Year-book 1905–07, 32 and 36.
[33] Year-book 1905–07, 44.

William the Conqueror. Therefore, Enander maintained "every attempt to make the 4th of July an exclusively Anglo-American holiday, when the deeds of the English puritans and the descendants of the cavaliers are honored, is an ignorance of justice, of history's witness."[34]

One high point in the Viking cult occurred in 1893, after the Columbian Exposition opened in Chicago, commemorating the 400th anniversary of Columbus' landing in the western hemisphere, when the A.B.C. timely enough published a book by Enander called *Nordmännen i Amerika eller Amerikas upptäckt* (The Norsemen in America or The Discovery of America).[35] The book gives a detailed description of the arrival of the Vikings and the subsequent settlements and takes issue with "Anglo-American" scholars who have disputed the Viking presence in America. In the conclusion, Enander laments the fact that his views have not been accepted and attributes this to the strong influence of the Italians in the U.S. and to the Pope who had declared "that the saint-like Columbus, inspired by the Holy Ghost and protected by the Virgin Mary," was the first European to reach America, which has resulted in a situation where it is "considered High Treason" to voice dissenting opinions. However, the "historic truth" lives on and long after the speeches to Columbus have been forgotten, the fact will remain "that the Norsemen discovered America and founded lasting colonies there 500 years before Columbus saw the light of day."[36] The book was reviewed favorably in *Augustana,* which called it "thorough" and "correct", recommending it for general reading.[37]

It is interesting to note that Enander is not only arguing the case for the early Viking presence, which in his view can be seen as "Swedish," but that he also places the issue in a contemporary context. Enander's attacks on the Italian Americans should be seen as one way in which the Swedish Americans were trying to establish superiority over another immigrant group in America, with which the Swedish Americans had to compete for economic and political influence. Enander's anti-Catholicism is not surprising, given both the strong anti-Catholic feelings in the Augustana Synod and in the United States in general at the time.[38]

Another example of framing the issue of the Viking landings in North America in contemporary terms comes from the Swedish-American educator J.S. Carlson, also associated with the Augustana Synod, and an active participant in Swedish-American cultural life around the turn of the century. Born in

---

[34] Enander 1892a, 261.

[35] Enander 1893.

[36] Enander 1893, 65–66.

[37] *Augustana,* 8 June 1893.

[38] For anti-Catholicism in the Augustana Synod from the period, see *Augustana* 7 April 1892, 23 June 1892, 15 December 1892, and 29 June 1893.

Sweden but educated at Augustana and Gustavus Adolphus Colleges, he became professor of Scandinavian languages at the University of Minnesota in the 1880s.[39] In 1908, a year after leaving his professorship at Minnesota, Carlson published a booklet called *Amerikas siste svensk* (America's Last Swede), based on a speech he had delivered on this topic in Minneapolis.[40] In it Carlson looks into the future, invoking the image of the last Swede in America, whom he defined as the last Swedish American interested in preserving a sense of Swedishness in the country. The last Swede in America reflects on the long and glorious history of his compatriots in the New World and on a history that spans almost a millenium, from the time of the arrival of the Vikings up to the present Swedish immigrants.

Like Enander before him, Carlson also uses the Vikings as an opportunity to comment on contemporary matters. Indeed, it might be difficult to decide which was more important to Carlson, to try to set the historical record straight or to show the superiority of the Swedish immigrant group, and Carlson seems to go further than Enander in his views.[41]

Carlson claims that as the "Nordic dragon ships set sails for the west" and landed in America, "the first white, a Nordic Viking, stepped on the shores of America; and the first foreign language to reach the ears of the Indians was the language of the North." He thunders: "Mark this, you smug Briton, you proud son of England, you who have never been first at anything, except pilfering that which others have discovered" and continues "[T]he birthright to the discovery of America is not yours; you cannot get it even by bribing the Italian, because he himself has borrowed it. The birthright to the discovery of America belongs to the North and to no one else."

Carlson goes one step beyond Enander, in that he not only attacks the Italians, but also criticizes the English, as he perceived the movement to Americanize immigrants in America as essentially the same as imposing English customs and values on the immigrant community.[42] An interesting parallel can be found in Anders Schön's discussion of the New Sweden colony in 1906, in which he says that the Swedish colonists came to America not in pursuit of freedom, but to rather to "transplant that freedom which they and their fathers had won themselves" in Sweden. Moreover, Schön states, they did not seek to inflict their religious beliefs on other early Americans, immigrants and natives alike, as had the Puritans at Plymouth Rock, who came to America seeking freedom but who were "spiritually narrow-minded" in imposing their religion on others.[43]

[39] Kastrup 1975, 413.
[40] Carlson, 1908.
[41] The following is based on Carlson 1908, 12.
[42] Hasselmo 1974, 52–54.
[43] Year-book 1905–07, 36–37.

The Viking tradition in America has remained strong up until the present time. The controversy over the so-called rune stone in Alexandria, Minnesota, which was discovered in 1898 and was claimed to have been erected in 1362 by Vikings on a mission from the king of Sweden and Norway, is an example of the longevity of the Viking heritage. Although it was declared to be a forgery immediately by prominent American and European scholars at the time, and by subsequent generations of scholars,[44] it has continued to have a great appeal to generations of Swedish and Scandinavian Americans, suggesting that the Vikings are still an important ingredient in Swedish- and Scandinavian-American identities.

Culture Heroes

The emphasis on the contributions by significant Swedish Americans to American history or by Swedes to world history was another characteristic of the creation of a Swedish-American history. Willi Paul Adams has called attention to what he terms the "culture-heroes" of different ethnic groups. They were not only important to the group itself but were also widely recognized by American society at large. "With or without their approval," Adams continues, "they are claimed by the group and held up to society at large as proof of its collective ability, its contribution to building America, and so forth."[45]

Given the different and sometimes competing cultural segments of the Swedish-American community, it seems likely to assume that the choice of "culture-heroes" was not uncontested. Just as there was a debate on what kind of literature should be read in Swedish America, the choice of historical heroes to represent the groups must have been equally important. Although little research has been done on these questions, the discussion of the statue of Linnaeus that was erected in Chicago in 1891 (see chapter two), provides one example of a discussion of a suitable historical candidate for the Swedish-American community.

An examination of specific culture heroes in the Augustana Synod shows that two persons were particularly important, namely the Swedish-born nineteenth-century engineer John Ericsson and King Gustavus Adolphus. They will be discused in the following sections.

John Ericsson

John Ericsson came to America in 1839. Ericsson had been a successful engineer who before his arrival in the U.S. had worked in the construction of canals

---

[44] Cf. Wahlgren 1958 and Blegen 1968.
[45] Adams 1985, 153.

in Sweden, and in building locomotives in Great Britain. During the Civil War his services were enlisted by the North. He designed a ship, the *Monitor*, which was put into battle against the Confederate *Merrimac* at the Battle of Hampton Roads in 1862, where it prevented the destruction of the Union fleet.[46] His ties to organized Swedish America were weak. It was instead the Swedish-American leadership who, in the manner suggested by Willi Paul Adams, claimed him as a symbol of the group, arguing that a Swede in a very significant way had contributed to the outcome of the Civil War. In 1926, following a decade-long fund raising campaign, a commemorative statue of John Ericsson was erected near the Lincoln Memorial in Washington, D.C., and was unveiled in a ceremony in the presence of the Swedish Crown Prince and President Coolidge, during which the president spoke in highly congratulatory terms of both Ericsson and Swedish Americans in general.[47] Moreover, the symbol of John Ericsson was exploited politically, at least in Illinois, where in the mid-1890s a Swedish-American Republican League was formed, using Ericsson as a symbol. This organization sought to ensure that the traditional Swedish support for the Republican party continue, at a time when Swedish voters had begun to be attracted by populist and Democratic political ideas.[48]

Ericsson was also a major figure within the Augustana Swedish-American cultural sphere, and a common historical topic in the Synod's two leading cultural publications *Prärieblomman* and *Ungdomsvännen*. In one article by Ernst Zetterstrand in *Prärieblomman* in 1904, Ericsson was labeled "a typical Swedish American,"[49] and the calendar also included several other articles on Ericsson and/or the Battle of Hampton Roads.[50] *Ungdomsvännen* carried a serialized biography of Ericsson in 1903, published an account of the Battle of Hampton Roads in 1911, and described the construction of the *Monitor* in 1912.[51] In 1893, *Augustana* reprinted a speech by the Augustana minister C.A. Blomgren, which talked about "great memories" providing inspiration to the Swedish Americans. One such memory dealt with the defense of the American union and the abolition of slavery, in both of which, Blomgren maintains, Ericsson was of crucial importance. Blomgren also draws a parallel between Ericsson's role for the United States and that of Gustavus Adolphus and Axel

---

[46] "John Ericsson," in Nationalencyklopedin 1991, 569.

[47] Proceedings 1926, Norman & Runblom 1988, 208.

[48] Proceedings 1896–97.

[49] Ernst A. Zetterstrand, "John Ericsson. En karekteristik af den store uppfinnaren," *Prärieblomman*, 1904, 4 (1903), 49.

[50] Hjalmar Edgren, "Sjöstriden på Hampton Roads 1862," *Prärieblomman*, 1903, 3 (1902); Wilhelm Reslow, "Monitor," *Prärieblomman*, 1905, 5 (1904); E.W. Olson, "John Ericsson March," *Prärieblomman*, 1907, 7 (1906); Jakob Bonggren, "John Ericsson," *Prärieblomman*, 1913, 13 (1912).

[51] "John Erickson," *Ungdomsvännen*, 1903, 249–50; "Sjöstriden på Hampton Roads," *Ungdomsvännen*, 1911, 241–44; "Huru Ericssons Monitor kom till," *Ungdomsvännen*, 1912, 89–93.

Oxenstierna for seventeenth-century Europe, stating that "A son of Svea" emerged to save the U.S., "like Gustavus Adolphus and Oxenstierna came forth and saved Europe," concluding that "in the Pantheon of America...his picture will be placed among the foremost, and the jubilations of the people will be mixed with the waves of the Atlantic and the Pacific in a song of praise of the greatest Swede in the New World."[52]

At Augustana College, the life of John Ericsson was celebrated several times. The 100th anniversary of Ericsson's birth was celebrated on July 24th, 1903. President Andreen spoke about "The life and significance of John Ericsson for us Swedes and for our native country," and Swedish folk songs were sung and 24 young girls performed a flag exercise.[53] When the 50th anniversary of the Battle of Hampton Roads was marked in March 1912, *Augustana* commented that it was an important date for the United States in general, and for "us Swedish-Americans in particular," and that it was "appropriate for us Swedes to honor a man whose life lends credit to Swedes wherever they live and work."[54] The 1906 article in the Augustana student newspaper about "Patriotism as Augustana," already referred to in chapter three, promoted a specific Swedish-American patriotism at the school, and held up John Ericsson as an example of this, who in the author's opinion was "a poor Swede [and] a poor American, [but] a splendid Swedish-American!"[55]

Gustavus Adolphus

The Swedish king Gustavus Adolphus occupied a special position at Augustana College, and throughout the years a number of celebrations in his memory took place. In his person the Augustana Swedish Americans could combine both the religious and ethnic elements of their identity, as they celebrated him both as a Lutheran and as a Swede. In fact, in several instances the Gustavus Adolphus celebration was called a reformation festivity. Because November 6th was the death date of the king, most of the celebrations at Augustana were held as close as possible to that date. This emphasis on Gustavus Adolphus was also paralleled in Sweden during the late nineteenth century, especially in conjunction with the 250th anniversary of the king's death in 1882. The king's significance for maintaining Lutheranism in Sweden and for defending Protestantism in Europe was emphasized by contemporary historians, as was the king's and Sweden's function as a Germanic barrier towards Russia.[56]

[52] *Augustana*, 10 October 1895.
[53] *Augustana*, 30 July 1903.
[54] *Augustana*, 14 March 1912.
[55] Augustana *Observer*, February 1906.
[56] Ordesson 1992, 100–05.

In 1891, the Gustavus Adolphus celebration was held on November 5. Johan Enander, who had recently assumed the professorship of Swedish, spoke on his view of Gustavus Adolphus in world history, outlining his intervention in the Thirty Years War, his role as a man of education (the university in Tartu in Estonia was founded during Gustavus' reign), and his interest in America's position in the development of civilization, where "a home for all poor and freedom loving persons" was eventually created (plans for the New Sweden Colony were made during his reign). Enander concluded that the king's life was an example of the life of a true Christian.[57]

Two years later, the day was celebrated on November 6, and *Augustana* reminded its readers that this date was of importance "to us as Swedes and Lutherans." The celebration took place in the afternoon with speeches about Gustavus Adolphus in both Swedish and English, and in the evening a "successful" concert was held.[58] In 1901, a Reformation festival was held in November in conjunction with the visit of Bishop von Schéele. References to Gustavus Adolphus do not seem to have been specifically included in the program. Still, the focus on the Reformation was sure to bring the king's name to mind. In addition, geology professor J.A. Udden spoke on the topic of "Augustana—the Center of Swedish-American Culture.[59] The celebration in 1902 included a speech in Swedish by seminary professor Nils Forsander on "the first and the most important Swedish Christian heroes," who, according to Forsander, were Ansgar (the first missionary to Sweden), and Gustavus Adolphus, respectively.[60]

In 1907, it had been 275 years since the king fell at the Battle of Lützen, and preparations were underway at Augustana for a commemoration. Johan Enander, who by now was both aging and physically weak, had heard of the plans for the festivity, and sent President Andreen several memorial medallions coined in Sweden for the occasion, and asked to be notified of the program for the celebration.[61] Held in the Augustana chapel, the program marked the anniversary of a king who died for "faith and freedom of thought," as the report in *Augustana* put it. As in 1902, seminary professor Nils Forsander spoke in Swedish on the topic "Our most glorious memory" and I.M. Anderson addressed the topic "Gustavus Adolphus. Why Honor Him?" in English.[62] The following year Professor Oscar Montelius, a leading Swedish archaelogist who was visiting the campus, spoke on the topic of Sweden during the Viking

[57] *Augustana*, 5 November 1891 and 12 November 1891.
[58] *Augustana*, 16 November 1893.
[59] *Augustana*, 21 November 1901.
[60] *Augustana*, 6 November 1902.
[61] ACL, GAP. Letters from Johan Enander to Gustav Andreen, 18 and 27 October 1907.
[62] *Augustana*, 14 November 1907.

Age on November 6, "Gustavus Adolphus Day" as *Augustana* now called it.[63]

The ethnic and religious aspects of celebrating Gustavus Adolphus were expressed in 1915. *Augustana* argued for the continued celebration of Gustavus Adolphus, and stated that by remembering the king, Swedish Americans would combined a pride in their "ancestral faith" with "the glorious history, language, and literature" of our ancestral country.[64] The celebration at Augustana College, which *Augustana* called "a commemoration of our ancestry," also combined religion with ethnicity, as hymns were sung and G.N. Swan spoke on Tegnér and *Fritiofs saga*.[65]

Even when formal celebrations did not take place, comments and articles about Gustavus Adolphus were often published in Augustana publications during the month of November. In 1900, for example, Gustaf N. Swan presented the king to readers of *Augustana*, concluding that every Swede in Sweden is familiar with the life of the king through the public schools, and that it ought to be a "happy duty" (*kär plikt*) for the Swedish-American youth to read about him as well. "Who can read about his life without feeling proud to be Swedish?" he asked.[66] A 1909 editorial comment in *Augustana* maintained that the 6th of November was a day that should be celebrated, preferably with the same patriotism that American holidays were marked. The paper linked Gustavus Adolphus and Lincoln by suggesting that the king fought for the same principles as the president, namely political freedom and freedom of thought.[67] In its comment in 1913, *Augustana* emphasized the fact that the power of the Pope had diminished as a result of Gustavus' actions, and also added that it ought to be of great interest to the Swedish people that the king's memory was still highly regarded by Swedish Americans.[68]

The significance of the Gustavus Adolphus celebrations is also shown in a booklet of "dialogues and monologues" for youth groups in the Augustana Synod, published by Augustana pastor and author C.W. Andeer in 1904. In a dialogue concerning the reasons why Swedish Americans ought to celebrate the king, Person A asks why he as an American should celebrate a Swedish king. The answer given by Person B is that Gustavus is celebrated because of his historical significance in defending freedom of religion and the Protestant cause during the Thirty Years War. Moreover, in a vein similar to the editorial comment in *Augustana* from 1909, Person B also links Gustavus Adolphus and his grandfather, the sixteenth-century king Gustav Vasa, to prominent

[63] *Augustana*, 19 November 1908.
[64] *Augustana*, 4 November 1915.
[65] *Augustana*, 11 November 1915. Cf. also SSIRC, GNS, Letter from Jules Mauritzson to G.N. Swan, 16 October 1915.
[66] *Augustana*, 8 November 1900.
[67] *Augustana*, 4 November 1909.
[68] *Augustana*, 30 October 1913.

American historical persons, by saying that Gustav Vasa fought for political freedom for Sweden in the same way as George Washington and Abraham Lincoln advocated the same principles for the United States. Gustavus Adolphus, however, went even further in espousing the cause of religious freedom, which makes him even more worthy of celebrations.[69]

By November 1915, *Augustana* could thus happily conclude that "Gustavus Adolphus days" were celebrated more and more throughout the Augustana Synod, including in its congregations and in its youth groups. These celebrations contributed both towards the preservation of a "great national memory" in Swedish America, as well as an appreciation of "what we as a people have in common." The two most important elements in this Swedish-American commonality which, according to *Augustana*, served to "hold us together as a people" were, again, "our ancestral faith," to which Gustavus Adolphus dedicated his life, and "the glorious history, literature, and language of our ancestral country."[70]

Two leading culture heroes in the Augustana Synod were thus John Ericsson and Gustavus Adolphus. John Ericsson represented a Swede who had played an important part in American history, while Gustavus Adolphus' significance rested with his role as a defender of Lutheran religion. By celebrating the lives of these individuals, the ethnic and religious elements of the Synod's identity were combined. It also meant that the Augustana Swedish Americans appropriated the positive characteristics ascribed to two individuals with no immediate connections to the Synod, thus making John Ericsson and Gustavus Adolphus a part of their Swedish-American identity.

Founders Day and the Golden Anniversary

Celebrations which focused more specifically on the history of the ethnic group itself provide yet another way of examining the growth of a sense of history among the Swedish Americans. At Augustana a commemoration of what was called Founders Day took place during a few years in the beginning of the first decade of this century, and in 1910 the Synod observed its fiftieth anniversary in a week-long celebration. Both Founders Day and the fiftieth anniversary of 1910 provided the Augustana Swedish Americans with opportunities to reflect on their characteristics and history in America.

[69] Andeer 1904b, 39–41.
[70] *Augustana*, 4 November 1915.

Founders Day

In March of 1901, the student association Svenska Vitterhetssällskapet at Augustana College suggested that a "Swedish Day" should be observed at the school. It was argued that it was "only fair that we...have a Swedish day of such nature," as Washington's birthday was celebrated on February 22. It was also suggested that May 1 would be an appropriate date for such a day.[71] The matter was discussed by the Board of Directors, and in May 1901 it was announced that the student proposal had been granted.[72] When the first day was celebrated the following year, it was called Founders Day to honor the founders of the Synod, college, and seminary, and was, according to President Andreen to be marked every April 27 henceforth. This would be an opportunity, said Andreen, to "build our own traditions, to celebrate the arrival of spring in a dignified manner, and to not forget the most important ingredient from the May celebrations in Sweden, the white student cap."[73] Andreen asserted that this day would be Swedish in nature, regardless of the language used, as the founders of the school and Synod were Swedish, and would help fulfil "the mission God has given us as a Swedish-American people in the New World."[74]

The first Founders Day events took place at the end of April 1902, and lasted from a Thursday evening until Sunday afternoon. The main focus of this celebration was on the history of the Augustana Synod and on the early founding fathers, and included speeches by Synod leaders, visitors, singing, and a visit "by street car" to the graves of former presidents T.N. Hasselquist and Olof Olsson at Riverside Cemetery in Moline. Several hundred persons were in attendance.[75]

The main speech was delivered by Erik Norelius, one of the founding fathers from 1860 who was often called the patriarch of the Augustana Synod, and dealt with the events that led up to the founding of the Synod. In Norelius' estimation, the decision to break with the Synod of Northern Illinois in 1860 and among other things, to establish the Augustana Seminary, was a "declaration of independence" which was necessary to "save the faith and the creed and to make the Swedish-American cultural development (*den svensk-amerikanska odlingen*)" possible.[76] A festive poem was then read by Ludvig

---

[71] ACL, CFC, Augustana College Faculty Minutes, 8 February 1901. Cf. also Augustana, 7 March 1901.

[72] *Augustana*, 30 May 1901.

[73] *Augustana*, 27 February 1902.

[74] *Augustana*, 27 February 1902.

[75] "Grundläggarnes dag vid Augustana College och Teologiska Seminarium," *Augustana*, 1 May 1902.

[76] *Augustana*, 24 April 1902.

Holmes,[77] which, according to Carl Sundbeck who attended the celebration, was equal to the poetry of Johan Olov Wallin.[78]

As a member of the Patriotic Student Association (*Fosterländska student-förbundet*) in Uppsala, Sundbeck also received a delegation of Augustana students who sent back a greeting to Sweden in poetic form. In it, the old homeland is assured that the Swedish Americans, even those "born and raised under the Star Spangled Banner" still use the Swedish language, still love the music of the north, and still have not "sold" their "inheritance" and "childhood faith" for the "gold of a foreign land."[79]

A week after this celebration, *Augustana* echoed opinions similar to those of Erik Norelius, emphasizing the "independent men" who formed the Synod and suggesting that their motives were to preserve "their religious faith, their language, and their ancestral way of thinking." This was a feeling shared by other Swedes in America, *Augustana* continued, and it did not take them long to understand that "here in America [it] was possible to maintain all of their ancestral good and still be just as good American citizens" because it was not in their "nature" to "without further ado shed what over the trial of centuries had been judged to be of inestimable value."[80]

Founders Day was celebrated in 1903 and 1904 in a similar manner as in 1902.[81] After those years, no sources mention continued celebrations. Apparently, the day never achieved the status of a Swedish-American national day, as some had hoped.

The Golden Anniversary

In June of 1910, the Augustana Synod commemorated its fiftieth anniversary with a grand celebration in Rock Island. In 1905 a committee had been appointed to plan these observances, commemorating the history of both the Synod and Augustana College and Theological Seminary.[82] This "golden anniversary" became, in Conrad Bergendoff's words, "the greatest event in Augustana history,"[83] providing opportunities to look back and ponder the accomplishments of the past half century, as well as to look ahead to the future. The celebrations began on June 5 and lasted for a full ten days. During the first five days the semi-centennial of Augustana College and Theological Seminary was commemorated, including the commencement exercises for the

---

[77] Ludvig Holmes, "Festdikt" in Holmes 1904, 304–12.
[78] Sundbeck 1904a, 159.
[79] Sundbeck 1904a, 163–64.
[80] *Augustana*, 8 May 1902.
[81] *Augustana*, 30 April 1903 and 5 May 1904 report on celebrations in 1903 and 1904.
[82] Bergendoff 1969, 120.
[83] Bergendoff 1969, 121.

classes of 1910 for both institutions, whereas the second part of the program was devoted to the Augustana Synod.[84]

The events were directed towards both an American and a Swedish audience, as the list of official participants in and the greetings at both the college and synodical anniversary celebrations demonstrate. As noted in chapter two, the audience naturally enough included representatives from the Augustana Synod in general, but also other American Lutheran denominations, and non-Swedish-American colleges and universities (primarily in Illinois). Governor of Eberhard of Minnesota, who was of Swedish descent, was also in attendance.

The *rapprochement* between official Sweden and the Augustana Synod resulted in three Swedish official delegates: Henrik Schück, professor of literature and *rector magnificus* at Uppsala University representing Uppsala and Lund universities, Bishop von Schéele representing the Church of Sweden, and the Rev. Per Pehrsson of the Swedish pastoral association. In addition, telegrams and greetings were received from more than fifty other individuals and organizations in Sweden. Greetings from both President Taft and King Gustav V further illustrate the dual emphasis in the Golden Anniversary, and the official nature of the event.[85]

Many speeches were held during the celebration, focusing on what had been achieved during the past five decades, and in them two themes characteristic of the Synod's purpose emerge. In his presidential report to the Synod, held at the Synodical annual meeting at the same time, Erik Norelius looked back on the denomination's history, something which he was uniquely qualified to do, since he was one of the few persons present at the denomination's founding in 1860 who was still alive. He spoke of the growth of the Synod, its institutions, and its influence throughout Swedish America. He concluded that the Augustana Synod was the Swedish-American denomination which best "had preserved the faith of our fathers and their special Swedish culture and language,"[86] thus emphasizing the Synod's dual religious and ethnic significance. The ethnic emphasis represented a change of opinion for Norelius, as he had been one of the advocates for the movement to prepare for the disappearance of Swedish five decades earlier.

In one of the main addresses at the Synod jubilee, Pastor J.A. Krantz spoke on the topic of "the mission of the Augustana Synod," a talk which can serve as an illustration of the Synod's dual mission. According to Krantz, the Synod's most important tasks were religious, namely to "reestablish and cher-

[84] Minnen 1911 provides an extensive account of the celebrations and form the basis for the following discussion.
[85] Minnen 1911, 5–8.
[86] Referat 1910, 32.

ish a true and confessional Lutheran Christianity," to "be a true evangelical free church," and to "gather our Swedish people in [the church's] bosom."[87]

However, Pastor Krantz also stated that another important task for the Synod was to "preserve the Swedish language and cherish Swedish culture" in America. The Swedish culture to be maintained by the Augustana Synod would also, according to Pastor Krantz, represent "the noblest, purest, and most useful dimensions" of the ancestral traditions brought to America by the Swedish immigrants, and the main vehicle for its preservation was the language.[88] Krantz' argument thus not only shows the significance of the ancestral culture for the Synod, but also reflects the general tendency to emphasize certain suitable dimensions of the Swedish cultural baggage available to the Augustana Swedish Americans.

What was celebrated during Founders Day and at the Golden Anniversary in Rock Island during the first decade of this century? Clearly, the focus was on what had been achieved since the founding of the Synod in 1860, focusing on the denomination's religious heritage. In addition to the religious heritage, however, the ethnic element also played an important role. The student association that initially proposed the idea of Founders Day spoke of celebrating a "Swedish day," explicitly linking it to such an American celebration as Washington's birthday. The greeting from the Augustana students to their compatriots in Uppsala with its assurances that their heritage had not been sold for the gold of a foreign land also underscores this interpretation and in 1910 Pastor Krantz explicitly spoke of maintaining the Swedish culture and language as one of the main tasks of the Augustana Synod. The dual emphasis on the Synod's religious and ethnic identity had thus developed fully by the Golden Anniversary in 1910.

Swedish-American History According to Johan Enander and the Augustana Synod

History was thus an important ingredient in the creation of an ethnic identity among the Augustana Swedes, and it is possible to discern a specific Swedish-American historical tradition created within the Augustana Synod. This section will summarize the sense of a Swedish-American history, as it was formulated by leading representatives of the Augustana Synod.

As has been noted many times, Johan Enander was crucial in the formulation of a Swedish-American history. Born in Sweden in 1842, he emi-

[87] Minnen 1911, 187–93.
[88] Minnen 1911, 194–95.

grated at the age of 27 in 1869, having attended the *läroverk* in Vänersborg for a few years. He enrolled at Augustana College with the intent of becoming a minister, but after a brief time was appointed editor of the Augustana Synod's most influential newspaper, *Hemlandet*. In 1872, he bought the paper together with G.A. Bohman, and remained editor and owner until 1890. He served as professor of Swedish language and literature at Augustana College from 1890 to 1893, edited *Svenska Journalen* in Omaha, Nebraska 1893–1896, and took over *Hemlandet* again from 1896 to his death in 1910. Enander also served as editor of the family magazine *När och fjerran* 1877–1879. He worked actively within the Republican Party, and was in 1889 appointed U.S. minister to Denmark, a post he could not accept for medical reasons.[89] When he died in 1910, one obituary recognized his importance by saying that "one of the chieftains of Swedish culture has fallen" who had devoted his entire life to "the preservation of Swedishness in America" and to whom "being a Swedish American was second only to being a human being."[90] His opinions on Swedish America and Swedish-American history also provided a sounding board for others discussing this topic. Enander's significance for the Augustana Synod was also great—Ulf Beijbom has called him the Synod's "foremost layman."[91] Given Enander's centrality, it seems useful to focus on his ideas and to summarize them, in order to provide an illustration of the view of Swedish-American history within the Augustana Synod.

One of the central themes running through Enander's historical thinking is the role of Sweden, Swedes, and Swedish Americans in the development of the American republic. The Viking journeys and the New Sweden colony were particularly important elements in Enander's conception of a Swedish-American history. His intention in writing history is clear from his first significant historical work, a Swedish-language survey of American history up until 1763, the above-mentioned *Förenta Staternas historia utarbetad för den svenska befolkningen i Amerika* (1874–77).[92] Even though American colonial history in its entirety is presented in Enander's book, a fifth of the book deals with the Viking journeys to North America as well as with the background of Scandinavia at the time. In this section Enander claims that the "Norsemen" not only discovered America, but also founded colonies there "with which Greenland and Iceland maintained contacts until 1347."[93] Enander realized that his strong emphasis on the "life and culture of the Norsemen" was open to criticism but defended his decision by saying that his intended audience, "a

---

[89] Skarstedt 1897, 51–53.
[90] Schön 1910, 372. For comments on Enander in Swedish America, see e.g., Beijbom 1980, 263–70, Barton 1994, 64–67.
[91] Beijbom 1980, 264.
[92] Enander 1874–77.
[93] Enander 1874, 50.

Swedish-American public" ought to be aware of the "child of Norse culture" which "had been planted on American soil more than five centuries before Columbus landed there." His main intention in writing the book was, he declares in the preface, to ensure that the memory of "our heroic distant past never would fade among those Scandinavian descendants who inhabit American soil."[94]

Enander continued to express his opinions both in writing and as a public speaker up until the first decade of the twentieth century, and his publications and speeches also continued to be informed by an emphasis on the contributions of Sweden and Swedish-Americans to the American republic.

Enander's view of the full scope of Swedish-American history was well formulated in a 1890 speech given in Chicago. The occasion was a celebration of what was called "Our Forefathers' Day," an attempt to establish a Swedish-American "national day" of celebration, following the successful 1888 New Sweden jubilee.[95] The festivity was arranged by an organization called "Friends of our Forefathers" in which Enander was the driving force.[96] As Ulf Beijbom has pointed out, a celebration like "Our Forefathers's Day" provided Swedish Americans with both an opportunity to stake out their historical claims in the American republic, and a way of asserting the contemporary cultural work in Swedish America.[97] An editorial comment in *Hemlandet* from 1890 also underscores this dual dimension of "Our Forefathers' Day" as the paper commented that the celebration was intended not only to remember the old, but that "the rich inheritance, given to us by our fathers" is a valuable "treasure," worth preserving for "our nationality" and "for the benefit and advantage of our adopted fatherland."[98]

In his speech, called "En dröm" (A Dream), Enander outlined his version of Swedish-American history, from the arrivals of Nordic Vikings under the leadership of Leif Eriksson to what the Vikings called Vinland on the North American continent up to the present time.[99] According to Enander, the Viking settlements in North America continued to thrive, despite various hardships, and in 1121 the settlements, where the inhabitants were dressed in similar costumes to what "we still today can see in the memory-rich Dalarna, parts of the beautiful Södermanland, in Norway's valleys or on Iceland"[100], were visited by a bishop from Iceland, "America's first ordained bishop"[101]. Eventu-

---

[94] Enander 1874, preface.
[95] Similar celebrations had been arranged throughout Swedish America in 1889. [*Hemlandet*, 7 September and 18 September 1889.]
[96] *Våra Förfäders Dag*, vol 1, no 1, (6 September 1890), 1.
[97] Beijbom, 1980, 268.
[98] *Hemlandet*, 4 September 1890.
[99] The following is based on Enander 1892a, 13–28.
[100] Enander 1892a, 19.
[101] Enander 1892a, 20.

ally, however, the Viking settlements in America went under, and the memories of these settlements faded in Europe. It was only in Iceland that the memories of the Viking journeys lingered, and provided Columbus who visited the island in 1477 the information he needed for his journey to America.[102] According to Enander, the Vikings thus both directly and indirectly discovered America.

The next installment in Enander's Swedish-American history is the New Sweden colony on the Delaware River, which he describes in glowing terms. Here life is characterized by religious and political freedom "clearly of a higher nature than in the English colonies founded by the Puritans, and the Qaukers," hard work, frugal and Christian lifestyles, and happiness.[103]

The Delaware phase in Swedish-American history is followed by the Swedish part in the American revolution. According to Enander, the deciding vote in favor of the adoption of the Declaration of Independence in Philadelphia in July 1776 was cast by a delegate from Pennsylvania, "the respectable Swedish-American John Morton," thus placing that state on the affirmative side and "determining the future of the fatherland." Moreover, Enander maintains, during the War of Independence "Swedish-American troops" were in the forefront at the Battle of Trenton, and their outstanding performance caused George Washington to reflect: "If only all my troops were such heroes as these descendants of Swedes, to whom no undertaking is too difficult, no obstacle insurmountable or no duty too heavy."[104]

Enander concluded by addressing the contemporary situation. This phase of Swedish-American history included the hardworking, religious, industrious, and honorable immigrants of the nineteenth century, who with "labor and prayers" are establishing themselves in America, and who eventually will "reclaim their share of Vinland the Good, that once was their fathers' settlement."[105] The most prominent representatives of this era of Swedish-American history were the Swedish soldiers in the Union Army and John Ericsson, who, when called upon, would rally to the defense of their new homeland, ensuring the preservation of freedom and human rights.[106]

Enander's conception of Swedish-American history, from the Vikings via New Sweden and the American Revolution to the present time, became very influential in Swedish America. In 1913, Augustana pastor Alfred Bergin out-

[102] Enander 1892a, 22.

[103] Enander 1892a, 23.

[104] Enander 1892a, 24–25. Morton's Swedish ancestry seems certain. An ancestor, Mårten Mårtensson, born in Sweden c. 1645, had emigrated to the New Sweden colony as a child. [Craig 1996, 2–3.] According to Peter Stebbins Craig, a leading expert on the New Sweden colony, it is not unlikely that John Morton could have had some knowledge of Swedish. (Personal communication from Peter Stebbins Craig, April 1997.)

[105] Enander 1892a, 25.

[106] Enander 1892a, 26.

lined a historical conception similar to that of Enander's, including a query about the possible Swedish ancestry of George Washington.[107] In 1916, the editor of *Ungdomsvännen* published an article entitled "Några bindestreck mellan Sverige och Amerika" (Some Hyphens Between Sweden and America), in which he encourages his readers to study history. Anyone browsing the annals of Swedish America will find that the long Swedish-American history, from the Vikings to the present time, does not make the Swedes aliens in America, but will have to conclude that "America belongs to the Swede."[108]

A final example of the Swedish role in the adoption of the Declaration of Independence comes from the poem "Ett fosterländskt minne" (A Patriotic Memory) by Ludvig Holmes, written in 1896. Holmes conjures up the scene of the final vote on the Declaration, which was tied when John Morton cast the deciding vote in favor of adopting the Declaration, causing Holmes to comment that "John Morton was Swedish, and the vote he gave was Swedish, because it put an end to the oppression." The poem ends with a small Swedish boy running to ask his Swedish father to ring the bell when the vote is final. In the last stanza of the poem, the boy tells his father in "pure Swedish": "Now ring Father! Now ring Father! It is done!/America has taken leave from England!"[109]

Conclusion

History was a significant element in the creation of a Swedish-American identity in the Augustana Synod. Certain individuals and events from both the Swedish and Swedish-American pasts were given special prominence and became a part of the Swedish-American tradition that emerged within the Synod. The establishment of an early presence in America, the highlighting of significant Swedish and Swedish-American contributions to the American republic, and the emphasis on certain positive character traits from Swedish and Swedish-American history became particularly important in this process. We have also seen how a specific Swedish-American history was established, beginning with the Viking journeys to America and ending with the Swedish immigrants of the nineteenth and twentieth centuries.

It is also evident that this conception of Swedish-American history gained influence not only within the Augustana Synod. The celebration of the New Sweden colony in 1888, for example, attracted a wide spectrum of the Swe-

---

[107] Alfred Bergin, "Hafva vi som svenskar några gemensamma lifsintressen?", *Ungdomsvännen*, 1913, 86.
[108] E.W. Olson, "Några bindestreck mellan Sverige och Amerika,"*Ungdomsvännen* 1916, 113–15. Quotation from p. 115.
[109] Holmes 1896, 42–43.

dish-American community, and *Svensk-amerikanska historiska sällskapet*, established with Johan Enander as its first president in 1905, included both Augustana and non-Augustana persons among its early leadership.[110] The New York-based cultural magazine *Valkyrian* also expressed views of Swedish-American history that follow the same pattern which we have seen in the Augustana Synod, from the Vikings to John Ericsson.[111]

Other ethnic groups were also engaged in the creation of their own histories. John Bodnar has called American history "replete with examples of minority groups mounting spirited defenses of their own versions of the past," labeling the role played by the past for American ethnic groups "ethnic memory."[112] Some examples will illustrate this point.

To the Norwegian Americans, the Vikings were of equal, if not greater, importance than to the Swedes. One of the most active Norwegian-American apologists, Rasmus Bjørn Anderson—in some ways a parallel to Johan Enander among the Swedes—devoted much of his life as an educator and newspaperman to advancing the cause of the Viking discovery of America, pre-dating the Swedish efforts under Enander. Already in May 1868 he presented a "Leif Eriksson Lecture" in the Norwegian-American community Decorah, Iowa, which was to become one of his standard lectures.[113] In 1874 Anderson published the book *America Not Discovered By Columbus*, in which he not only argued that the Vikings had been the first Europeans in the New World, but also that the Viking spirit of freedom via the English Magna Charta had found its way into the American Declaration of Independence. This became an important element in a Norwegian-American conception of history, or, as Orm Øverland has noted, a "myth of the Norse origins of British and American democracy" which had developed fully around the turn of the century.[114]

Since the Norwegians lacked a colonial experience in America, the coming of the sloop *Restaurationen* in 1825 has been important in establishing an early, and undebatable Norwegian presence in America. In 1925 the Norse-American centennial was celebrated in Minneapolis and St. Paul, lasting for

[110] Representatives from the Augustana sphere on the first board of directors included Gustav Andreen, Johan Enander, C.W. Foss (professor of history at Augustana College), and the editor of *Prärieblomman* Anders Schön. Other sections of Swedish America were also represented, such as David Nyvall, president of the Mission Covenant North Park College, C.G. Lagergren, dean of the Swedish Baptist Seminary, C. G. Wallenius, the head of the Swedish Methodist Seminary in Evanston, Illinois, and Charles Johansen, the editor of the New York-based cultural magazine *Valkyrian*. [Year-book 1905–07, 59.]

[111] Thander 1996, 190–211.

[112] Bodnar 1992, 43.

[113] Hustvedt 1966, 57–60, 143.

[114] Øverland 1996, 9. Johan Enander expressed almost identical views in an undated speech, most likely held in the 1890s. Cf. Blanck 1989, 142–45.

several days, and providing Norwegian Americans with an opportunity to emphasize both their ethnicity and their full status as Americans.[115]

Similar examples can also be found in the Slavic groups. In a discussion of the creation of a Slavic nationalism in the U.S., Victor Greene has shown that the Poles in America "promoted ... symbolic heroes" from the Polish past in their "desire to reach their proper place in American society."[116] From the available Polish national and cultural heroes the Poles emphasized two in particular, Thaddeus Kosciuszko and Casimir Pulaski.[117] Both men had served in Washington's army during the War of Independence, and Pulaski's efforts were especially noteworthy, as he had sacrificed his life for his adopted land and leader at Savannah in 1779. Statues of the men were erected in both Chicago, the capital of "Polonia" (Polish America) and in Washington, D.C.. In Chicago 100,000 Polish Americans attended the unveiling of the Kosciuszko statue in 1904, and in 1910 statues of both Kosciuszko and Pulaski were set up in the capitol. The Washington statues were given to the United States by the Polish National Alliance on behalf of "all Americans of Polish extraction" as a sign of "loyalty and devotion to our adopted country" and willingness of the Polish Americans like their eighteenth-century forebears, to "shed our blood" for American liberty, welfare, and safety.[118]

[115] Schulz 1994, 128–29 is a perceptive discussion of the celebrations.
[116] Greene 1973, 202.
[117] The following is based on Greene 1973, 203–04.
[118] Quoted in Greene 1973, 203. Irish-American conceptions of history are discussed in Bodnar 1992, 69–70.

Chapter Six

Concluding Remarks

What did it mean to be Swedish-American in the Augustana Synod around the turn of the century? This has been the fundamental question throughout this study. This concluding chapter will summarize the previous chapters and discuss the nature of this Swedish-American identity. Some of the study's general starting points will first be discussed, after which the three central questions of *how* a Swedish-American identity was created in the Augustana Synod, *what* it consisted of, and *why* it came into being will be discussed.

The construction of a Swedish-American identity in the Augustana Synod was not unique. Other immigrant and ethnic groups in the United States were also engaged in similar processes. Indeed, the nineteenth century in both Europe and America was characterized by the growth of national feelings and traditions which were, in the words of Eric Hobsbawm, being "invented." Although different in nature, the nation-building processes in Sweden and the United States in the late nineteenth century provide the framework within which the ethnic identity of the Augustana Synod was created. The developments in the Augustana Synod are thus an example of this larger process, providing an illustration of how one particular group fashioned an answer to the question of who they were.

The significance of ethnicity varied greatly among Swedish immigrants and their children in late nineteenth- and early twentieth-century America. To some, it meant nothing or very little, while the opposite was true of a small group of cultural activists or ethnic leaders who formulated a sense of Swedishness. Thus, there arose a range of possible identifications, varying from a weaker ethnic awareness to a fully developed ethnic identity. This study has concentrated on the more developed identity, on the group and institutional level, in that it is the ethnic identity of the Augustana Synod and its leadership that has been the focus of analysis.

This study has also argued that the nature of ethnic identities can vary from an everyday level, often rooted in the daily lives of members of the ethnic community, up to what has been called an elite level. This elite level has formed the basis for the discussion of the ethnic identity in the Augustana Synod. Moreover, this ethnic identity is seen as something new and specific to the American context in which the members of the ethnic community lived. It was constructed or invented through a gradual selection process, consisting of cultural elements from both old and new world experiences. This duality means that the new ethnic identity which emerged in America, was, literally, Swedish-American.

As we have seen, the Swedish-American community was divided along several fault lines. Religion, social status, and cultural and political opinions were important characteristics that further sub-divided the Swedish-American group, and we have also seen that at times quite a keen competition for influence in the community took place between these groups. Although not exclusively concerned with the issue of ethnic identity, these many Swedish-American organizations were important in the creation of a Swedish-American identity. Given the split nature of the Swedish-American community, different versions of a Swedish-American identity were advocated, sometimes opposing each other, so it is possible to speak of a struggle for cultural hegemony in Swedish America.

However, Swedish America was not only characterized by division. At times the community—or at least parts of it—was also able to unite. Public manifestations such as the 1888 New Sweden Jubilee in Minneapolis, the campaign for the Linnaeus statue in Chicago, or the 1893 Columbian Exposition show that differences within the community could be overcome when the group was presenting itself to the larger American community.

All this said, the Augustana Synod was the leading organization in Swedish America. The Synod's membership was between a fifth and a third of all persons of Swedish descent in the United States during the period of investigation, but the Synod clearly also reached beyond its membership proper in terms of influence in Swedish America, as many non-members also availed themselves of the Synod's services. Looked at from the perspective of the number of Swedish Americans who belonged to one of the many Swedish-American organizations that existed over time, the Synod's dominance was even greater, and in 1920 sixty percent of all members in a Swedish-American organization belonged to the Augustana Synod. By the turn of the century, its network of congregations, educational and benevolent institutions, its publishing house, bookstores, and publications spanned the entire American continent, making it possible to speak of an Augustana sphere of influence in Swedish America, in which a Swedish-American identity was both created and maintained.

In examining the nature and characteristics of the Swedish-American identity in the Augustana Synod, the first question to be discussed is *how a Swedish-American identity was created* in the denomination. There was obviously an important temporal dimension to the development of a Swedish-American identity in the Augustana Synod, and a definite turning point occurred during the last decade of the nineteenth century. During the early years of the Synod's history there seems to have been a relatively small concern with the preservation or the contents of a sense of Swedishness in the Augustana Synod. Instead, a great deal of importance was placed on the "Americanization" of the Swedish immigrants, a discussion which was largely couched in terms of the use and role of the Swedish and English languages. As we have seen, such influential Synod leaders as Erland Carlsson, T.N. Hasselquist, and Erik Norelius spoke about the futility of preserving the Swedish language in America and instead underscored the necessity of learning English.

This attitude was also reflected in the emphasis on the English language at Augustana College, the constitution of which from the very beginning called for one of the three professorships to be filled by an English-speaking instructor. From the late 1880s and onward Swedish was also used only rarely as the language of instruction in the college, and as a result of a series of curricular reforms beginning in the mid-1880s, it even became possible to graduate from Augustana without having studied the Swedish language at all. In addition, the curriculum had already in 1869 been organized along American lines with four student classes, and the addition of the different vocational programs of study at the college, such as the "commercial school" which primarily attracted students from the immediate vicinity of non-Swedish background, also shows how important the American context was at Augustana during the early years.

From *circa* 1890, however, a noticeable change with regard to the position of Swedish in the Augustana Synod can be observed. At Augustana College, official pronouncements from the college leadership, statements in the college catalogs, and comments from visitors and observers of the contemporary Swedish-American scene all emphasize the importance of Swedish at Augustana at this time. In 1891 the professorship of Swedish and Christianity was separated into two positions, and the first instructor to teach exclusively Swedish in the college was, significantly enough, Johan Enander, one of the leading Swedish-American cultural activists. The college actively sought to hire well-qualified teachers of Swedish during the following years.

Moreover, from 1902 the college catalogs singled out Swedish as a subject of particular importance, and encouraged all students of Swedish parentage to enroll in the courses. We have also seen that there was a substantial interest among students in studying Swedish as well as in engaging in Swedish-related extra-curricular activities. Several Swedish literary societies were started at the school during the years around the turn of the century, including Svenska Vitterhetssällskapet from 1896, Tegnér-förbundet from 1901, and Iduna from 1902. The discussions in the Phrenokosmian Society, which had been established in 1860, also show a greater interest in topics relating to the college's ethnic background from around 1890. Swedish and Swedish-American-related celebrations began to be observed, and several visitors from Sweden were received on the campus.

We can find further examples of an emphasis on the Synod's interest in its ethnic background among its publishing activities. Although the great majority of the publications at the Augustana Book Concern up until 1915 were in Swedish, those publications that dealt with topics relating to Swedish or Swedish-American culture began appearing in earnest precisely during the latter part of the 1890s. *Prärieblomman* and *Ungdomsvännen*, A.B.C's leading cultural periodicals, first appeared under A.B.C. imprint in 1900, and during the following two decades they were followed by a number of books of prose and poetry by a group of Swedish-American authors, such as C.W. Andeer, Vilhelm Berger, Jakob Bonggren, Ludvig Holmes, C.A. Lönnqvist, Anna Olsson, and Johan Person.

The emphasis on Swedish conditions at the A.B.C. at this time can also be seen in a content analysis of two of the leading primers at the A.B.C., *Församlingsskolans läsebok* and *Tredje läseboken* from 1891 and 1917. The latter book put much greater weight on both Swedish and Swedish-American topics than the former, evidence for a very noticeable change of stress over a twenty-six-year period. In addition, Swedish literature also began to be published at the A.B.C. after the turn of the century, including *Ur svenska sången* (1901), *Fritiofs saga* (1914), and *Fänrik Ståls sägner* (1915).

The years around 1890 thus appear to be something of a watershed for the significance of a Swedish ethnicity both at Augustana College and in the denomination at large. Prior to that time, Swedishness played a relatively small role, at least judging from official pronouncements, and from the activities at Augustana College. The situation was quite different after 1890, when both the Swedish and Swedish-American nature of the Augustana Synod was underscored. A growing sense of ethnicity was expressed in what has been called a Swedish-American cultural tradition which was being constructed or invented, providing the foundations for the Synod's Swedish-American identity. Although there were some parallels to the ways in which Swedish nationalism of the 1890s was formulated, the emergence of the Swedish-American tradition in the Augustana Synod is better understood within its American context, especially in light of the generational change and the varying significance of religion and ethnicity in the Augustana Synod.

Two phases can be discerned in the Synod's early history that help to explain this development. The first phase was the period from 1860 to about 1890, when relatively small significance was attached to the denomination's ethnicity. Two main explanations can be given for this. As has been shown in chapter two, the period 1860-1890 was a phase of rapid growth and institution building. The Synod grew quickly from its original thirty-six Midwestern congregations with a few thousand members in 1860 to close to eight hundred congregations with over 175,000 members and a number of educational and benevolent institutions, spanning the entire American continent in the mid-1890s. This period of institution building created tensions within the Synod, as the relative independence of individual congregations and regional conferences resulted in decentralizing tendencies. It was not until 1894 that a Synodical constitution was adopted, creating a lasting balance between the central, regional, and local elements in the Synod. The Synod was also challenged from the outside, for example through the conflict with the followers of what became the Mission Covenant Church in the 1870s as well as with secular, more urban-based groups in the 1870s and 1880s. Much of the work of the Augustana Synod during this first period was thus focused on building and maintaining the denomination, as well as meeting challenges from the outside. Maintaining a Lutheran faith among Swedish immigrants in America was paramount to the Synod, which also meant that the religious dimension of the Synod's life became central during this first phase, helping to explain the relative indifference the denomination seems to have shown for its ethnicity.

A second explanation deals with the generational composition of the Augustana Synod. Although the Synod statistics do not include any specific information on the birth place of its members, it seems evident that the Augustana Synod was dominated by Swedish-born members during the 1860s, 70s, and 80s. The immigration of Swedes on a large scale began in earnest after the Civil War, which means that at least two decades would have to pass before an American-born generation would become dominant. The analysis of the student body at Augustana College confirms this assumption. The dominance of Swedish-born individuals provides the second explanation for the lack of interest in the Synod's ethnicity during this first phase of the institution's history. These Augustana Swedes, born in Sweden, of rural background, and with roots in the Swedish religious revival movement of the mid-nineteenth century, were grounded in Swedish circumstances where a sense of national Swedish identity was weak. In leaving for America, they sought emancipation from the Swedish economic, social, and even religious conditions, rather than the opportunity to express national feelings. Once in America, characterized by great ethnic, religious, and cultural variety, the Augustana Synod provided these Swedes with mostly a religious continuity, which was, however, expressed in familiar Swedish forms, particularly in terms of the language. During this first phase of the Synod's history, then, the sense of Swedish ethnicity was an unreflected or taken-for-granted part of the Synod's religious identity, a fact which further helps to explain the weak position of the denomination's ethnic background during this time.

The second phase of the denomination's history lasted between *circa* 1890-1917. By this time, the Synod was well established as the dominant force in Swedish America, and although there were still distinct religious and ideological differences between the Augustana Synod and other Swedish-American groups, conflicts of the kind noticeable in the 1870s and 1880s seem to have been fewer.

Moreover, the Synod was dominated by the children and the grandchildren of the Swedish immigrants during the second phase, a group which had different national and ethnic needs than their parents and grandparents. At Augustana College, the American-born students were rapidly becoming a majority after 1890, something which also seems to have been true for the Synod as a whole. The analysis of the student body at Augustana College also shows that the Augustana Swedish Americans were leaving the farms and entering white collar professions and that the majority of them remained within the Augustana sphere of Swedish America upon graduation.

As we have seen, it was during this second phase that the Synod's ethnic identity began to be emphasized and co-exist with its religious identity. Thus, a window of opportunity was opened and it became possible to formulate a sense of Swedishness within the Augustana Synod. Given the significance of generational change for the character of ethnic identities, it can furthermore be argued that, as the American-born generations of Swedish Americans in the Augustana Synod with no personal experience of Sweden and with limited knowledge of the Swedish language or Swedish cultural traditions in general became dominant, the nature of their ethnic identity changed. It became, in the words of Joshua Fishman "a transmuted past" or an ethnic ideology, which was something that had to be learned. This reflected and actively formulated ethnicity of the second phase was thus radically different from the unreflected and taken-for-granted sense of Swedish identity presumed during the first period of the Synod's history, and we can thus say that the Augustana Synod went from being Swedish to Swedish-American.

The second question deals with *what the Swedish-American identity consisted of*. The analysis of the ethnicity in the Augustana Synod has been based on a variety of materials, including Augustana College with its curriculum, student organizations, and general cultural activities; the Augustana Book Concern and its publishing profile; and a discussion of the growth of a specific Swedish-American history within the Synod.

The ingredients in Augustana's Swedish-American identity consisted of both Swedish and Swedish-American elements, and it expressed in itself in a classroom at Augustana College, at a Swedish-American celebration on campus, or a publication from the Augustana Book Concern, and often in a highly idealized and romantic manner. The sense of self drew on selected cultural elements from a Swedish and Swedish-American, and to a lesser extent American, repertoire of "high culture," such as literature, history, and religion. It emphasized great Swedish and Swedish-American accomplishments and underscored character traits, such as freedom, bravery, and religiosity thought to be characteristic of both Swedes and Swedish-Americans.

The turning point with regard to the significance given to ethnicity in the Augustana Synod around 1890 also meant that the nature of the ethnicity changed. Prior to that time the sense of Swedishness at Augustana College, as expressed through the authors studied in the Swedish classes or discussed in the literary societies, to a large degree mirrored the contemporary literary selections in the Swedish secondary schools. Relatively little attention was paid to specific Swedish-American cultural conditions, which also confirms this pattern.

The advent of the second phase meant an affirmation of ethnicity within the Augustana Synod. As the American-born generations began to dominate the Synod, their Swedishness was no longer taken for granted, but had to be learned or constructed. What I have called a Swedish-American cultural tradition began to emerge, consisting of both Swedish and Swedish-American cultural elements. The selection of Swedish literature and history continued to reflect an idealized, romantic, and patriotic view of the Swedish past. At Augustana College, for example, Swedish history was most often represented by King Gustavus Adolphus, and the Swedish authors most frequently studied and discussed were drawn from the Romanticism of the nineteenth century, with Johan Ludvig Runeberg and Esaias Tegnér as by far the two most popular authors. The Swedish literary selections at the Augustana Book Concern also show an emphasis on Romanticism and critically established authors of the nineteenth century.

A fairly careful selection process was also at work with regard to those cultural elements from Sweden that were included in the Synod's view of Swedish culture. Although the Synod's ethnic identity was being affirmed and given possibilities to develop in its own right, religious concerns still set clear boundaries for the cultural expressions in the Augustana Synod. We have seen how a particular view of literature and culture was encouraged. Some examples of Augustana's role as a gatekeeper include the debate over the selection of poems for Johan Enander's anthology of Swedish poetry *Ur svenska sången* (where we have found a specific "Augustana point of view"), the discussions about *smutslitteraturen* (trash literature) in which the Augustana Synod objected to the importation of certain popular Swedish fiction to Swedish America, or in the way the Augustana Book Concern carefully examined, rejected, or sent back for rewriting some of the manuscripts it received for consideration. The absence of a number of authors of popular fiction at the A.B.C., who were frequently read in both Sweden and elsewhere Swedish America, and August Strindberg's weak position in the Augustana Synod's view of Swedish literature is also illustrative of this process.

Furthermore, it must be strongly underscored that the contents of this ethnic identity that emanated from Sweden, took on a meaning that was specific to its new American context. The Swedish cultural symbols that were included in Augustana College's version of a Swedish-American identity, such as *Fritiofs saga, Fänrik Ståls sägner*, or Gustavus Adolphus, were all given a new significance in their American context. Even though Augustana College's Swedish curriculum and general view of Swedish culture to a large degree echoed cultural patterns in Sweden as they were expressed, for example, in the Swedish secondary schools, the meaning of *Fritiofs saga* or the achievements of Gustavus Adolphus in Swedish America around 1900 was shaped by the American and Swedish-American context in which these cultural elements functioned, and appropriated by the Augustana community.

The kings Gustavus Adolphus and Charles XII were both prominent parts of the Swedish national movement associated with the 1890s, symbolizing Sweden's era of greatness and successes on the European political theater. At Augustana, however, it was Gustavus Adolphus who dominated the stage in numerous contexts during the two first decades of the twentieth century. He became a perfect symbol for the Augustana Synod, as he embodied both the religious and ethnic dimensions of the denomination. The emphasis on independence and freedom discerned in the writings of Runeberg and Tegnér also provided an opportunity to assign such characteristics to members of the Augustana Swedish-American community, qualities which could also be communicated to the larger Swedish-American and American communities.

In addition to the cultural elements drawn from the national Swedish cultural repertoire, the Swedish-American identity of the second phase also meant a strong awareness of a sense of a specific Swedish-American culture emerging in the Synod. The Augustana Swedish Americans now began to see themselves as different from the homeland Swedes, with their own culture and history. From 1903, the Augustana College catalogs stated that one of the missions of the school was to be an "exponent of Swedish-American culture," and President Andreen spoke of the importance of the Swedish-American colleges in making "thoroughly dedicated" Swedish Americans out of their students. As we have seen, many aspects of Swedish-American culture were also discussed in the college literary societies or celebrated on the campus during the first two decades of the twentieth century.

Several of the Swedish-American authors whose fiction or poetry were published by the A.B.C. after the turn of the century also specifically dealt with the nature of this new Swedish-American identity. In his *Svensk-amerikanska studier* from 1912, Johan Person argued that the Swedish Americans were becoming a separate "people," which was "neither Swedish, nor American, but a combination of both." In the works of C.W. Andeer, moreover, Swedish-American life is portrayed in highly positive terms, especially within the sphere of the Augustana Synod. Andeer contrasts Swedish Americans and Swedish-American culture against conditions in Sweden, a comparison which is favorable to Swedish America. The two leading cultural periodicals published by the A.B.C., *Ungdomsvännen* and *Prärieblomman*, also became important vehicles in promoting Swedish-American culture and identity.

The comparison between the A.B.C.'s two primers *Församlingsskolans läsebok* from 1891 and *Tredje läseboken* from 1917 also illustrates the shift in emphasis from Swedish to Swedish-American in Augustana's sense of Swedish ethnicity. In the first book, the national or ethnic elements dealt almost exclusively either with national Swedish conditions, such as Swedish history or literature, or with cultural aspects of the immigrants' adopted homeland, such as selections of American poetry in Swedish translation. Twenty-six years later, when *Tredje läseboken* appeared, the Augustana Synod's Swedish-American identity was fully developed and a large part of the book was devoted to accounts of the life and times of Swedes in America, from the New Sweden colony up until what was then the present time.

This sense of a specific Swedish-American identity also included the construction and celebration of a specific Swedish-American history. We have seen how a concern for recording and writing the history of the Swedes in America in general and the Augustana Synod in particular developed from an early date. The historical consciousness among the Augustana Swedes also manifested itself in the creation of special celebrations of the Synod's history. Founders' Day was established in 1902 to commemorate the founders of the Synod, and the fiftieth anniversary celebration in 1910 also became an opportunity to look back at half a century of work in the new land and to celebrate the Synod's achievement.

Moreover, we have also seen how the attempts to write a Swedish-American history focused not only on the nineteenth and twentieth centuries. Johan Enander's historical writings provide a particularly good example of the tendency to establish, in Orm Øverland's words, a Swedish-American "homemaking myth," in which the establishment of an early presence in America became particularly important. Here, the New Sweden colony from the seventeenth century was of central significance. Although no connections existed between the colony and the Swedish immigrants of some two hundred years later, the latter still sought to establish an historical continuity between the colony and themselves, providing them with an opportunity to become a "colonial people," in an attempt to place themselves on the same level as the seventeenth-century New England colonists. Moreover, the many positive characteristics given to life in the New Sweden colony, such as freedom, religiosity, and hard work, were also characteristics that by extension were applied to the Swedish immigrants of the late nineteenth and early twentieth centuries.

In addition to the New Sweden colony, the life and achievements of John

Ericsson was central to Augustana's conception of a Swedish-American history, and his life and achievements were praised and celebrated throughout the Augustana Synod. Given Ericsson's role in the construction of the *Monitor* which played a significant part on the Union side in the Battle of Hampton Roads during the Civil War, he became, in the words of Willi Paul Adams, an excellent "culture-hero" for the Augustana Synod. Although his connections to organized Swedish America were weak, the Swedish-American ethnic leadership still used him, making him into one of their own. The achievements of John Ericsson and his contributions to the American republic became those of other Swedish immigrants of the nineteenth and twentieth centuries; as John Ericsson was, in the words of Ernst Zetterstrand in a 1904 article about him in *Prärieblomman*, a "typical Swedish American."

Other elements in the creation of a Swedish-American history included such Swedish contributions to the growth of the American republic, participation in the Revolutionary War, and at the signing of the Declaration of Independence in 1776. As we have seen, the Vikings were necessary in the creation of Swedish-American history. Although no direct Viking impact on the history of the United States could be found, the case for the Viking landing on the North American continent had to do with establishing that the true "discoverers" of America were Scandinavians, and not Italians or Spaniards. To some Augustana authors, such as Johan Enander and E.W. Olson, this history of a Swedish presence in North America extending back almost a millenium gave the Swedes a special status or birthright in America, making it possible for E.W. Olson to claim that "America belongs to the Swede!"

The cultural elements in the Swedish-American identity of the Augustana Synod were thus based on selective parts of both the Swedish and Swedish-American past and cultural traditions. An idealized and romantic Swedish-Americanism was born, emphasizing famous persons, Swedish and Swedish-American accomplishments and achievements, enviable and lofty character traits, supposedly characteristic of both Swedes and Swedish Americans. Thus, readers of *Ungdomsvännen*, would be exposed to fiction and poetry by notable Swedish writers, such as Johan Ludvig Runeberg and Esaias Tegnér as well as stories and poetry by Swedish-American authors like C.W. Andeer or Ludvig Holmes. They would marvel at the achievements of Gustavus Adolphus and his defense of the Lutheran religion during the Thirty Years War, at the establishment of a Swedish colony on the Delaware River in 1638, and at John Ericsson's genius during the Civil War. In this way a separate Swedish-American canon evolved, with its own history, literature, heroes, and heroines.

Although a systematic examination of the cultural expressions of other parts of Swedish America is outside the focus of this study, evidence suggests that the Augustana version of a Swedish-American identity became the preeminent one in the cultural struggle in the Swedish-American community, and other factions of the community seem to have accepted at least some parts of the Augustana Swedish-American identity. This is not surprising, given the dominant position the Synod had in Swedish America in terms of the number of members and synod institutions. The need to establish an early presence in America seems to have transcended the ideological divisions of the Swedish-American community, and we have seen that the 250th anniversary celebration of the New Sweden colony in 1888 also managed to bring together large parts of the Swedish Americans. The same can be said of the significance attached to the Vikings. Still, as the example of the Linnaeus statue in Chicago shows, historical symbols could be contested, and in order to maintain a united Swedish-American community, compromises had to be made.

Finally, some answers to the question of *why this Augustana version of a Swedish-American identity developed* will be offered. Obviously, the generational shift was of great significance. The Swedish-born generation, with religious rather than ethnic priorities, was succeeded by American-born Swedish Americans to whom ethnicity was more important. To them, the development of the ethnic identity became a strategy for interacting with the American society. Augustana's Swedish-American identity placed emphasis on such positive traits as religiosity, freedom, and independence, characteristics that were also central in the American republic. In addition, it underscored how both Swedes and Swedish Americans had contributed significantly to the development of the American nation. This conception can be seen as one way of promoting the integration and acceptance of the Swedish Americans by convincing the American host society that the Swedish Americans were a group particularly suited for membership in the American republic. The construction of a Swedish-American history, ranging from the Vikings, via the colonial Swedish experience of the seventeenth century and Swedish contributions to the establishment of the American republic, to John Ericsson's significant contributions to the victory of the Union in the Civil War are examples of how the formulators of the ethnic identity of the Augustana Swedish Americans sought to portray the group as especially appropriate for becoming Americans.

It is also possible to see the ethnic identity as one element in the competition between Swedish Americans and other ethnic groups with whom they were competing for resources, influence, and a place in the American social fabric. Ethnic identity became one way of establishing superiority over other groups, and as we have seen, Johan Enander's case for the Viking discovery of America was explicitly cast in terms of the contemporary American ethnic situation with noticeable anti-Catholicism, as he suggested that Italian Catholics and the Pope had sought to prevent the recognition of the Viking claim as the first Europeans in the New World. The growing nativist sentiments around the turn of the century most likely also provided an important impetus for the Swedish Americans to use their ethnicity as a way of emphasizing their proximity to mainstream America and of distancing themselves culturally from the new immigrants from southern and eastern Europe.

Another way of looking at this question has to do with the nature of American nationalism, and as a part of the on-going nation building process in nineteenth-century America. As has been suggested by Lawrence Fuchs, the American conception of nationalism allowed for a "voluntary pluralism" for most European groups, including the Swedish Americans. As long as the members of an ethnic group loyally adhered to the abstract political philosophies that formed the basis for the United States, the American national idea allowed for the maintenance of the groups' ancestral cultures. It was thus possible for the Swedish immigrants and their children to affirm and even develop their ethnic identities and express support for Swedish and Swedish-American cultural symbols, while at the same time remaining loyal Americans.

In fact, it can be argued that the creation of hyphenated ethnic identities, be they German-American, Italian-American, Norwegian-American, or Swedish-American, was a logical consequence of American nationalism. Other groups also developed conceptions of ethnicity, stressing similar traits as did the Swedish Americans. The relative lack of emphasis on ethnicity in the conception of American nationalism thus provided an opportunity for those European-American ethnic groups who chose to do so, to use their respective ethnic identities as building blocks in the construction of their American national identity. Looked at from this perspective, the Swedish immigrants and their children living in turn-of-the-century America were, by becoming Swedish Americans, also becoming Americans.

Bibliography[1]

Unpublished Primary Sources

USA

Chicago, Illinois

Archives of the Evangelical Lutheran Church in America (ELCA)
C.J. Bengtson Collection (CJB)

Minneapolis, Minnesota

Archives of the Augsburg Fortress Publishing House (AFP)
Augustana Book Concern Collection (uncataloged)
    Board of Directors, Minutes (ABCMin)

Rock Island, Illinois

Augustana College Library, Special Collections (ACL)
Augustana College & Theological Seminary
    Board of Directors, (BdDir)
    College Faculty & Committees (CFC)
    Registration Forms (uncataloged) (RF)
Gustav Andreen Papers (GAP)
Phrenokosmian Society (PS)
Svenska Vitterhetssällskapet (SV)

Swenson Swedish Immigration Research Center, Augustana College (SSIRC)
Ernst Skarstedt Collection (ESC)
G.N. Swan Collection (GNS)

Sweden

Uppsala

Uppsala University Library (Uppsala universitetsbibliotek, UUB)
Adolf Noreen Collection (ANC)

---

[1] The alphabetization follows Swedish practice.

Published Primary Sources

Official Statistics

Bureau of the Census, *Ninth Census of the United States 1870* (Washington, D.C., 1872) [Census 1870]

Bureau of the Census, *Tenth Census of the United States 1880* (Washington, D.C., 1883) [Census 1880]

Bureau of the Census, *Thirteenth Census of the United States 1910* (Washington, D.C., 1913) [Census 1910]

Bureau of the Census, *Fourteenth Census of the United States, 1920* (Washington, D.C., 1922) [Census 1920]

Bureau of the Census, *Religious Bodies: 1906* (Washington, D.C. 1910) [Religious Bodies 1906]

Bureau of the Census, *Religious Bodies: 1926* (Washington, D.C. 1929) [Religious Bodies 1926]

Augustana Synod Minutes

The titles for the minutes of the Augustana Synod vary somewhat over the years. For the sake of consistency I will use the short reference form of *Referat* plus the year to refer Augustana Synod Minutes. The minutes 1860–1878 were reprinted and published by the Augustana Book Concern in 1917. All references from those years are quoted from this reprint edition.

Titles:

1860–1883: *Protokoll hållet vid Skandinaviska Ev. Lutherska Augustana Synodens (numeral) årsmöte i (place)*

1884–1890: *Officiellt referat öfwer förhandlingarna wid Skandinaviska Ev. Lutherska Augustana Synodens (numeral) årsmöte i (place)*

1891–94: *Referat öfwer förhandlingarna wid Skandinaviska Evangelisk Lutherska Augustana Synodens (numeral) årsmöte i (place)*

1895–1900: *Referat öfwer förhandlingarna wid Evangelisk Lutherska Augustana Synodens (numeral) årsmöte i (place)*

1901–05: *Referat öfver förhandlingarna vid Augustana Synodens (numeral) årsmöte i (place)*

1906–11: *Referat af förhandlingarna vid Augustana Synodens (numeral) årsmöte i (place)*

1912–19: *Augustana-synodens referat (numeral) årsmöte hållet i (place)*

Places and dates of publication:

Chicago: 1860–1872
Red Wing, Minn.: 1873
Rock Island: 1874
Moline, Ill.: 1875
Chicago: 1876
Red Wing, Minn.: 1877
Chicago: 1878–79
Moline, Ill.: 1880–83
Rock Island: 1884–

Catalogs and Reference Works

Bergendoff, Conrad, *The Augustana Ministerium* (Rock Island, 1980)

Catalog of Augustana College and Theological Seminary (Rock Island and year) [Catalog and year]

Dalkullan. Almanack och Kalender för 1910 (Chicago, 1910) [Dalkullan, 1910]

Doderer, Klaus, hrsg., *Lexikon der Kinder- und Jugendliteratur*, 4 vols. (Weinheim & Basel, 1973–1982)

Engberg, Holmberg & Lindells Bokförteckning (Chicago, n.d. [1876?]) [Engberg, Holmberg & Lindell, 1876]

The Engberg-Holmberg Publishing Company's Bokförteckning N:o 5 (Chicago, n.d.) [Engberg-Holmberg Catalog]

Evangeliska Fosterlandsstiftelsens 50-åriga verksamhet 1856–1906. En minnesskrift (Stockholm, 1906) [EFS 1906]

Förlags-katalog från Augustana Book Concern (Rock Island, 1912) [ABC Catalog, 1912]

Förteckning å böcker som finnas i Nya Svenska Bokhandeln i St. Paul (St. Paul, Minn., n.d.) [Nya Svenska Bokhandeln]

Katalog från Lutheran Augustana Book Concern. 1900 (Rock Island, 1900) [ABC Catalog 1900]

Katalog från Augustana Book Concern (Rock Island, 1920) [ABC Catalog 1920]

Katalog öfver Böcker och Musikalier som finnas i A. Österholm & Co.'s bokhandel. No. 13 State Street, N.Y, N.Y. (New York, n.d. (1890/91?) [Österholm Catalog]

Katalog öfver den svenska afdelningen af I.T. Relling & Co.'s Boklager 226 Milwaukee Avenue, Chicago (Chicago, 1878) [Relling katalog, 1878]

Korsbaneret (Rock Island, 1881–1915)

Larsson, Gunilla & Eva Tedenmyr, eds., *Svenskt tryck i Nordamerika. Katalog över Tell G. Dahllöfs samling* (Stockholm, 1988) [Larsson & Tedenmyr 1998]

Linnström, Hjalmar, ed., *Svenskt boklexikon åren 1830–1865*, 1–2, (Uppsala, 1961)

Nationalencyklopedin, vol 5. (Höganäs, 1991) [Nationalencyklopedin 1991]

N.W. Ayer and Son's American Newspaper Annual and Directory (Philadelphia, 1910) [N.W. Ayer 1910]

Skarstedt, Ernst, *Våra pennfäktare*, (San Franciso, 1897)

Svensk Bok-Katalog för åren 1866–1875 (Stockholm, 1878) [Bok-Katalog 1866–75]

Svensk Bok-Katalog för åren 1876–1885 (Stockholm, 1890) [Bok-Katalog 1876–85]

Svensk Bok-Katalog för åren 1886–1895 (Stockholm, 1900) [Bok-Katalog 1886–95]

Svensk Bok-Katalog för åren 1896–1900 (Stockholm, 1904) [Bok-Katalog 1896–1900]

Svensk Bok-Katalog för åren 1901–1905 (Stockholm, 1908) [Bok-Katalog 1901–05]

Svensk Bok-Katalog för åren 1906–10 (Stockholm, 1913) [Bok-Katalog 1906–10]

Svensk Bok-Katalog för åren 1911–15 (Stockholm, 1919) [Bok-Katalog 1911–15]

Svensk Bok-Katalog för åren 1916–20 (Stockholm, 1923) [Bok-Katalog 1916–20]

Svensk Katalog från C. Rasmussens Bokhandel (Minneapolis, 1907) [Rasmussen Catalog, 1907]

Svenskt litteraturlexikon (Lund, 1970)

Who is Who Among the Alumni? (Rock Island, 1923)

Wilstadius, Paul, *Smålands nation i Uppsala. Biografiska och genealogiska anteckningar, II 1845–1950* (Uppsala, 1961)

Åhlén, Bengt, ed., *Svenskt författarlexikon 1900–1940. Biobibliografisk handbok till Sveriges moderna litteratur*, 2 vols. (Stockholm, 1942)

224

Document Collections, Memorial volumes, Official histories

Ander, Fritiof & Oscar Nordstrom, eds., *The American Origin of the Augustana Synod* (Rock Island, 1942)

Augustana Book Concern 1889–1914 samt Augustanasynodens tidigare förlagsverksamhet: festskrift med anledning af verksamhetens 25-årsjubileum (Rock Island, 1914) [Augustana Book Concern 1914]

Dahl, K.G. William, *Letters Home from the Prairie Priest*, transl. by Rev. Earl Helge Byleen (privately printed, no date). Available at Special Collections, Augustana College Library. [Dahl no date]

Minnen från Jubel-festen. Program, predikningar och tal vid Augustana Colleges och Augustana-synodens Femtio-års-jubileum den 5–15 juni 1910 (Rock Island, 1911) [Minnen 1911]

Minnesskrift med anledning af Augustana-synodens femtioåriga tillvaro. Historisk översikt af hvad som uträttats under åren 1860–1910 (Rock Island, 1910) [Minnesskrift 1910]

Nothstein, Ira O., ed., *Selected Documents Dealing with the Organization of the First Congregations and the First Conferences of the Augustana Synod* (Rock Island, 1944) [Nothstein 1944]

Olson, Ernst W., *En bokhandelshistoria* (Chicago, 1910)

Proceedings of the Conventions of the Swedish-American Republican League of Illinois 1896–1897 (n.p., n.d. [Chicago 1897?]) [Proceedings 1896–97]

Proceedings at the Unveiling of the Statue of John Ericsson in Potomac Park, Washington, D.C. (Washington, D.C., 1926) [Proceedings 1926]

The Augustana Synod. A Brief Review of its History, 1860–1910 (Rock Island, 1910) [Augustana History 1910]

Year-Book of the Swedish-American Historical Society 1905–1907/Svensk-Amerikanska Historiska Sällskapets Årsbok (Chicago 1907) [Year-book 1905–07]

Westin, Gunnar, ed., *Emigranterna och kyrkan. Brev till och från svenskar i Amerika, 1849–1892* (Stockholm, 1932)

Contemporary Publications

[Holmes, Ludvig], *Dikter af Ludvig* (Rock Island, 1896) [Holmes 1896]

[Holmes, Ludvig], *Nya dikter af Ludvig* (Rock Island, 1904) [Holmes 1904]

[Holmes, Ludvig], *Ludvigs dikter. 1:a bandet.* (Rock Island, 1911) [Holmes 1911]

[Lönnqvist, C.A.], *Dikter af Teofilus* (Rock Island, 1907) [Lönnqvist 1907]

[Olson, E.W.] Döbbelju, E., *Charley Washington. Studentkomedi* (Rock Island, n.d. [1917?]) [Charley Washington 1917]

Andeer, C.W., *I brytningstid. Skisser från det svensk-amerikanska folklivet* (Rock Island, 1904) [Andeer 1904a]

Andeer, C.W., *Augustanafolk. Bilder och karaktärer ur vårt kyrkliga arbete* (Rock Island, 1911)

Andeer, C.W., *Augustanafolk. Andra samlingen. Flera bilder och karaktärer ur vårt kyrkliga arbete* (Rock Island, 1914)

Berger, Vilhelm, *Vårt språk* (Rock Island, 1912)

Berger, Vilhelm, *Svensk-amerikanska meditationer* (Rock Island, 1916)

Bjursten, Herman, *Två flammor* (Minneapolis, 1898)

Bonggren, Jakob, *Sånger och sagor* (Rock Island, 1902)

Carlson, J.S., *Amerikas siste svensk* (Minneapolis, 1908).

Enander, Johan Alfred, *Förenta Staternas historia utarbetad för den svenska befolkningen i Amerika* (Chicago, 1874–1877)
Enander, Johan Alfred, *Valda Skrifter*, I (Rock Island, 1892) [Enander 1892a]
Enander, Johan Alfred, *Nordmännen i Amerika eller Amerikas upptäckt. Historisk afhandling med anledning af Columbiafesterna i Chicago 1892–1893* (Rock Island, 1893)
Fries, Nikolaus, *Vid fyrelden* (Rock Island, 1904)
Fries, Nikolaus, *Vid fyrbåken* (Stockholm, 1908)
Guds vägar. Berättelser för ungdom av M.L. m.fl. (Rock Island, 1908) [Guds vägar 1908]
Linder, Oliver, *I Västerled. Stycken på vers och prosa* (Rock Island, 1914)
Lönnqvist, C.A., *Vildros. Ett nytt knippe dikter* (Rock Island 1916)
Mattson, Hans, ed., *250th Anniversary of the First Swedish Settlement in America, September 14, 1888* (Minneapolis, 1888),
Norelius, Erik, *De svenska lutherska församlingarnas och svenskarnes historia i Amerika*, 2 vols. (Rock Island, 1891 and 1916)
Norelius, Erik, *T.H. Hasselquist. En lefnadsteckning* (Rock Island, 1900)
Olsson, Anna, *Från solsidan* (Rock Island, 1905)
Olsson, Anna, *En prärieunges funderingar* (Rock Island, 1917)
Olsson, Olof, *A Pilgrim Story from Augustana College* (Rock Island, 1896)
Pehrsson, Per, *Råd och anvisningar till utvandrare* (Stockholm, 1912)
Person, Johan, *Svensk-amerikanska studier* (Rock Island, 1912)
Peterson, C.F., *Sverige i Amerika. Kulturhistoriska och biografiska teckningar* (Chicago, 1898)
Stein, Armin, *August Herman Franke. En lifsbild från den tyska pietismens tid* (Rock Island, 1893)
Stein, Armin, *August Herman Franke. En lifsbild från den tyska pietismens tid* (Stockholm, 1911)
Sundbeck, Carl, *Svensk-amerikanerna. Deras materiella och andliga sträfvanden* (Rock Island, 1904) [Sundbeck 1904a]
Sundbeck, Carl, *Svensk-Amerika lefve! Några tal hållna i Amerika* (Stockholm, 1904) [Sundbeck 1904b]
Swensson, Carl A., *I Sverige. Minnen och bilder från mina fäders land* (Stockholm, 1891)
Vid Jesu Krubba (Rock Island, 1907)

Schoolbooks

Andeer, C.W., *Dialoger och monologer för ungdomsföreningar* (Rock Island, 1904) [Andeer 1904b]
Bersell, A.O. ed., *Församlingsskolans läsebok* (Rock Island, 1890) [FL 1890]
Bersell, A. O. ed., *Barnens andra bok för skolan och hemmet* (Rock Island, 1897) [Bersell 1897]
Bersell, A.O. ed., *Församlingsskolans läsebok* (Rock Island, 1898) [FL 1898]
Edqvist, Märta, "Svenskarna i Nya Sverige" in her *Bilder ur fädernas kyrka för barn och ungdom* (Stockholm, 1915)
Enander, Johan, ed., *Eterneller och vårblommor. Deklamationsstycken och dialoger för föreningar och sällskap samt för läsning i hemmet* (Rock Island, 1892) [Enander 1892b]
Enander, Johan, ed., *Ur svenska sången under det nittonde seklet samt blad ur den*

svenska sångens historia. Poetisk läsebok för de svensk-amerikanska hemmen, ungdomsföreningarna och litterära sällskapen (Rock Island, 1901)
Hammer, Bertil & Andr. Wallgren, eds., *Första läseboken*, 15th ed., (Stockholm, 1915) [FL 1915]
Hammer, Bertil & Andr. Wallgren, eds., *Andra läseboken*, 11th ed., (Stockholm 1916) [AL 1916]
Läsebok för folkskolan, 8th edition, (Stockholm, 1878) [LfF 1878]
Masterpieces from Swedish literature, vols. 1–2, (Rock Island, 1906–08) [Masterpieces 1906, 1908]
Mauritzson, Jules, ed., *Tredje läseboken för skolan och hemmet* (Rock Island, 1917) [TL 1917]
Runeberg, Johan Ludvig, *Fänriks Ståls sägner*, edited by A. Louis Elmquist (Rock Island, 1915)
Tegnér, Esaias, *Fritiofs saga*, edited by Andrew A. Stomberg (Rock Island, 1914)
Vickner, E.J., *A Brief Swedish Grammar* (Rock Island, 1917)

Newspapers and Periodicals

Aftonbladet (Stockholm), 1903
Augustana. Tidning för den Swenska luterska kyrkan i Amerika (Rock Island), 1889–1918 [Augustana]
Augustana Observer (Rock Island), 1903–1916
Fosterlandet (Chicago), 1901
God Jul (Rock Island), 1916
Hemlandet. Det gamla och det nya (Chicago), 1860, 1890, 1901
Julrunan 1905, 1911, 1912
Prärieblomman 1899 (Chicago) and 1900–1913 (Rock Island)
Svenska Amerikanaren (Chicago), 1901
Svenska Dagbladet (Stockholm), 1913
Svenska Journalen (Rockford, Ill.), 1913
Svenska Kuriren (Chicago), 1901
Svenska Socialisten (Chicago), 1913
Svenska Tribunen (Chicago), 1901
Ungdomsvännen 1899 (St. Paul, Minn.), 1900–1918 (Rock Island)
Veckojournalen (Stockholm), 1912
Vid Juletid (Rock Island), 1896–1910
Våra förfäders dag (Chicago), 1890
Vårt Land (Stockholm), 1903

Personal communications

Bruce Karstadt, Minneapolis, March 1992
Peter Stebbins Craig, Philadelphia, April 1997.

Secondary Sources

Abramson, Harold J., "Religion," in Stephan Thernstrom, ed., *Harvard Encyclopedia of American Ethnic Groups* (Cambridge, Mass., 1980)

Adams, J.R.R., *The Printed Word and the Common Man: Popular Culture in Ulster 1700–1900* (Belfast, 1987)

Adams, Willi Paul, "Ethnic Leadership and the German-Americans" in Frank Trommler & Jospeh McVeigh, eds., *America and the Germans*, vol 1. (Philadelphia, 1985)

Albrecht, Esther Andreen, *Gustav Andreen and the Growth of Augustana College and Theological Seminary* (Rock Island & Minneapolis, 1950)

Ander, O. Fritiof, *T.N. Hasselquist. The Career and Influence of a Swedish-American Clergyman, Journalist, and Educator* (Rock Island, 1931)

Anderson, Benedict, *Imagined Communities. Reflections on the Origin and Spread of Nationalism* (London, 1991)

Anderson, Philip J., "Paul Peter Waldenström and America. Influence and Presence in Historical Perspective," *Covenant Quartely*, 52 (November 1994)

Anderson, Philip J., "Education and Identity Formation Among Swedish-American Mission Friends: The Case of Ansgar College, 1873–1884" in Philip J. Anderson et al., eds., *Scandinavian Immigrants and Education in North America* (Chicago, 1995)

Anderson, Philip J. & Dag Blanck, eds., *Swedish-American Life in Chicago: Cultural and Urban Aspects of an Immigrant People 1850–1930* (Uppsala, 1991) [Anderson & Blanck 1991a]

Anderson, Philip J. & Dag Blanck, "Introduction," in Philip J. Anderson & Dag Blanck, eds., *Swedish-American Life in Chicago: Cultural and Urban Aspects of an Immigrant People 1850–1930* (Uppsala, 1991) [Anderson & Blanck 1991b]

Anderson, Philip J., et al., eds., *Scandinavian Immigrants and Education in North America* (Chicago, 1995)

Andersson, Inger, *Läsning och skrivning. En analys av texter för den allmänna läs- och skrivundervisningen 1842–1982* (Umeå, 1986)

Andræ, Carl-Göran, "Ett socialhistoriens dilemma. Några försök att definiera sociala grupper och klasser i svensk historia," *Historisk Tidskrift*, 98 (1978:1).

Andreen, Gustav, *Det svenska språket i Amerika* (Stockholm, 1900)

Andreen, Gustav, "Jules Mauritzson," *Korsbaneret*, 52 (1931)

Andrén, Carl-Gustaf, *Kyrkokunskap* (Lund, 1971)

Appel, John, "Hansen's Third Generation Law," *Jewish Social Studies*, 23 (January, 1961)

Appleby, Joyce, Lynn Hunt & Margaret Jacob, *Telling the Truth About History* (New York, 1994)

Arden, G. Everett, *The School of the Prophets. The Background and History of Augustana Theological Seminary 1860–1960* (Rock Island, 1960)

Arden, G. Everett, *Augustana Heritage. A History of the Augustana Lutheran Church* (Rock Island, 1963)

Barth, Fredrik, "Introduction", in his *Ethnic Groups and Boundaries. The Social Organization of Culture Difference* (Boston, 1969)

Barton, H. Arnold, "Clio and Swedish America: Historians, Organizations, Publications" in Nils Hasselmo, ed., *Perspectives on Swedish Immigration* (Chicago, 1978)

Barton, H. Arnold, "The Life and Times of Swedish America," *Swedish-American Historical Quarterly*, 35 (July 1984)

Barton, H. Arnold, "Förord" in Gunilla Larsson & Eva Tedenmyr, *Svenskt tryck i Nordamerika. Katalog över Tell G. Dahllöfs samling* (Stockholm, 1988)

Barton, H. Arnold, "Cultural Interplay between Sweden and Swedish America," *Swedish-American Historical Quarterly*, 43 (1992)

Barton, H. Arnold, "Swedish Reactions to the Emigration Question Around the Turn of the Century," *Swedish-American Historical Quarterly*, 45, (April 1993)

Barton, H. Arnold, *A Folk Divided: Homeland Swedes and Swedish Americans, 1840–1940* (Carbondale, Illinois, 1994)

Barton, H. Arnold, "Swedish Visitors' Views of Swedish-American Education," in Philip J. Anderson et al., eds., *Scandinavian Immigrants and Education in North America* (Chicago, 1995)

Bates, Barbara Snedeker, "Denominational Periodicals: The Invisible Literature," *Phaedrus*, 7 (Spring/Summer 1980)

Beck, L.H., "Upsala College. Kort historik", *Prärieblomman*, 1908, 8 (1907)

Beck, Walter H., *Lutheran Elementary Schools in the United States* (St. Louis, 1939)

Beijbom, Ulf, *Swedes in Chicago. A Demographic and Social Study of the 1846–1880 Immigration* (Uppsala, 1971)

Beijbom, Ulf, "The Historiography of Swedish America", *Swedish Pioneer Historical Quarterly*, 31, (October, 1980)

Beijbom, Ulf, "Vilhelm Berger, en skildrare av emigranternas hundår," *Personhistorisk tidskrift*, 77 (1981)

Beijbom, Ulf, "Swedish-American Research: Its Standing Today and Perspectives for Tomorrow", *Swedish-American Historical Quarterly*, 34 (April, 1983)

Beijbom, Ulf, *Utvandrarna och Svensk-Amerika* (Växjö, 1986)

Beijbom, Ulf, "Svensk etnicitet i Amerika och Australien. Några iakttagelser från den svenska utvandringens vanligaste respektive mest perifera mål 1846–1930," *Rig*, 71 (1988)

Beijbom, Ulf, *Svenskamerikanskt. Människor och förhållanden i Svensk-Amerika* (Växjö, 1990) [Beijbom 1990a]

Beijbom, Ulf, "Swedish-American Organizational Life" in Harald Runblom & Dag Blanck, eds., *Scandinavia Overseas. Patterns of Cultural Transformation in North America and Australia* (Uppsala, 1990) [Beijbom 1990b]

Beijbom, Ulf, ed., *Swedes in America: Intercultural and Interethnic Perspectives on Contemporary Research* (Växjö, 1993)

Bennich-Björkman, Bo & Lars Furuland, "Vad folket sjöng och läste," in Lars Lönnroth & Sven Delblanc, eds., *Den svenska litteraturen. De liberala genombrotten 1830–1890* (Stockholm, 1988)

Benson, Adolph & Naboth Hedin, eds., *Swedes in America 1638–1938* (New Haven, Conn., 1938)

Berg, Bodil, "Svedvi sockenbibliotek. En undersökning av bokbestånd, boklån och låntagare med huvudvikten lagd på tiden 1886–1890" in Lars Furuland & Bengt Brundin, eds., *En bok om biblioteksforskning* (Uppsala, 1969)

Bergendoff, Conrad, "The Role of Augustana in the Transplanting of a Culture Across the Atlantic," in J. Iverne Dowie & J. Thomas Tredway, eds., *The Immigration of Ideas. Studies in the North Atlantic Community* (Rock Island, 1968)

Bergendoff, Conrad, *Augustana ... A Profession of Faith. A History of Augustana College 1860–1935* (Rock Island, 1969)

Bergendoff, Conrad, "Augustana in America and in Sweden," *Swedish Pioneer Historical Quarterly*, 24 (October, 1973)

Bergendoff, Conrad, "Fritiof Fryxell and Augustana" in David A. Schroeder & Rich-

229

ard C. Anderson, eds., *Earth Interpreters. F.M. Fryxell, Geology, and Augustana* (Rock Island, 1992)

Berger, Vilhelm, *Svensk-Amerika i målbrottet* (New York, 1933)

Bercovitch, Sacvan, *The American Jeremiad* (Madison, Wisc., 1978)

Björck, Staffan, *Heidenstam och sekelskiftets Sverige. Studier i hans nationella och sociala författarskap* (Stockholm, 1946)

Björk, Ulf Jonas, "The Swedish-American Press. Three Newspapers and Their Communities," Unpublished Ph.D. dissertation, University of Washington, 1987

Björk, Ulf Jonas, "Making Swedish-America Visible. The Fiction and Essays of Johan Person", in Poul Houe, ed., *Out of Scandinavia*, (Minneapolis, 1993)

Blanck, Dag, "'A Language Does Not Die Easily': Swedish at Augustana College, 1860–1900," *Swedish-American Historical Quarterly*, 33 (October 1982)

Blanck, Dag, "Svensk eller amerikan. Till frågan om Augustana College och assimileringen av svenskar i USA 1860–1900," Unpublished seminar paper, Department of History, Uppsala University, 1983.

Blanck, Dag, "History at Work: The 1888 New Sweden Jubilee," *Swedish-American Historical Quarterly*, 39 (1988)

Blanck, Dag, "Constructing an Ethnic Identity: The Case of the Swedish-Americans" in Peter Kivisto, ed., *The Ethnic Enigma. The Saliency of Ethnicity for European-Origin Groups* (Philadelphia, 1989)

Blanck, Dag, "The Swedish Americans and the 1893 Columbian Exposition" in Philip J. Anderson & Dag Blanck, eds., *Swedish-American Life in Chicago: Cultural and Urban Aspects of an Immigrant People 1850–1930* (Uppsala, 1991)

Blanck, Dag, "Guest Editor's Introduction to Special Swedish Issue", *Swedish-American Historical Quarterly*, 43 (July 1992)

Blanck, Dag, "Growing Up Swedish in America: The Construction of a Swedish-American Ethnic Consciousness" in Poul Houe, ed., *Out of Scandinavia* (Minneapolis, 1993)

Blanck, Dag, "Introduction," in Ann Boaden & Dag Blanck, eds., *Looking West. Three Essays on Swedish-American Life by Jules Mauritzson* (Rock Island, 1994)

Blanck, Dag, "North Stars and Vasa Orders: On the Relationship Between Sweden and Swedish America," *Swedish-American Historical Quarterly*, 46 (July 1995)

Blanck, Dag, "Five Decades of Transatlantic Research on Swedish Emigration to North America" in P. Sture Ureland & Ian Clarkson, eds., *Language Contact Across the North Atlantic* (Tübingen, 1996)

Blanck, Dag & Harald Runblom, eds., *Swedish Life in American Cities* (Uppsala, 1991)

Blegen, Theodore, *The Kensington Rune Stone* (St. Paul, Minn., 1968)

Bodnar, John, *The Transplanted. A History of Immigrants in Urban America* (Bloomington, Ind., 1985)

Bodnar, John, *Remaking America. Public Memory, Commemoration, and Patriotism in the Twentieth Century* (Princeton, N.J., 1992)

Boëthius, Ulf, *När Nick Carter drevs på flykten: Kampen mot "smutslitteraturen" i Sverige 1908–1909* (Stockholm, 1989)

Breton, Raymond, "Institutional Completeness of Ethnic Communities and the Personal Relations of Immigrants," *American Journal of Sociology*, 70 (September, 1964)

Breton, Raymond, "Collective Dimensions of the Cultural Transformation of Ethnic Communities and the Larger Society," in Jean Burnet et al., eds., *Migration and the Transformation of Cultures* (Toronto, 1992)

230

Brink, Lars, "Vad läste studenterna vid college? En granskning av den litterära kanon vid Gustavus Adolphus College, 1890–1950," Unpublished seminar paper, Department of Literature, Uppsala University, 1988

Brink, Lars, *Gymnasiets litterära kanon. Urval och värderingar i läromedel 1910–1945* (Uppsala 1992)

Burke, Peter, *Popular Culture in Early Modern Europe* (New York, 1978)

Carlson, Leland H., *A History of North Park College* (Chicago, 1941)

Carlsson, Sten, "Chronology and Composition of Swedish Emigration to America," in Harald Runblom & Hans Norman, eds., *From Sweden to America. A History of the Migration* (Uppsala & Minneapolis, 1976)

Carlsson, Sten, "Augustana Lutheran Pastors in the Church of Sweden," *Swedish-American Hisorical Quarterly*, 35 (July 1984).

Chapman, Malcolm, Mary McDonald & Elizabeth Tonkin "Introduction" in Tonkin, McDonald, and Chapman, eds., *History and Ethnicity* (London, 1989)

Christianson, J.R., "Shaping the Culture of an Immigrant College Town: Decorah, Iowa, 1850–1890," in Philip J. Anderson et al., eds., *Scandinavian Immigrants and Education in North America* (Chicago, 1995)

Cipolla, Carlo, *Literacy and Development in the West* (Harmondsworth, 1969)

Cohen, Abner, ed., *Urban Ethnicity* (London, 1974)

Commager, Henry Steele, "The Search for a Usable Past" in his *The Search for a Usable Past* (New York, 1967)

Connor, Walker, "When is a Nation?" *Ethnic and Racial Studies*, 13 (January 1990)

Conzen, Kathleen Neils, "German-Americans and the Invention of Ethnicity," in Frank Trommler & Jospeh McVeigh, eds., *America and the Germans. An Assessment of a Three-Hundred-Year History*, vol 1. (Philadelphia, 1985)

Conzen, Kathleen Neils, *Immigrant Milwaukee, 1836–1860: Accomodation and Community in a Frontier City* (Cambridge, Mass., 1976)

Conzen, Kathleen Neils, "Mainstream and Side Channels: The Localization of Immigrant Cultures," *Journal of American Ethnic History*, 11 (Fall, 1991)

Conzen, Kathleen Neils, "The Stories Immigrants Tell," *Swedish-American Historical Quarterly*, 46 (January 1995)

Conzen, Kathleen Neils et al., "The Invention of Ethnicity. A Perspective from the U.S.A.," *Journal of American Ethnic History*, 12 (Fall 1992)

Craig, Peter Stebbins, "Mårten Mårtensson & His Morton Family," *Swedish Colonial News*, (Philadelphia), 1 (Spring 1996)

Cremin, Lawrence, *American Education. The National Experience 1783–1876* (New York, 1984)

Davies, Wallace Evan, *Patriotism on Parade. The Story of Veterans' and Hereditary Organizations in America 1783–1900* (Cambridge, Mass., 1955)

Elson, Ruth, *Guardians of Tradtion. American Schoolbooks of the Nineteenth Century* (Lincoln, Nebr., 1964)

Elvander, Nils, *Harald Hjärne och konservatismen. Konservativ idédebatt i Sverige 1865–1922* (Uppsala, 1961)

Erickson, Scott E., *David Nyvall and the Shape of an Immigrant Church: Ethnic, Denominational, and Educational Priorities among Swedes in America* (Uppsala, 1996)

Erling, Bernhard, "Augustana, Bishops, and the Church of Sweden," *Lutheran Forum*, 26 (February 1992)

Erling, Bernhard, "The Augustana Synod and Sweden. Changes and Influences," in Scott E. Erickson, ed., *American Religious Influences in Sweden* (Uppsala, 1996)

Estus, Charles W. & John F. McClymer, *Gå Till Amerika. The Swedish Creation of An Ethnic Identity for Worcester, Massachusetts* (Worcester, Mass., 1994)

Fischer, Michael M.J., "Ethnicity and the Post-Modern Arts of Memory" in James Clifford & George E. Marcus, eds., *Writing Culture: The Poetics and Politics of Ethnography* (Berkeley, Calif., 1986)

Fishman, Joshua, *Language Loyalty in the United States* (The Hague, 1966)

Fishman, Joshua & Vladimir Nahirny "American Immigrant Groups: Ethnic Identification and the Problem of Generations", *Sociological Review*, 13 (1965)

Fishman, Joshua & Vladimir Nahirny, "Ukranian Language Maintenance Efforts in the United States" in Joshua Fishman, *Language Loyalty in the United States* (The Hague, 1966)

Florin, Christina & Ulla Johansson, *"Där de härliga lagrarna gro ..." Kultur, klass och kön i det svenska läroverket 1850–1914* (Stockholm, 1993)

Fuchs, Lawrence, *The American Kaleidoscope. Race, Ethnicity, and the Civic Culture* (Hanover, N.H., 1990)

Furuland, Lars, *Statarna i litteraturen. En studie i svensk dikt och samhällsdebatt* (Stockholm, 1962)

Furuland, Lars, "Öresskrifter för folket", *Dagens Nyheter*, 2 September 1972

Furuland, Lars, "The Swedish-American Press as a Literary Institution of the Immigrants," in Harald Runblom & Dag Blanck, eds., *Scandinavia Overseas. Patterns of Cultural Transformation in North America and Australia* (Uppsala, 1990)

Furuland, Lars, "From *Vermländingarne* to *Slavarna på Molokstorp*. Swedish-American Theater in Chicago" in Philip J. Anderson & Dag Blanck, eds., *Swedish-American Life in Chicago: Cultural and Urban Aspects of an Immigrant People 1850–1930* (Uppsala, 1991) [Furuland 1991a]

Furuland, Lars, "'Lyssna till den granens susning ...' Om en läsebok som folkuppfostrare" in his *Ljus över landet och andra litteratursociologiska uppsatser* (Hedemora & Uppsala, 1991) [Furuland 1991b]

Furuland, Lars, "Rättvikskullans sångbok i USA," in *Rättvikskrus. Rättviks hembygsförenings årsskrift 1996*, 16 (1996)

Gerber, David A., *The Making of An American Pluralism. Buffalo, New York 1825–1860* (Urbana, Ill., 1989)

Glazer, Nathan, "Ethnic Groups in America: From National Culture to Ideology," in Morroe Berger et al., *Freedom and Control in Modern Society* (New York, 1954)

Glazer, Nathan, *We Are All Multiculturalists Now* (Cambridge, Mass., 1997)

Glazer, Nathan, & Daniel Patrick Moynihan, *Ethnicity. Theory and Experience* (Cambridge, Mass., 1975)

Gleason, Philip, "American Identity and Americanization," in Stephan Thernstrom, ed., *Harvard Encyclopedia of American Ethnic Groups* (Cambridge, Mass., 1980)

Granquist, Mark, "Swedish- and Norwegian-American Religious Traditions, 1860–1920," *Lutheran Quarterly*, 8 (Autumn 1994)

Greene, Victor, "Slavic American Nationalism: Poles, Czechs and Slovaks, 1918–1921" in Anna Cienciala, ed., *American Contributions to the Seventh International Congress of Slavists. Volume III: History* (The Hauge, 1973)

Greene, Victor, *For God and Country. The Rise of Polish and Lithuanian Ethnic Consciousness in America, 1860–1910* (Madison, Wisc., 1975)

Greene, Victor, *American Immigrant Leaders 1800–1910. Marginality and Identity* (Baltimore, Md., 1987)

Grönberger, Robert, *Svenskarna i St. Croix-dalen, Minnesota* (Minneapolis, 1879)

Gustafsson, Berndt, *Svensk kyrkohistoria* (Stockholm, 1966)

Hamrin, Margareta, "A Study of Swedish Immigrant Children's Literature Published in the United States, 1850–1920", *Phaedrus*, (Spring, 1979)

Handlin, Oscar, *The Uprooted* (Boston, 1951)

Hansen, Marcus Lee, *The Problem of the Third Generation Immigrant* (Rock Island, 1938)

Hasselmo, Nils, *Amerikasvenska. En bok om språkutvecklingen i Svensk-Amerika* (Stockholm, 1974)

Hasselmo, Nils, "The Language Question," in Nils Hasselmo, ed., *Perspectives on Swedish Immigration* (Chicago, 1978)

Higham, John, "Leadership" in Stephan Thernstrom, ed., *Harvard Encyclopedia of American Ethnic Groups*, (Cambridge, Mass., 1980)

Hilen, Andrew, *Longfellow and Scandinavia. A Study of the Poet's Relationship with the Northern Languages and Literature* (New Haven, Conn., 1947)

Hill, S.M., "Nebraska-svenskarnas bildningssträfvanden. Ett litet stycke svensk-amerikansk kulturhistoria", *Prärieblomman*, 1907, 7 (1906)

Hobsbawm, Eric, "Introduction: Inventing Traditions", in Hobsbawm & Terence Ranger, eds., *The Invention of Tradition* (Cambridge, 1983)

Hobsbawm, Eric, *Nations and Nationalism since 1780. Programme, Myth, Reality* (Cambridge, 1990)

Hoglund, A. William, *Immigrants and Their Children in the United States. A Bibliography of Doctoral Dissertations, 1885–1982* (New York, 1986)

Hroch, Miroslav, *Social Preconditions of National Revival in Europe. A Comparative Analysis of the Social Composition of Patriotic Groups Among the Smaller European Nations* (Cambrige, Engl., 1985)

Hustvedt, Lloyd, *Rasmus Bjørn Anderson. Pioneer Scholar* (Northfield, Minn., 1966)

Hvenekilde, Anne, "'Hvad gjør vi saa med arven?' En studie av abc-er og lesebøker utgitt til norsk morsmålsundervisning i Amerika," Unpublished Ph.D. dissertation, University of Oslo, 1992

Isaacs, Harold, *Idols of the Tribe. Group Identity and Political Change* (New York, 1975)

Isajiw, Wsevolod, "Definitions of Ethnicity", *Ethnicity*, 1 (1974)

Jansson, Torkel, *Samhällsförändring och sammanslutningsformer. Det frivilliga föreningsväsendets uppkomst och spridning i Husby-Rekarne från omkring 1850 till 1930* (Uppsala, 1982)

Jansson, Torkel, *Adertonhundratalets associationer. Forskning och problem kring ett sprängfullt tomrum eller sammanslutningsprinciper och föreningsformer mellan två samhällsformationer c:a 1800–1870* (Uppsala, 1985)

Jansson, Torkel, "En historisk uppgörelse. När 1800-talsnationen avlöste 1600-tals-staten," *Historisk Tidskrift,* 110 (1990 : 1)

Jansson, Torkel, "Från stormakt till smånation. En väv av ekonomisk-politiska och sociokulturella trådar" in Stellan Dahlgren et al. eds., *Från stormakt till smånation. Sveriges plats i Europa från 1600-tal till 1900-tal* (Stockholm, 1994)

Jarvi, Raymond, "The Rise and Fall of Engberg-Holmberg" in Philip J. Anderson & Dag Blanck, eds., *Swedish-American Life in Chicago: Cultural and Urban Aspects of an Immigrant People 1850–1930* (Uppsala, 1991)

Jenswold, John R., "The Rise and Fall of Pan-Scandinavianism in Urban America," in Odd Lovoll, ed., *Scandinavian and Other Immigrants in Urban America. The Proceedings of A Research Conference, October 26–27, 1984* (Northfield, Minn., 1985)

233

Johannesson, Eric, *Den läsande familjen. Familjetidskriften i Sverige 1850–1880* (Stockholm, 1980)

Johannesson, Eric, "The Flower King in the American Republic: The Linnaeus Statue in Chicago, 1891," in Philip J. Anderson & Dag Blanck, eds., *Swedish-American Life in Chicago: Cultural and Urban Aspects of an Immigrant People 1850–1930* (Uppsala, 1991) [Johannesson 1991a]

Johannesson, Eric, "Scholars, Pastors and Journalists: The Literary Canon of Swedish-America," in Dag Blanck & Harald Runblom, eds, *Swedish Life in American Cities* (Uppsala, 1991) [Johannesson 1991b]

Johansson, Egil, "Literacy studies in Sweden. Some examples" in Egil Johansson, ed., *Literacy and Society in a Historical Perspective. A Conference Report* (Umeå, 1973)

Johansson, Egil, "Literacy Campaigns in Sweden," in Robert F. Arnove & Harvey J. Graff, eds., *National Literacy Campaigns: Historical and Comparative Perspectives* (New York, 1987)

Johnson, Eric & C.F. Peterson, *Svenskarne i Illinois. Historiska anteckningar* (Chicago, 1880)

Kammen, Michael, *Mystic Chords of Memory. The Transformation of Tradition in American Culture* (New York, 1991)

Kantowicz, Edward, "Polish Chicago. Survival Through Solidarity," in Melvin Holli & Peter d'A. Jones, eds., *The Ethnic Frontier. Essays in the History of Group Survival in Chicago and the Midwest* (Grand Rapids, Mich., 1977)

Karsten, Peter, *Patriot-Heroes in England and America. Political Symbolism and Changing Values over Three Centuries* (Madison, Wisc., 1978)

Kastrup, Allan, *The Swedish Heritage in America* (St. Paul, Minn., 1975)

Keillor, Steven J, "Rural Norwegian-American Reading Societies in the Late Nineteenth Century," *Norwegian-American Studies*, 1992

Kivisto, Peter, "Overview: Thinking about Ethnicity", in Peter Kivisto, ed., *The Ethnic Enigma. The Salience of Ethnicity for European-Origin Groups* (Philadelphia, 1989)

Kivisto, Peter & Dag Blanck, eds., *American Immigrants and Their Generations. Studies and Commentaries on the Hansen Thesis after Fifty Years* (Urbana, Ill., 1990)

Klingberg, Göte, *Das deutsche Kinder- und Jugendbuch im schwedischen Raum* (Weinheim & Basel, 1973)

Kussak, Åke *Författaren som predikant. Ett frikyrkosamfunds litterära verksamhet 1910–1939* (Stockholm, 1982)

Kälvemark, Ann-Sofie, *Reaktionen mot utvandringen. Emigrationsfrågan i svensk debatt och politik 1901–1904* (Uppsala, 1971)

Landelius, Otto Robert, "Några anteckningar till den svensk-amerikanska bokhandelns historia", *Bokhandlaren*, 44 (No. 33, 1951)

Lange, Anders & Charles Westin, *Etnisk diskriminering och social identitet* (Stockholm, 1981)

Lazowitz, Bernard & Louis Rowitz, "The Three-Generation Hypothesis," *American Journal of Sociology*, 69 (March 1964)

Legreid, Ann M., "'By the Oaks of Mamre': Swedish Lutheran Colonization on the Frontiers of Southwestern Iowa, 1870–1900," *Swedish-American Historical Quarterly*, 44 (April 1993)

Lewan, Bengt, "Tegnér i skolan. Målsättningar i litteraturundervisningen 1840–1970," in *Vetenskapssociteten i Lund Årsbok 1972* (Lund, 1972)

Linder, Oliver, "Svensk-amerikanska litteraturen," in Karl Hildebrand & Axel Fredenholm, eds., *Svenskarna i Amerika*, vol 2. (Stockholm, 1925) [Linder 1925a]

Linder, Oliver A., "Svensk-amerikanska tidningspressen" in Karl Hildebrand and Axel Fredenholm, eds., *Svenskarna i Amerika*, vol 2. (Stockholm, 1925) [Linder 1925b]

Lindmark, Sture, *Swedish America 1914–1932. Studies in Ethnicity with Emphasis on Illinois and Minnesota* (Stockholm, 1971)

Lindquist, Emory, *Smoky Valley People* (Lindsborg, Kansas, 1953)

Lindquist, Emory, *Bethany in Kansas* (Lindsborg, Kansas, 1975)

Lipset, Seymour Martin, *The First New Nation. The United States in Historical and Comparative Perspective* (New York, 1963)

Ljungmark, Lars, *For Sale—Minnesota. Organized Promotion of Scandinavian Immigration, 1866–1873* (Göteborg, 1971)

Lo-Johansson, Ivar, "Folkskolans läsebok" in *Litteraturens vägar. Litteratursociologiska studier tillägnade Lars Furuland* (Stockholm, 1988)

Lovoll, Odd, ed., *Scandinavians and Other Immigrants in Urban America* (Northfield, Minn,. 1985)

Lovoll, Odd, ed., *Nordics in America. The Future of Their Past* (Northfield, Minn., 1993)

Lowenthal, David, *Possessed by the Past. The Heritage Crusade and the Spoils of History* (New York, 1996)

Lund, Doniver A., *Gustavus Adolphus College. A Centennial History 1862–1962* (St. Peter, Minn., 1963)

Lundevall, Karl-Erik, *Från åttital till nittital. Om åttitalslitteraturen och Heidenstams debut och program* (Stockholm, 1953)

Lyle, Guy R., "College Literary Societies in the Fifties," *The Library Quarterly*, 4 (1934)

Lyons, Martyn, *Le Triomphe du Livre. Une histoire sociologique de la lecture dans la France du xixième siècle* (N.p.: Promodis, 1987)

Lönnroth, Lars & Sven Delblanc, eds., *Den svenska litteraturen. Vol 2. Upplysning och romantik* (Stockholm, 1988) [Lönnroth & Delblanc 1988a]

Lönnroth, Lars & Sven Delblanc, eds., *Den svenska litteraturen. Vol 3. De liberala genombrotten 1830–1890* (Stockholm, 1988) [Lönnroth & Delblanc 1988b]

Lönnroth, Lars & Sven Delblanc, eds., *Den svenska litteraturen. Vol 4. Den storsvenska generationen* (Stockholm, 1989)

Martinsson, Bengt-Göran, *Tradition och betydelse. Om selektion, legitimering och reproduktion av litterär betydelse i gymnasiets litteraturundervisning 1865–1968* (Linköping, 1989)

Marty, Martin E., "Religion: The Skeleton of Ethnicity in America", *Church History*, 41 (March 1972)

Mattson, A. D., *Polity of the Augustana Synod* (Rock Island, 1941)

McKay, James & Frank Lewins, "Ethnicity and the Ethnic Group: A Conceptual Analysis and Reformulation," *Ethnic and Racial Studies*, 1 (October 1978)

Medelius, Hans & Sten Rentzhog, eds., *90–tal. Visioner och vägval. Fataburen 1991. Nordiska Museets och Skansens Årsbok* (Stockholm, 1991)

Moody, J., "Northwestern College", *Prärieblomman,* 1909, 9 (1908)

Mählqvist, Stefan, *Böcker för svenska barn 1870–1950. En kvantitativ analys* (Stockholm, 1977)

Nelson, Frank, "Minnesota College", *Prärieblomman,* 1912, 12 (1911)

Nelson, Helge, *The Swedes and the Swedish Settlements in North America*, 2 vols. (Lund, 1943)

Nilsson, Hjalmar & Eric Knutson, *Svenskarne i Worcester 1868–1898* (Worcester, Mass., 1898)

Nordahl, Per, *Weaving the Ethnic Fabric. Social Networks Among Swedish-American Radicals in Chicago 1890–1940* (Umeå, 1994)

Nordgren, J. Vincent, "Elementary Christian Education in the Augustana Synod" in *After Seventy-five Years, 1860–1935. A Jubilee Publication* (Rock Island, 1935)

Nordlinder, Eva, *Sekelskiftets svenska konstsaga och sagodiktaren Helena Nyblom* (Stockholm, 1991)

Nordstrom, Byron, "The Sixth Ward. A Minneapolis Swede Town in 1905" in Nils Hasselmo, ed., *Perspectives on Swedish Immigration* (Chicago, 1978)

Norman, Hans, *Från Bergslagen till Nordamerika. Studier i migrationsmönster, social rörlighet och demografisk struktur med utgångspunkt från Örebro län 1851–1915* (Uppsala, 1974)

Norman, Hans, "The New Sweden Colony and the Continued Existence of Swedish and Finnish Ethnicity", in Carol E. Hofecker et al., eds, *New Sweden in America* (Newark, Delaware, 1995)

Norman, Hans & Harald Runblom, *Transatlantic Connections. Nordic Migration to the New World after 1800* (Oslo, 1988) [Norman & Runblom 1988a]

Norman, Hans & Harald Runblom, "Research on Overseas Migration from the Nordic Countries. A Bibliographical Essay" in Hans Norman & Harald Runblom, *Transatlantic Connections. Nordic Migration to the New World after 1800* (Oslo, 1988) [Norman & Runblom 1988b]

Nothstein, Ira O., "The Language Transition in the Augustana Synod," *The Augustana Quarterly,* 24 (July, October 1945)

Nyberg, Janet, "Swedish Language Newspapers in Minnesota" in Nils Hasselmo, ed., *Perspectives on Swedish Immigration* (Chicago, 1978)

Nystrom, Daniel, *A Ministry of Printing. History of the Publication House of Augustana Lutheran Church 1889–1962* (Rock Island, 1962)

Olneck, Martin & Marvin Lazerson, "Education," in Stephan Thernstrom, ed., *Harvard Encyclopedia of American Ethnic Groups* (Cambridge, Mass., 1980)

Olson, Anita Ruth "Swedish Chicago: The Extension and Transformation of an Urban Immigrant Community, 1880–1920," Unpublished Ph.D. dissertation, Northwestern University, 1990

Olson, Ernst, Anders Schön & Martin J. Engberg, *History of the Swedes of Illinois*, 2 vols. (Chicago, 1908)

Olson, Oscar N., "Cultural Life in the Synod," in *After Seventy-five Years 1860–1935. A Jubilee Publication* (Rock Island, 1935)

Olson, Oscar N., *The Augustana Lutheran Church in America 1860–1910. The Formative Period* (Rock Island, 1956)

Olsson, Karl A., *By One Spirit. A History of the Evangelical Covenant Church of America* (Chicago, 1962)

Olsson, Karl A., "Paul Peter Waldenström and Augustana" in J. Iverne Dowie & Ernest M. Espelie, eds., *The Swedish Immigrant Community in Transition* (Rock Island, 1963)

Olsson, Karl A., "Kontinuitet och förvandling inom svenska immigrantsamfund i USA," *Kyrkohistorisk årsskift,* 82 (1982)

Ordesson, Sverker, *Gustav Adolf, Sverige och Trettioåriga kriget. Historieskrivning och kult* (Lund, 1992)

Ostergren, Robert, "Swedish Migration to North America in Transatlantic Perspective" in Ira Glazier & Luigi de Rosa, eds., *Migration Across Time and Nations: Population Mobility in Historical Contexts* (New York, 1986)

Ostergren, Robert, *A Community Transplanted. The Trans-Atlantic Experience of a*

Swedish Immigrant Settlement in the Upper Middle West, 1835–1915 (Uppsala, 1988)

Park, Robert, *The Immigrant Press and Its Control* (New York, 1922)

Patterson, Orlando, "Context and Choice in Ethnic Allegiance: A Theoretical Framework and Caribbean Case Study" in Nathan Glazer & Daniel Patrick Moynihan, eds., *Ethnicity. Theory and Experience* (Cambridge, Mass., 1975)

Person, Peter P., "A History of Higher Education Among the Swedish Immigrants in America," Unpublished Ed.D. dissertation, Harvard University, 1941

Peterson, Brent, *Popular Narratives and Ethnic Identity. Literature and Community in Die Abendschule* (Ithaca, N.Y., 1991)

Petterson, Lars, *Frihet, jämlikhet, egendom och Bentham. Utvecklingslinjer i svensk folkundervisning mellan feodalism och kapitalism, 1809–1860* (Uppsala, 1992)

Pleijel, Hilding, "Bibeln i svenskt fromhetsliv" in Pleijel, Bror Olsson & Sigfrid Svensson, *Våra äldsta folkböcker* (Lund, 1967)

Posern-Zielinski, Aleksander, "Ethnicity, Ethnic Culture and Folk Tradition in the American Society (On the Example of Polonia Collectivity in the USA)," *Ethnologia Polonia*, 4 (1978)

Rice, John G. "Marriage Behavior and the Persistence of Swedish Communities in Rural Minnesota" in Nils Hasselmo, ed., *Perspectives on Swedish Immigration* (Chicago, 1978)

Rudolph, Frederick, *The American College and University. A History* (New York, 1962)

Runblom, Harald, "Chicago Compared: Swedes and Other Ethnic Groups in American Cities" in Philip J. Anderson & Dag Blanck, eds., *Swedish-American Life in Chicago: Cultural and Urban Aspects of an Immigrant People 1850–1930* (Uppsala, 1991)

Runblom, Harald & Hans Norman, eds., *From Sweden to America. A History of the Migration* (Uppsala & Minneapolis, 1976)

Runblom, Harald & Lars-Göran Tedebrand, "Future Research in Swedish-American History: Some Perspectives", *Swedish Pioneer Historical Quarterly*, 30, (April, 1979)

Runeby, Nils, *Den nya världen och den gamla. Amerikabild och emigrationsuppfattning i Sverige 1820–1860* (Uppsala, 1969)

Rydbeck, Kerstin, *Nykter läsning. Den svenska godtemplarrörelsen och litteraturen 1896–1925* (Uppsala, 1995)

Sanders, Hanne, "Om fanatiske sværmere og sande kristne. Den offentlige debat om den religiose vækkelse i Danmark og Sverige 1800–1850," *Historisk Tidskrift*, 112 (1992 : 2)

Sanders, Hanne, *Bondevækkelse og sekularisering. En protestantisk folkelig kultur i Danmark og Sverige 1820–1850* (Stockholm, 1995)

Sarna, Jonathan, "From Immigrants to Ethnics: Toward a New Theory of 'Ethnicization,'" *Ethnicity*, 5 (December 1978)

Saveth, Edward N., *American Historians and European Immigrants, 1875–1925* (New York, 1948)

Schersten, Albert Ferdinand, *The Relation of the Swedish-American Newspaper to the Assimilation of Swedish Immigrants* (Rock Island, 1935)

Schultz, April, *Ethnicity on Parade. Inventing the Norwegian American through Celebration* (Amherst, Mass., 1994)

Schön, Anders, "Joh. A. Enander. Kort minnesruna för Ungdomsvännen", *Ungdomsvännen*, 1910, 10 (1909)

Scott, Larry E., *The Swedish Texans* (San Antonio, Texas, 1990)

Seller, Maxine, "The Education of Immigrants in the United States: An Introduction to the Literature," *Immigration History Newsletter*, 13 (1981)

Severin, Ernest, *Svenskarne i Texas i ord och bild*, 2 vols. (Austin, Texas, 1919)

Skarstedt, Ernst, *Svensk-amerikanska folket i helg och söcken* (Stockholm, 1917)

Smith, Anthony D., "Ethnic Myths and Ethnic Revivals," *European Journal of Sociology*, 25 (1984) [Smith 1984a]

Smith, Anthony D., "National Identity and Myths of Ethnic Descent," *Research in Social Movements, Conflict and Change*, 7 (1984) [Smith 1984b]

Smith, Anthony D., *National Identity* (Hardmondsworth, 1991)

Smith, Anthony D., "Introduction: Ethnicity and Nationalism," *International Journal of Comparative Sociology*, 33 (1–2, 1992)

Smith, Timothy, "Immigrant Social Aspirations and American Education, 1880–1930," *American Quarterly*, 21 (Fall 1969)

Smith, Timothy, "Religion and Ethnicity in America", *American Historical Review*, 83 (December 1978)

Sollors, Werner, "Literature and Ethnicity" in Stephan Thernstrom, ed., *Harvard Encyclopedia of American Ethnic Groups* (Cambridge, Mass., 1980)

Sollors, Werner, *Beyond Ethnicity. Consent and Descent in American Culture* (New York, 1986)

Sollors, Werner, ed., *The Invention of Ethnicity* (New York, 1989)

Staionos, Kathryn Vance, "Ethnicity as Process. The Creation of an Afro-American Identity," *Ethnicity*, 7 (1980)

Stephenson, George, *The Religious Aspects of Swedish Immigration. A Study of Immigrant Churches* (Minneapolis, 1932)

Stockenström, Göran, "Sociological Aspects of Swedish-American Literature" in Nils Hasselmo, ed., *Perspectives on Swedish Immigration* (Chicago, 1978)

Stolarik, M. Mark, "Immigration and Education: Some Ethnic and National Comparisons," in Philip J. Anderson et al., eds., *Scandinavian Immigrants and Education in North America* (Chicago, 1995)

Strand, Algot E., ed., *A History of the Swedish-Americans in Minnesota*, vol 1 (Chicago, 1910), 289–298

Svedjedal, Johan, "Bokmarknaden," in Lars Lönnroth & Hans-Erik Johannesson, eds., *Den svenska litteraturen. Bokmarknad, bibliografier, samlingsregister* (Stockholm, 1990)

Svedjedal, Johan, *Bokens samhälle. Svenska bokförläggareföreningen och svensk bokmarknad 1887–1943*, I (Stockholm, 1993)

Svedjedal, Johan, "Kvinnorna i den svenska bokbranschen," in his *Författare och förläggare och andra litteratursociologiska studier* (Hedemora, 1994)

Svensson, Birgitta, *Den omplanterade svenskheten. Kulturell självhävdelse och etnisk medvetenhet i den svensk-amerikanska kalendern Pärieblomman 1900–1913* (Göteborg, 1994)

Svensson, Sonja, *Läsning för folkets barn. Folkskolans Barntidning och dess förlag 1892–1914* (Stockholm, 1983)

Swan, G.N., "En återblick," *Year-Book of the Swedish Historical Society of America/ Svenska Historiska Sällskapets i Amerika Årsbok 1914–1915* (Chicago, 1915).

Swanson, Mary Towley, *Elusive Images of Home. Stories of Swedish-American Art* (Stockholm, 1996)

Swedish-American Historical Quarterly, 43 (July, 1992)

Söderström, Axel, *Minneapolis-minnen* (Minneapolis, 1899)

Söderström, Axel, *Blixtar på tidningshorisonten* (Warroad, Minnesota, 1910)

Söderström, Hugo, *Confession and Cooperation. The Policy of the Augustana Synod in Confessional Matters and the Synod's Relations with other Churches up to the Beginning of the Twentieth Century* (Lund, 1973)

Tarschys, Karin, *"Svenska språket och litteraturen." Studier över modersmålsundervisningen i högre skolor* (Stockholm, 1955)

Taylor, Philip, *The Distant Magnet. European Emigration to the U.S.A.* (London, 1971)

Tedebrand, Lars-Göran, *Västernorrland och Nordamerika 1875–1913. Utvandring och återinvandring* (Uppsala, 1972)

Thander, Gunnar, "Valkyrian 1897–1909: A Study in Swedish-American Ethnicity," Unpublished Ph.D. dissertation, University of Minnesota, 1996

Thernstrom, Stephan, *The Other Bostonians. Poverty and Progress in the American Metropolis 1880–1970* (Cambridge, Mass., 1973)

Thistlethwaite, Frank, "Migration from Europe Overseas in the Nineteenth Century" in *Comité International des Sciences Historiques. XIième Congrès Internationale des Sciences Historiques, Stockholm 21–28 Août 1960, Rapports, V,* (Stockholm, 1960)

Thomas, William & Florian Znaniecki, *The Polish Peasant in Europe and America*, edited and abridged by Eli Zaretsky, orig. published 1918–1920 (Urbana, Ill., 1985)

Tingsten, Herbert, *Gud och fosterlandet. Studier i hundra års skolpropaganda* (Stockholm, 1969)

Ulrich, Robert, *The Bennet Law of 1889: Education and Politics in Wisconsin* (New York, 1980)

Vecoli, Rudolph, *"Contadini* in Chicago: A Critique of *The Uprooted"*, *Journal of American History*, 51 (December 1964)

von Schéele, K.G.H., *Hemlandstoner. En hälsning från modern Svea till dotterkyrkan i Amerika* (Stockholm, 1894)

Wahlgren, Erik, *The Kensington Stone. A Mystery Solved* (Madison, Wisc., 1958)

Weiss, Bernard J., ed., *American Education and the European Immigrant, 1840–1940* (Urbana, Ill., 1982)

Wendelius, Lars, *Kulturliv i ett svenskamerikanskt lokalsamhälle: Rockford, Illinois* (Uppsala, 1990)

Westerberg, Kermit, "Books and Reading in a Swedish-American Immigrant Community: A Case Study of the Lending Library of the Vega Litterära Förening (Vega Literary Society), St. Paul, from 1881 to 1948, With an Emphasis on Bookstock Characteristics, Patronage, and Circulation Statistics, and Popular Reading Tastes," Unpublished Master's Paper, University of Minnesota School of Library Science, 1977

Westerberg, Kermit B., "In Private and Public: The Dialogue of Libaries, Immigrants, and Society," in Philip J. Anderson et al., eds., *Scandinavian Immigrants and Education in North America* (Chicago, 1995)

Widén, Albin, "Svenska böcker i USA," *Konung Oscar II:s Vandringsbibliotek Årsbok 1950* (Lund, 1950)

Williams, Anna, *Skribent i Svensk-Amerika. Jakob Bonggren, journalist och poet* (Uppsala, 1991)

Williams, Anna, Review of Birgitta Svensson, *Den omplanterade svenskheten, Samlaren*, 116, (1995)

Yancey, William, Eugene P. Erickson and Richard N. Juliani, "Emergent Ethnicity: A Review and Reformulation," *American Sociological Review*, 41 (June 1976)

Yinger, J. Milton, *Ethnicity. Source of Strength? Source of Conflict?* (Albany, N.Y., 1994)

Zelinsky, Wilbur, *Nation Into State. The Shifting Symbolic Foundations of American Nationalism* (Chapel Hill, N.C., 1988)

Åkerman, Sune, "From Stockholm to San Francisco: The Development of the Historical Studies of External Migrations", *Annales Academiæ Regiæ Scientiarum Upsaliensis*, 19 (1975)

Øverland, Orm, *Home-Making Myths: Immigrants' Claims to a Special Status in Their New Land* (Odense, 1996)

Acta Universitatis Upsaliensis
STUDIA HISTORICA UPSALIENSIA

Editores: Rolf Torstendahl, Torkel Jansson & Jan Lindegren

37. *Sture Lindmark:* Swedish America 1914–1932. Studies in Ethnicity with Emphasis on Illinois and Minnesota. 1971.

38. *Ulf Beijbom:* Swedes in Chicago. A Demographic and Social Study of the 1846–1880 Immigration. 1971.

39. *Staffan Smedberg:* Frälsebonderörelser i Halland och Skåne 1772–76. 1972.

40. *Björn Rondahl:* Emigration, folkomflyttning och säsongarbete i ett sågverksdistrikt i södra Hälsingland 1865–1910. Söderala kommun med särskild hänsyn till Ljusne industrisamhälle. 1972.

41. *Ann-Sofie Kälvemark:* Reaktionen mot utvandringen. Emigrationsfrågan i svensk debatt och politik 1901–1904. 1972.

42. *Lars-Göran Tedebrand:* Västernorrland och Nordamerika 1875–1913. Utvandring och återinvandring. 1972.

43. *Ann-Marie Petersson:* Nyköping under frihetstiden. Borgare och byråkrater i den lokala politiken. 1972. (Ej i bokhandeln)

44. *Göran Andolf:* Historien på gymnasiet. Undervisning och läroböcker 1820–1965. 1972.

45. *Jan Sundin:* Främmande studenter vid Uppsala universitet före andra världskriget. En studie i studentmigration. 1973.

46. *Christer Öhman:* Nyköping och hertigdömet 1568–1622. 1973. (Ej i bokhandeln)

47. *Sune Åkerman, Ingrid Eriksson, David Gaunt, Anders Norberg, John Rogers & Kurt Ågren:* Aristocrats, Farmers and Proletarians. Essays in Swedish Demographic History. 1973.

48. *Uno Westerlund:* Borgarsamhällets upplösning och självstyrelsens utveckling i Nyköping 1810–1880. 1973. (Ej i bokhandeln)

49. *Sven Hedenskog:* Folkrörelserna i Nyköping 1880–1915. Uppkomst, social struktur och politisk aktivitet. 1973. (Ej i bokhandeln)

50. *Berit Brattne:* Bröderna Larsson. En studie i svensk emigrantagentverksamhet under 1880-talet. 1973.

51. *Anders Kullberg:* Johan Gabriel Stenbock och reduktionen. Godspolitik och ekonomiförvaltning 1675–1705. 1973.

52. *Gunilla Ingmar:* Monopol på nyheter. Ekonomiska och politiska aspekter på svenska och internationella nyhetsbyråers verksamhet 1870–1919. 1973.

53. *Sven Lundkvist:* Politik, nykterhet och reformer. En studie i folkrörelsernas politiska verksamhet 1900–1920. 1974.

54. *Kari Tarkiainen:* "Vår gamble Arffiende Ryssen". Synen på Ryssland i Sverige 1595–1621 och andra studier kring den svenska Rysslandsbilden från tidigare stormaktstid. 1974.

55. *Bo Öhngren:* Folk i rörelse. Samhällsutveckling, flyttningsmönster och folkrörelser i Eskilstuna 1870–1900. 1974.

56. *Lars Ekholm:* Svensk krigsfinansiering 1630–1631. 1974.

57. *Roland Nordlund:* Krig på avveckling. Sverige och tyska kriget 1633. 1974.

58. *Clara Nevéus:* Trälarna i landskapslagarnas samhälle. Danmark och Sverige. 1974.

59. *Bertil Johansson:* Social differentiering och kommunalpolitik. Enköping 1863–1919. 1974.

60. *Jan Lindroth:* Idrottens väg till folkrörelse. Studier i svensk idrottsrörelse till 1915. 1974.

61. *Richard B. Lucas:* Charles August Lindbergh, Sr. A Case Study of Congressional Insurgency, 1906–1912. 1974.

62. *Hans Norman:* Från Bergslagen till Nordamerika. Studier i migrationsmönster, social rörlighet och demografisk struktur med utgångspunkt från Örebro län 1851–1915. 1974.

63. *David Gaunt:* Utbildning till statens tjänst. En kollektivbiografi av stormaktstidens hovrättsauskultanter. 1975.

64. *Eibert Ernby:* Adeln och bondejorden. En studie rörande skattefrälset i Oppunda härad under 1600-talet. 1975.

65. *Bo Kronborg & Thomas Nilsson:* Stadsflyttare. Industrialisering, migration och social mobilitet med utgångspunkt från Halmstad, 1870–1910. 1975.

66. *Rolf Torstendahl:* Teknologins nytta. Motiveringar för det svenska tekniska utbildningsväsendets framväxt framförda av riksdagsmän och utbildningsadministratörer 1810–1870. 1975.

67. *Allan Ranehök:* Centralmakt och domsmakt. Studier kring den högsta rättskipningen i kung Magnus Erikssons länder 1319–1355. 1975.

68. *James Cavallie:* Från fred till krig. De finansiella problemen kring krigsutbrottet år 1700. 1975.

69. *Ingrid Åberg:* Förening och politik. Folkrörelsernas politiska aktivitet i Gävle under 1880-talet. 1975.

70. *Margareta Revera:* Gods och gård 1650–1680. Magnus Gabriel De la Gardies godsbildning och godsdrift i Västergötland. I. 1975.

71. *Aleksander Loit:* Kampen om feodalräntan. Reduktionen och domänpolitiken i Estland 1655–1710. I. 1975.

72. *Torgny Lindgren:* Banko- och riksgäldsrevisionerna 1782–1807. "De redliga män, som bevakade ständers rätt". 1975.

73. *Rolf Torstendahl:* Dispersion of Engineers in a Transitional Society. Swedish Technicians 1860–1940. 1975.

74. From Sweden to America. A History of the Migration. Red. Harald Runblom & Hans Norman. 1976.

75. *Svante Jakobsson:* Från fädernejorden till förfäders land. Estlandssvenskt bondfolks rymningar till Stockholm 1811–1834; motiv, frekvens, personliga konsekvenser. 1976.

76. *Lars Åkerblom:* Sir Samuel Hoare och Etiopienkonflikten 1935. 1976.

77. *Gustaf Jonasson:* Per Edvin Sköld 1946–1951. 1976.

78. *Sören Winge:* Die Wirtschaftliche Aufbau-Vereinigung (WAV) 1945–53. Entwicklung und Politik einer „undoktrinären" politischen

Partei in der Bundesrepublik in der ersten Nachkriegszeit. 1976.

79. *Klaus Misgeld:* Die „Internationale Gruppe demokratischer Sozialisten" in Stockholm 1942–1945. Zur sozialistischen Friedensdiskussion während des Zweiten Weltkrieges. 1976.

80. *Roland Karlman:* Evidencing Historical Classifications in British and American Historiography 1930–1970. 1976.

81. *Berndt Fredriksson:* Försvarets finansiering. Svensk krigsekonomi under skånska kriget 1675–79. 1976.

82. *Karl Englund:* Arbetarförsäkringsfrågan i svensk politik 1884–1901. 1976.

83. *Nils Runeby:* Teknikerna, vetenskapen och kulturen. Ingenjörsundervisning och ingenjörsorganisationer i 1870-talets Sverige. 1976.

84. *Erland F. Josephson:* SKP och Komintern 1921–1924. Motsättningarna inom Sveriges Kommunistiska Parti och dess relationer till den Kommunistiska Internationalen. 1976.

85. *Sven Lundkvist:* Folkrörelserna i det svenska samhället 1850–1920. 1976.

86. *Bo Öhngren:* GEOKOD. En kodlista för den administrativa indelningen i Sverige 1862–1951. 1977.

87. *Mike L. Samson:* Population Mobility in the Netherlands 1880–1910. A Case Study of Wisch in the Achterhoek. 1977.

88. *Ugbana Okpu:* Ethnic Minority Problems in Nigerian Politics: 1960–1965. 1977.

89. *Gunnar Carlsson:* Enköping under frihetstiden. Social struktur och lokal politik. 1977.

90. *Sten Carlsson:* Fröknar, mamseller, jungfrur och pigor. Ogifta kvinnor i det svenska ståndssamhället. 1977.

91. *Rolf Pålbrant:* Arbetarrörelsen och idrotten 1919–1939. 1977.

92. *Viveca Halldin Norberg:* Swedes in Haile Selassie's Ethiopia 1924–1952. A Study in Early Development Co-operation. 1977.

93. *Holger Wester:* Innovationer i befolkningsrörligheten. En studie av spridningsförlopp i befolkningsrörligheten utgående från Petalax socken i Österbotten. 1977.

94. *Jan Larsson:* Diplomati och industriellt genombrott. Svenska exportsträvanden på Kina 1906–1916. 1977.

95. *Rolf Nygren:* Disciplin, kritikrätt och rättssäkerhet. Studier kring militieombudsmannaämbetets (MO) doktrin- och tillkomsthistoria 1901–1915. 1977.

96. *Kenneth Awebro:* Gustav III:s räfst med ämbetsmännen 1772–1799 – aktionerna mot landshövdingarna och Göta hovrätt. 1977.

97. *Eric De Geer:* Migration och influensfält. Studier av emigration och intern migration i Finland och Sverige 1816–1972. 1977.

98. *Sigbrit Plaenge Jacobson:* 1766 års allmänna fiskestadga. Dess uppkomst och innebörd med hänsyn till Bottenhavsfiskets rättsfrågor. 1978.

99. *Ingvar Flink:* Strejkbryteriet och arbetets frihet. En studie av svensk arbetsmarknad fram till 1938. 1978.

100. *Ingrid Eriksson & John Rogers:* Rural Labor and Population Change. Social and Demographic Developments in East-Central Sweden during the Nineteenth Century. 1978.

101. *Kerstin Moberg:* Från tjänstehjon till hembiträde. En kvinnlig låglönegrupp i den fackliga kampen 1903–1946. 1978.

102. *Mezri Bdira:* Relations internationales et sousdéveloppement. La Tunisie 1857–1864. 1978.

103. *Ingrid Hammarström, Väinö Helgesson, Barbro Hedvall, Christer Knuthammar & Bodil Wallin:* Ideologi och socialpolitik i 1800-talets Sverige. Fyra studier. 1978.

104. *Gunnar Sundberg:* Partipolitik och regionala intressen 1755–1766. Studier kring det bottniska handelstvångets hävande. 1978.

105. *Kekke Stadin:* Småstäder, småborgare och stora samhällsförändringar. Borgarnas sociala struktur i Arboga, Enköping och Västervik under perioden efter 1680. 1979.

106. *Åke Lindström:* Bruksarbetarfackföreningar. Metalls avdelningar vid bruken i östra Västmanlands län före 1911. 1979.

107. *Mats Rolén:* Skogsbygd i omvandling. Studier kring befolkningsutveckling, omflyttning och social rörlighet i Revsunds tingslag 1820–1977. 1979.

108. *János Perényi:* Revolutionsuppfattningens anatomi. 1848 års revolutioner i svensk debatt. 1979.

109. *Kent Sivesand:* Skifte och befolkning. Skiftenas inverkan på byar och befolkning i Mälarregionen. 1979.

110. *Thomas Lindkvist:* Landborna i Norden under äldre medeltid. 1979.

111. *Björn M. Edsman:* Lawyers in Gold Coast Politics c. 1900–1945. From Mensah Sarbah to J.B. Danquah. 1979.

112. *Svante Jakobsson:* Osilia–Maritima 1227–1346. Studier kring tillkomsten av svenska bosättningar i Balticum, i synnerhet inom biskopsstiftet Ösel-Wiek. 1980.

113. *Jan Stattin:* Hushållningssällskapen och agrarsamhällets förändring – utveckling och verksamhet under 1800-talets första hälft. 1980.

114. *Bertil Lundvik:* Solidaritet och partitaktik. Den svenska arbetarrörelsen och spanska inbördeskriget 1936–1939. 1980.

115. *Ann-Sofie Kälvemark:* More children of better quality? Aspects on Swedish population policy in the 1930's. 1980.

116. *Anders Norberg:* Sågarnas ö. Alnö och industrialiseringen 1860–1910. 1980.

117. *Jan Lindegren:* Utskrivning och utsugning. Produktion och reproduktion i Bygdeå 1620–1640. 1980.

118. *Gustaf Jonasson:* I väntan på uppbrott? Bondeförbundet/Centerpartiet i regeringskoalitionens slutskede 1956–1957. 1981.

119. *Erland Jansson:* India, Pakistan or Pakhtunistan? The Nationalist Movements in the North-West Frontier Province, 1937–47. 1981.

120. *Ulla-Britt Lithell:* Breast-feeding and Repro-
duction. Studies in marital fertility and infant
mortality in 19th century Finland and Sweden.
1981.
121. *Svenbjörn Kilander:* Censur och propaganda.
Svensk informationspolitik under 1900-talets
första decennier. 1981.
122. *Håkan Holmberg:* Folkmakt, folkfront, folkde-
mokrati. De svenska kommunisterna och demo-
kratifrågan 1943–1977. 1982.
123. *Britt-Marie Lundbäck:* En industri kommer till
stan. Hudiksvall och trävaruindustrin 1855–
1880. 1982.
124. *Torkel Jansson:* Samhällsförändring och sammanslutningsformer. Det frivilliga föreningsväsendets uppkomst och spridning i Husby-
Rekarne från omkring 1850 till 1930. 1982.
125. *Per Jansson:* Kalmar under 1600-talet. Omland,
handel och krediter. 1982.
126. *Svante Jakobsson:* Fattighushjonets värld i
1800-talets Stockholm. 1982.
127. *Runo Nilsson:* Rallareliv. Arbete, familjemöns-
ter och levnadsförhållanden för järnvägsarbetare
på banbyggena i Jämtland–Härjedalen 1912–
1928. 1982.
128. *J. Alvar Schilén:* Det västallierade bombkriget
mot de tyska storstäderna under andra världskriget och civilbefolkningens reaktioner i de
drabbade städerna. 1983.
129. *Bodil Nävdal-Larsen:* Erik XIV, Ivan Groznyj
og Katarina Jagellonica. 1983.
130. *Birgitta Olai:* Storskiftet i Ekebyborna. Svensk
jordbruksutveckling avspeglad i en östgöta-
socken. 1983.
131. *Ann Hörsell:* Borgare, smeder och änkor. Eko-
nomi och befolkning i Eskilstuna gamla stad
och Fristad 1750–1850. 1983.
132. *Ragnar Björk:* Den historiska argumenteringen.
Konstruktion, narration och kolligation – för-
klaringsresonemang hos Nils Ahnlund och Erik
Lönnroth. 1983.
133. *Björn Asker:* Officerarna och det svenska
samhället 1650–1700. 1983.
134. *Erik Tiberg:* Zur Vorgeschichte des Livländi-
schen Krieges. Die Beziehungen zwischen Mos-
kau und Litauen 1549–1562. 1984.
135. *Bertel Tingström:* Sveriges plåtmynt 1644–
1776. En undersökning av plåtmyntens roll som
betalningsmedel. 1984.
136. *Curt Ekholm:* Balt- och tyskutlämningen 1945–
1946. Omständigheter kring interneringen i
läger i Sverige och utlämningen till Sovjetunio-
nen av f d tyska krigsdeltagare. Del 1: An-
komsten och interneringen. 1984. Andra upplagan 1995.
137. *Curt Ekholm:* Balt- och tyskutlämningen 1945–
1946. Omständigheter kring interneringen i
läger i Sverige och utlämningen till Sovjetunio-
nen av f d tyska krigsdeltagare. Del 2: Utlämningen och efterspelet. 1984. Andra upplagan
1995.
138. *Sven H. Carlson:* Trade and dependency. Studies in the expansion of Europe. 1984.

139. *Torkel Jansson:* Adertonhundratalets associationer. Forskning och problem kring ett sprängfullt tomrum eller sammanslutningsprinciper
och föreningsformer mellan två samhällsformationer, c:a 1800–1870. 1985.
140. *Bernt Douhan:* Arbete, kapital och migration.
Valloninvandringen till Sverige under 1600-
talet. 1985.
141. *Göran Rydeberg:* Skatteköpen i Örebro län
1701–1809. 1985.
142. *Habib Ben Abdallah:* De l'iqta' étatique à l'iqta'
militaire. Transition économique et change-
ments sociaux à Baghdad, 247–447 de l'Hégire/
861–1055 ap. J. 1986.
143. *Margot Höjfors Hong:* Ölänningar över haven.
Utvandringen från Öland 1840–1930 – bakgrund, förlopp, effekter. 1986.
144. *Carl Johan Gardell:* Handelskompani och bon-
dearistokrati. En studie i den sociala strukturen
på Gotland omkring 1620. 1986.
145. *Birgitta Olai:* "… till vinnande af ett redigt
Storskifte …". En komparativ studie av storskiftet i fem härader. 1987.
146. *Torkel Jansson:* Agrarsamhällets förändring
och landskommunal organisation. En kontur-
teckning av 1800-talets Norden. 1987.
147. *Anders Florén:* Disciplinering och konflikt.
Den sociala organiseringen av arbetet: Jäders
bruk 1640–1750. 1987.
148. *Tekeste Negash:* Italian Colonialism in Eritrea
1882–1941: Policies, Praxis and Impact. 1988.
149. *Lotta Gröning:* Vägen till makten. SAP:s organisation och dess betydelse för den politiska
verksamheten 1900–1933. 1988.
150. *Ove Pettersson:* Byråkratisering eller avbyrå-
kratisering. Administrativ och samhällsorgani-
satorisk strukturomvandling inom svenskt väg-
väsende 1885–1985. 1988.
151. *Knut Ohlsson:* Grosshandlare, bönder, småfolk.
Trönös skogsnäringar från och med det indus-
triella genombrottet. 1988.
152. *Eva Österberg & Dag Lindström:* Crime and
Social Control in Medieval and Early Modern
Swedish Towns. 1988.
153. *Marie C. Nelson:* Bitter Bread. The Famine in
Norrbotten 1867–1868. 1988.
154. *Gísli Ágúst Gunnlaugsson:* Family and Household in Iceland 1801–1930. Studies in the
relationship between demographic and socio-
economic development, social legislation and
family and household structures. 1988.
155. *Elsa Lunander:* Borgaren blir företagare. Studier kring ekonomiska, sociala och politiska
förhållanden i förändringens Örebro under
1800-talet. 1988.
156. *Ulla-Britt Lithell:* Kvinnoarbete och barntillsyn
i 1700- och 1800-talets Österbotten. 1988.
157. *Annette Thörnquist:* Lönearbete eller egen
jord? Den svenska lantarbetarrörelsen och jord-
frågan 1908–1936. 1989.
158. *Stefán F. Hjartarson:* Kampen om fackför-
eningsrörelsen. Ideologi och politisk aktivitet
på Island 1920–1938. 1989.

159. *György Nováky:* Handelskompanier och kompanihandel. Svenska Afrikakompaniet 1649–1663. En studie i feodal handel. 1990.

160. *Margareta Åman:* Spanska sjukan. Den svenska epidemin 1918–1920 och dess internationella bakgrund. 1990.

161. *Sven A. Nilsson:* De stora krigens tid. Om Sverige som militärstat och bondesamhälle. 1990.

162. *Birgitta Larsson:* Conversion to Greater Freedom? Women, Church and Social Change in Northwestern Tanzania under Colonial Rule. 1991.

163. *Dag Lindström:* Skrå, stad och stat. Stockholm, Malmö och Bergen ca 1350–1622. 1991.

164. *Svenbjörn Kilander:* Den nya staten och den gamla. En studie i ideologisk förändring. 1991.

165. *Christer Öhman:* Den historiska romanen och sanningen. Historiesyn, värdestruktur och empiri i Georg Starbäcks historiska författarskap. 1991.

166. *Maria Ågren:* Jord och gäld. Social skiktning och rättslig konflikt i södra Dalarna ca 1650–1850. 1992.

167. *Stina Nicklasson:* Högerns kvinnor. Problem och resurs för Allmänna valmansförbundet perioden 1900–1936/1937. 1992.

168. *Lars Petterson:* Frihet, jämlikhet, egendom och Bentham. Utvecklingslinjer i svensk folkundervisning mellan feodalism och kapitalism, 1809–1860. 1992.

169. *Alberto Tiscornia:* Statens, godsens eller böndernas socknar? Den sockenkommunala självstyrelsens utveckling i Västerfärnebo, Stora Malm och Jäder 1800–1880. 1992.

170. *Irène Artæus:* Kvinnorna som blev över. Ensamstående stadskvinnor under 1800-talets första hälft – fallet Västerås. 1992.

171. *Anders Fröjmark:* Mirakler och helgonkult. Linköpings biskopsdöme under senmedeltiden. 1992.

172. *Hernán Horna:* Transport Modernization and Entrepreneurship in Nineteenth Century Colombia. Cisneros & Friends. 1992.

173. *Janne Backlund:* Rusthållarna i Fellingsbro 1684–1748. Indelningsverket och den sociala differentieringen av det svenska agrarsamhället. 1993.

174. *Agneta Breisch:* Frid och fredlöshet. Sociala band och utanförskap på Island under äldre medeltid. 1994.

175. *Åsa Karlsson:* Den jämlike undersåten. Karl XII:s förmögenhetsbeskattning 1713. 1994.

176. *Elisabeth Elgán:* Genus och politik. En jämförelse mellan svensk och fransk abort- och preventivmedelspolitik från sekelskiftet till andra världskriget. 1994.

177. *Lennart Thorslund:* Humanism mot rationalism. Mora 1890–1970: Om två förhållningssätt och deras betydelse i småstadens planeringshistoria. 1995.

178. *Paul A. Levine:* From Indifference to Activism. Swedish Diplomacy and the Holocaust, 1938–1944. 1996.

179. *Bengt Nilsson:* Kvinnor i statens tjänst – från biträden till tjänstemän. En aktörsinriktad undersökning av kvinnliga statstjänstemäns organisering, strategier och kamp under 1900-talets första hälft. 1996.

180. *Tsegaye Tegenu:* The Evolution of Ethiopian Absolutism. The Genesis and the Making of the Fiscal Military State, 1696–1913. 1996.

181. *Sören Klingnéus:* Bönder blir vapensmeder. Protoindustriell tillverkning i Närke under 1600- och 1700-talen. 1997

ACTA UNIVERSITATIS UPSALIENSIS
Studia Historica Upsaliensia 182

Distributor: Uppsala University Library, Uppsala, Sweden

Dag Blanck

Becoming Swedish-American

The Construction of an Ethnic Identity in the Augustana Synod, 1860–1917.

Dissertation in history to be publicly examined in Room X, Uppsala University, on October 4, 1997, at 10.15 a.m., for the degree of Doctor of Philosophy. The examination will be conducted in English.

ABSTRACT

Dag Blanck (1997). Becoming Swedish-American. The Construction of an Ethnic Identity in the Augustana Synod, 1860–1917. Acta Universitatis Upsaliensis. *Studia Historica Upsaliensia* 182. 240 pp. Uppsala, ISBN 91-554-4027-4.

This dissertation examines the construction of an ethnic identity in the Swedish-American community around the turn of the century 1900. It takes its starting points in discussions of the nature of ethnic identity, the role of ethnic leadership, and the process of nation-building and nationalism in 19th-century Europe and America.

The study focuses on the largest organization founded by Swedish immigrants in the United States, the Lutheran denomination the Augustana Synod, and examines its role for the creation of an ethnic identity. Three fundamental questions are posed: How did an ethnic identity develop in the Augustana Synod, what did it consist of, and why did it come into being. Three main empirical areas are used to analyze the development and contents of the Swedish-American identity: the Synod's largest institution of higher education, Augustana College in Rock Island, Illinois; the Synod's publishing house, the Augustana Book Concern; and the way in which a Swedish-American history was fashioned within the Synod.

The results of the study show how a Swedish-American identity was constructed by a cultural leadership in the Augustana Synod. This idealized and romanticized identity included Swedish, Swedish-American, and American cultural elements. An awareness of a Swedish-American culture, separate from both Sweden and the United States, developed in which the construction of a Swedish-American history played an important role, emphasizing an early Swedish presence on the American continent and significant Swedish and Swedish-American contributions to the American republic. The reasons for the creation of the identity are seen in the light of the nature of American nationalism, which made it possible for European immigrant groups to develop and maintain ethnic identities and still be loyal Americans.

Dag Blanck, Department of History, Uppsala University, S:t Larsgatan 2, SE-753 10 Uppsala, Sweden